CHOOSING FOR CHILDREN

CHOOSING FOR CHILDREN
Parents' Consent to Surgery

PRISCILLA ALDERSON

Oxford   New York
OXFORD UNIVERSITY PRESS
1990

Oxford University Press, Walton Street, Oxford OX2 6DP

Oxford New York Toronto
Delhi Bombay Calcutta Madras Karachi
Petaling Jaya Singapore Hong Kong Tokyo
Nairobi Dar es Salaam Cape Town
Melbourne Auckland

and associated companies in
Berlin Ibadan

Oxford is a trade mark of Oxford University Press

First published 1990 as an Oxford University Press
paperback and simultaneously in a hardback edition

British Library Cataloguing in Publication Data
Alderson, Priscilla
Choosing for children.
1. Hospitals. Patients. Children. High risk
therapy. Consent by parents. Consent by parents to high
risk therapy for children in hospitals. Ethical aspects
I. Title
174.24
ISBN 0-19-217774-5
ISBN 0-19-286115-8 pbk

Library of Congress Cataloging in Publication Data
Alderson, Priscilla.
Choosing for children / Priscilla Alderson.
p. cm.   Includes bibliographical references.
1. Sick children—Hospital care—Decision-making.   2. Informed consent
(Medical law)   3. Sick children—Medical care—Moral and ethical aspects.
4. Parent and child.   I. Title.
174'.2—dc20   RJ242.A42   1990   90-7176
ISBN 0-19-217774-5
ISBN 0-19-286115-8 (pbk.)

Typeset by Rowland Phototypesetting Ltd.
Printed in Great Britain by
Biddles Ltd.
Guildford and King's Lynn

Seeing the world comprised of relationships rather than of people standing alone, a world that coheres through human connection rather than through a system of rules.

Carol Gilligan

Foreword

All surgeons, whether junior or senior, have to be given consent for surgery by patients, parents, or guardians. For logistic reasons that consent is very often sought from the family on the day before surgery and after the patient has been admitted for the operation to be performed. Surgeons who perform long operations such as cardiac surgery may be in the operating theatre all day and only find time to come and see the family in the evening before the operation. The family are tense, the surgeon tired, and the situation fraught with potential complications.

This is clearly not satisfactory, and this important book by Priscilla Alderson should point out to clinicians why this is so. Although I have always been concerned about the quality of information given to families and about their level of understanding, her book shows clearly how informed consent is a life event for a family. No longer am I able to feel comfortable with a few minutes with the family on the day before surgery in the hope that our previous preparations have been sufficient.

It is clear that practising surgeons and clinicians have a responsibility to provide information which goes back long before the patient is finally admitted for surgery. The process of consent is a long one with the consent form being only the last symbolic gesture for a worried and caring family. The book you are about to read makes this point very well using parents' comments.

There is more though to consent than just information and Priscilla Alderson defines more clearly what we mean by trust. It is I think true that a competent and confident surgeon could talk an ill-informed family into having any operation performed upon their child. This of course does not happen because of the establishment of trust. I suspect that many surgeons do not appreciate the level of this trust and I am sure that their sense of responsibility to the families' overall well-being will be improved by reading this important work.

This book will take an important place on my bookshelf and should be read by all surgeons involved in the taking of consent. Not only is it thought-provoking and challenging but it is full of practical suggestions for improving the ways in which consent is taken. I am very glad to have the opportunity to write this foreword and I hope you enjoy the book as much as I did.

Martin J. Elliott MD FRCS
Consultant Cardiothoracic Surgeon
Hospital for Sick Children
Great Ormond Street

Acknowledgements

Hundreds of people helped me with this book. I am grateful to all of them, especially to the children, their parents, and the hospital staff who generously allowed me to observe and talk with them. Many of them wanted to remain anonymous, and it is difficult to pick out just a few names. Yet the ideas of the following people, and the encouragement of many of them, made this book possible. So I would like to thank: Elliot Shinebourne, who saw the need to research parents' consent, and who asked me to do so at the Brompton Hospital, and Bridget Comer, Fran Cox (who has lately achieved so many changes in the unit), Paul Highton, Sandra Mattos, and Sue Rees, also at the Brompton; Philip Rees, who welcomed me to the Hospital for Sick Children, Great Ormond Street, and his colleague Martin Elliott; also Fiona Benson, Timothy Chambers, Dorothy and Arthur Clift, Jean Gaffin (for the book's title), Jean Lovell-Davis, Jenny Mauger, and Richard Nicholson; Caroline Ramazanoglu with Victor Seidler, and members of the Sociology Department at Goldsmiths' College, University of London; Jill Siddle, Margaret Stacey, and Richard Wilson; also Nicola Bion and Heather Watson of Oxford University Press.

Thanks are also due to the Economic and Social Research Council for a three-year research grant, and the Harold Hyam Wingate Foundation for a scholarship to write the book.

The librarians of Goldsmiths' College, King's College Laws Library, and the National Association for the Welfare of Children in Hospital were very helpful.

Lastly I thank Juliet, Harriet, William, and Anna for all that I learned while I was their parent in hospital.

Contents

Medical terms

anaesthesia	loss of sensation
analgesia	pain relief
aneurysm	localized swelling of a blood vessel or heart chamber; some may burst
aorta	main artery taking blood from heart to body
aortic valve	one of four heart valves
arrest	heart stops beating
arrhythmias	irregular heart beats
ASD	atrial septal defect, hole between the two upper chambers of the heart
atresia	blocked or missing
atrioventricular septal defect (or canal defect)	the central part of the heart is missing so that the four chambers of the heart work as one. This defect occurs most often in children with Down's syndrome.
band	cord tied round the artery to the lungs to reduce excessive blood flow to the lungs and lower pressure on the small blood vessels
barium	chemical used for X-ray investigations
bypass	during open-heart surgery, the heart and lungs are stopped; the patient's blood passes through the heart-lung bypass machine which acts as artificial heart and lungs
cardiac catheterization	investigations carried out by passing a narrow tube through a vein or artery in the groin or arm up into the heart

diuretic	drug to increase the production of urine by the kidneys, used to reduce body fluid and hence reduce the work-load for the heart
doctors in order of seniority are:	consultant senior registrar (SR) registrar senior house officer (SHO)
ECG	electrocardiograph, an electrical recording of the heart by a machine which prints out the heart rhythms as patterns
echocardiography	scanning system in which a transducer placed on the chest emits sound-waves through the chest which are converted into images on a television screen. The same system is used for scanning pregnant women.
'Fallot'	Tetralogy of Fallot, a combination of four heart defects
Fontan operation	surgery in which the right atrium (upper chamber) is connected to the artery to the lungs
homograft	grafted human tissue
ICU	intensive care unit
IV line	narrow tube inserted and left in the vein for administering intravenous (through vein) nutrition and drugs
mitral valve	one of four heart valves
paediatric cardiologist	children's heart doctor concerned mainly with congenital heart defects
palliative surgery	aims to relieve the effects of disease but by definition does not correct or cure it; later corrective surgery may or may not be possible
pulmonary artery	artery from heart to lungs
pulmonary valve	one of the four heart valves

shunt operation	usually a cloth tube is placed between an arm artery and the right or left artery to the lungs to increase the blood flow to the lungs. This is usually a lower risk operation than open-heart surgery.
stenosis	narrowing in the blood vessel or valve
suction	secretions are sucked out of the respiratory tract. If the patient is on a ventilator this is briefly disconnected.
switch	see transposition
tertiary care	the British health service has three levels: primary or non-hospital care; secondary or local hospital care; tertiary care in a few specialized centres such as the nine designated centres in England for children's heart surgery. There is no designated centre in Wales.
transposition of the great arteries	the two major arteries from the heart are transposed, each arises from the other's place. Earlier operations, the Mustard's and the Senning's, altered the blood flow in the upper heart chambers. The switch operation disconnects the arteries and switches them over to be reconnected to their correct chambers.
tricuspid	one of the four heart valves
truncus	aorta and pulmonary artery arise from a single trunk
unit	each hospital had a paediatric cardiac unit, with one ward (mainly for admission and recovery) and one intensive care unit. Unit has been used in two senses.
ventilator	or respirator, machine for patients

	who cannot breathe adequately unaided
VSD	ventricular septal defect, hole between the two lower chambers of the heart

I

Introduction

Lauren was suddenly admitted to hospital from home when she was two weeks old. A few days after the emergency operation, her parents talked about giving proxy consent to heart surgery for their first child.

Lauren's mother: It hit me when we were waiting for her to come back from the operation. I think we were both expecting her to be dead. We'd prepared ourselves, been home and walked round, just the two of us. All her bits from a normal day were all left there.

Father: I tidied a little. Things that might be too painful to tidy later on. We talked about being only two again. So shattered. We couldn't express it properly to each other. The doctors were very honest, they told us she might not survive.

You hear of things happening to other people but it will never happen to you. Then sad things start happening to your friends. It comes nearer home. Then it hits you. You have a child with a heart defect. You begin to realize that statistics mean you, and you begin to dread what will happen next. You stop believing in good luck.

Mother: I was trying to be rational. Even if she died, we'd had thirteen very good days together at home as a family. It's funny you can get incredibly close to a child that's just a few days old. Shattering that it can just go. Life seems more precious. You get a period of being very elated. I felt almost godlike four days after the operation. You go right to the bottom, then up again. You've faced that, and you feel you can go through anything at all.

But I don't want her to suffer. We know she'll need more surgery later. I have a nagging doubt whether it would be better to let her quietly die. There are certain things I don't want to subject her to. I don't know whether it's just adults projecting their feelings about pain on to a baby, but what are we keeping her alive for?

Father: We see her wound and we feel funny about it. Obviously she feels pain, but we're putting our feelings on to her to some extent. And are we keeping her alive just for us? Not for her benefit? I felt strange giving consent. Should we let her die? But I can only vocalize this now, I felt too emotionally confused at the time.

Problems with proxy consent

Many parents giving proxy consent for their child share the questions facing Lauren's parents. Modern medicine forces doctors and families to make hard choices for patients. Much has been written about the choices adult patients make, but less is said about making proxy decisions on behalf of those too young or too ill to decide for themselves. Can parents and doctors be trusted to make wise decisions for children? Do parents who abuse and neglect their children, or who do not seem to understand medical information, have any right to share in making medical decisions for them?

'Children' refers to patients below the age at which they automatically have the legal right to give or withhold their consent. In the examples, all the children's names have been changed. The words 'parents' and 'families' are used interchangeably with 'patients' when they share experiences similar to those adult patients would have when considering consent. 'Parents' denotes the parents or guardian, the adults legally entitled to give proxy consent for the child. Consent for children in care was given by the natural parents (even for a child who had lived in a foster home for years and never saw her natural parents) or by social services.

Consent is supposed to be voluntary, not enforced. Yet there are the unavoidable constraints, such as a child's illness, and the limitations of medical skill. Some parents reluctantly have to consent to very high-risk treatment, knowing that it may hasten their child's death. There may also be constraints of limited time, severe shock, and desperate anxiety to preserve life at almost any cost.

About one child in ten died in the unit where Lauren was nursed. Almost all of them would have died if their defects had been left untreated. The hardest questions concern when hoped-for benefits justify the risks, and who can and should decide when this is so. Surgeons might achieve better results by introducing new techniques earlier. Yet there is criticism that some new drugs and operations are introduced too quickly, and that children endure much suffering while techniques are being developed, such as with bone marrow transplants. Heart-lung transplants for children with cystic fibrosis are another example of high-risk treatment which appears to have limited benefit.[1] Attempts to cure terminal illness can be taken to cruel extremes.[2] Should children, parents, nurses, and doctors have greater freedom to stop certain kinds of treatment?

The psychological harms also need to be taken into account.[3] In some organ transplant units, the whole family have psychological tests to assess whether they will be able to manage the strain of the surgery and long-term treatment afterwards. Six months after her son Christopher died, his mother was still distraught with guilt. He had not been accepted for the heart transplant waiting-list. His mother understood that Christopher had been rejected because her marriage was thought by the psychiatrist to be unstable, and she felt that the death was entirely her fault. Services intended to help families to make the best choice can have the reverse effect.

Consent is supposed to be informed. However, both parents and doctors may have little idea of what the surgeon will discover during an exploratory operation like Lauren's, what action will be taken, and what the short and long-term effects may be. There is also the difficulty of understanding the experiences, and best interests of very ill patients, especially of babies who have never been able to express an opinion.

Parents' distress tends to be seen as a disadvantage, crippling their thinking and understanding. I think this is a mistaken view. Lauren's parents were 'shattered' *because* they understood the danger she was in. Moral feelings, such as of anxiety and compassion, need to be seen as a vital part of informed proxy consent. They deepen understanding. Indeed, parents who do not show any emotional response to news of their child's dangerous condition would imply that they do not have any clear rational understanding.

Informed consent is often discussed as a one-way process of doctors informing families. It is better understood as a two-way exchange of information. Families, too, have important knowledge which doctors need to learn if they are to make informed judgements. However, the many difficulties for families and professionals attempting to share knowledge can be increased by the ways in which busy, noisy clinics and wards are organized. This book is about the importance of listening to children and their parents, and of trying to make decisions with them, not just for them. If decisions are to be shared, and children are to be heard, then the ways in which hospitals are organized have to change.

When decisions are made partly in ignorance, trust becomes very important. Yet trust is a complex emotion which cannot and should not just be switched on. Problems for some families in trusting doctors are reflected by some doctors' reluctance to trust families.

These problems need to be understood more clearly before they can be at least partly resolved, which is why they will be described in some detail.

Surgery involves many procedures from putting on a nameband at admission to the final examination before discharge. Some minor interventions distress children far more than the actual operation. Children benefit when consent to surgery is not one overall agreement to all the tests and treatment, and when parents share in making daily interim decisions, such as how much pain relief a child needs. Parents can only be involved in this way when they are present, and able to share in providing their child's daily care, and when their views are respected. This respect depends on a partnership of trust between parents and professionals, which is not easy to achieve.

Lawcourt cases on consent, such as when a patient sues a surgeon for giving too little warning of the risks of an operation, tend to imply that consent is an agreement between two individuals: the patient and the doctor. In reality, consent is a process often influenced by many individuals: surgical, medical, nursing, and paramedical teams, the patient, and the family. This team-work has advantages but also disadvantages for consent, when information is discussed by many individuals.

Three threads run through all the aspects of proxy consent just mentioned. These are:

  moral feelings (such as compassion and trust);
  medical and parental power;
  and countless, practical details in the design and running of wards
    and clinics which encourage or exclude families.

Examples throughout this book show that it is essential to review these three matters critically if the conditions which influence proxy consent are to improve. We need to know far more about the emotional as well as the rational elements of coming to an informed decision. The egalitarian idea of consent in which doctors and families share decisions is practised only when medical power is questioned and changed, and when doctors allow or encourage families to take on more authority. Attitudes and practices change when old, unhelpful customs are questioned and new ways of providing hospital care are adopted.

Yet the three issues of emotion, power imbalance, and practical context tend to be neglected in debates in law and medical ethics.

Both disciplines favour highly rational, impersonal, abstract discussion. The aim, through their imposed rules and reasoned argument, is to raise standards in the area of informed consent. Rules and reasoning are important ways of preventing harm to patients. Yet it is psychologically naïve to suppose that high standards are created by these approaches. Parents and professionals do not strive to offer the best care to sick children simply because they think they ought to, or from fear of litigation. They are also influenced by their own motives. Consent as informed and voluntary commitment pervades our everyday choices and actions, and is not limited to consent to surgery. The rules and duties of ethics, law, medicine, and nursing are like the external informed part of consent. Children also depend on the adults' inner, willing commitment to care for them, which cannot be enforced.

Much attention is now paid to assessing standards and quality in the health services. Yet the vital but invisible response of personal care cannot be measured in this way, and it is being damaged by so called cost-effectiveness which can be very wasteful. Many highly trained nurses are leaving children's intensive care units, partly because their poor pay and working conditions make them feel undervalued. Operations are cancelled for lack of nurses. Waiting children become more ill and, when they later have surgery, more difficult to nurse by the fewer, overworked nurses who are left. In this downward spiral, information and choice for families are affected by the support given to nurses and other professionals. The quality of consent is influenced by the political and economic context.

Some arguments dominating medical ethics are hostile to very young and very sick patients. In answer to the question, 'Why should doctors request patients' consent?' ethicists reply that the request *respects the rational person*, or that it acknowledges *the rights of the autonomous person*. These reasons are valuable for patients who are recognized as rational, as autonomous, and as persons. Yet many patients are too dependent, too young or old, too ill or mentally affected to be wholly rational or autonomous, and ethicists regard some of these as non-persons. Proxy consent on their behalf is not about rights and respect but, for these most vulnerable patients, it is at least as important as the direct consent of independent patients. Requesting consent is not just a minor afterthought of polite doctors, but new approaches are needed in discussion in medical ethics in order to appreciate the value of proxy consent.

Observing proxy consent

This book is based on three years of research in two children's heart surgery units. I observed the out-patient clinics, wards, intensive care units, X-ray and other departments, medical and nursing meetings. I interviewed parents in ninety-five families at length, between one and five times, and talked with many other families and staff members. The semi-structured interviews invited parents to give their account of their child's illness and treatment, and how much they thought they were, or could have been, informed and involved in medical and nursing decisions. Parents described how the whole family was affected by the child's heart condition and treatment, and talked of their hopes for the future.

Interviews were usually tape recorded if parents agreed. Some preferred me to write notes, and while I wrote a few would say, 'No, I haven't said the right word, I want to change that', and would do so. I hoped that they felt they had some control over the interview, the choice of topics, how far they wanted to speak about difficulties, and how much they wanted to revise their accounts as new thoughts occurred to them. I tried one home interview, but it seemed no more revealing than interviews in the wards where the parents were frank and critical. It seemed important to listen to them while they were going through the time of surgery when they were searching for words and making sense of the crisis, rather than to hear a well-rehearsed account sometime after they had gone home. Two parents said they did not wish to talk, a few said they were busy and, unsure whether this indicated reluctance, I did not approach them again. Several parents asked to talk to me. If parents looked upset I avoided them in case I added to the pressures on them, so I talked mainly to parents who seemed to be coping fairly well.

The hospitals asked me to carry out a survey of parents' views on the information and the facilities for families. Giving out 415 questionnaires opened up conversations with 200 families. With a nurse teacher and social worker in one hospital, I carried out surveys on nurses' satisfaction and stress, and on the views of bereaved parents. These all gave useful background information. My research was mainly of a kind described by the sociologist Margaret Stacey, writing about children in hospital.

We believe our skills as social scientists make it possible for us to point out the unintended suffering inflicted, suffering which is unrecognised and

which may perhaps be unnecessary or avoidable. Our claim . . . is to be able
to observe and analyse such sufferings in dimensions where doctors and
nurses are unsighted by virtue of their training. Their gaze is directed to the
mysteries of physiology and anatomy. . . . Our gaze has been trained to look
at the workings of the mind and of society . . . to look below the surface of
the commonsensical and see the deeper implications.[4]

My aim was to look at the deeper implications, at visible and
invisible aspects of proxy consent. For this I used mainly the case-
study method of examining a few detailed examples. This method
does not summarize themes and statistics from hundreds of cases,
although observing the many unreported cases helped me to understand the ones presented here. A comparable medical method would
be to look at the structure of an organ and its defects, rather than to
measure how often each defect occurs. The case-study method does
not deal with representative samples, or attempt to report the success
rate of informed consents. It aims to see how each example can tell us
more about the whole consent process. Most chapters will therefore
give a few examples which are similar to many others observed. A
few cases are used because they are rare, and these will be described
an unusual. In the family's view, proxy consent is about trying to
make the best decision in the context of their child's personal and
medical past and future. Case-studies can convey something of this
continuing narrative view.

Tables of figures cannot do this, and are better suited to the
professional view which assesses groups of patients relatively briefly
and occasionally. Attitudes to science, research, and, in some ways,
to ethics may very broadly be divided into two kinds which can be
called the detached and attached views.[5] The detached view aims to
be objective and rational, and to organize data precisely in order to
prove hypotheses or to solve problems. It has five underlying
assumptions.[6]

1. Everything is made up of separate parts.
2. We understand objects when we take them apart.
3. Then we can see the theoretical laws by which they work.
4. We learn by examining each precise part, extracted from its
   context. (The higher the level of learning, the smaller the part.)
5. Knowledge enables us to predict and control natural or moral
   activity.

So, for instance, patients having surgery are extracted from their
everyday life, and admitted to hospital. A small part of their anatomy

is studied in order to treat them. Medical knowledge is composed of many separate specialties, some of which take little note of other aspects of the patients' body, psyche, or daily life. One example is medical research about premature birth which concentrates on separate, possible, physiological causes, their prevention and control.

This approach is being questioned by women who relate premature birth to the mother's social and psychological state. Prematurity is most likely to occur among isolated, depressed mothers who are on a low income; it may be possible to 'talk up the baby's weight' through offering friendly, practical support.[7] This alternative approach reflects the second, attached view which sees being subjective, personal, and emotionally involved as a valid response. The attached view connects thinking with feeling, values with facts, and prefers to observe and respond rather than to predict and control. I suggest that there are five underlying assumptions of attachment.

1. Everything is made up of related parts.
2. We understand objects when we see them together.
3. Then we can see their complexity and interactions.
4. We learn by examining whole objects and persons in their context.
5. Then we can begin to discover an appropriate response.

Each approach has advantages and limitations. Scientific medicine could not have developed without the detached approach. In reality, detachment and attachment usually overlap, and no one is purely rational or objective. The two approaches have been separately identified because later chapters look at the tension between them in medical treatment and research, in parents' and professionals' attitudes, and in medical ethics. Case-studies are useful for examining families' experiences because they allow for the personal, attached approach within which the families tend to think.

The case-study method risks being unfairly selective, enlarging on problems and overlooking the many satisfied and grateful patients. This is partly because much can be learned when difficulties arise; each stage is less obvious when everything goes smoothly and can be taken for granted. Tolstoy's happy families 'are all more or less like one another' whereas each unhappy experience or family 'is unhappy in its own particular way'.[8] This variety takes longer to describe, and so can easily exaggerate the overall picture.

The families studied were in crisis, distressed by serious illness and treatment. To outline their basic experiences conveys a depressing account and may imply blame, where none is intended, of the professionals who work intensely hard to help them. Much of the families' distress was unavoidable, but some was linked to the ways health services are provided, ways which can be altered in order to reduce avoidable distress. Often these routines were not set up by individuals, but evolved through hospital systems. So in describing routines which frustrated both families and staff, the intention is not to criticize but to show the problems and to suggest ways of solving them.

Children's heart surgery units are among the most difficult settings possible for informed consent. Children's heart surgery is complex, dangerous, highly technical, sometimes experimental, or at least uncertain in the long-term effects. Each patient is cared for by teams of professionals, who work in a range of settings: wards, clinics, theatres, laboratories, at medical and other staff meetings. While heart surgery is not typical, it does clearly illustrate the practical problems for proxy consent which may be less obvious in routine, low-risk surgery.

Some of the families' difficulties are a sign of success. They arise because parents are now so much more involved in these two units (far more than in some hospitals providing lower risk surgery) and because new standards of family-centred care, shared discussion, and informed consent are being worked out between parents and staff. This book is not intended to be a description of two hospitals, since they have already changed very much. The aim is to show how people respond within certain, fairly common practices.

Problems of trust between families and professionals is a theme throughout this book. Similar problems are shared by anyone doing research, and writing or reading about it. Questions of trust in research include: How valid are the accounts of the researcher and of the people interviewed? How can they be verified? How can the privacy, dignity, and confidentiality of the people studied be respected? What theories and methods can be used for selecting, reporting, and interpreting the material honestly and fairly? How much can anyone reading a book trust it, or be trusted not just to dismiss it but to attend to the meaning despite all the limitations of the account? Readers considering how much of this book to accept are like patients and, to a less extent, doctors considering information about proposed surgery. Much information, even in reports of the most rigorous statistical study, has partly to be taken on trust, without demonstrable proof, if it is to be accepted at all.

Many people I interviewed said, 'I hope that what I am telling you will help to change things and make it easier for other people in future.' The distress of some families over avoidable events was intense (it is impossible to convey this intensity on paper) and therefore needed to be taken seriously. Because they were so grateful for the excellent medical and nursing care, parents hesitated to explain other difficulties to the hospital staff, although some of the junior staff were very aware of these problems. The parents entrusted me with their personal thoughts. In return I owe it to them to represent their views as clearly and fairly as possible, especially as the views of patients and parents are seldom heard in discussions about consent. Personal problems may seem remote from informed consent. However, they are central to proxy consent, which can only be understood through its personal context.

I also have another set of obligations, to the hospital staff. They, too, generously allowed me to observe them, and many of them talked to me very openly, and greatly helped my research. One hospital asked me to do the research because they are so concerned about informed consent, and have long been working to achieve higher standards. The main aims of the units are to save life and improve physical health. Since this book is not centrally about reporting successes in these priorities, but looks at the minefield of problems surrounding proxy consent, again it may give an unintentionally negative picture. Omissions generally resulted from lack of time and knowledge, certainly not from intention to hurt.

This has therefore been an extremely difficult book to write, to try to present each view fairly, to consider the difficulties which everyone shared in trying to achieve informed consent, yet not to overstate them.

Attitudes to consent

'Consent', meaning the whole process of being informed and coming to a voluntary decision, will be examined mainly in the following ways. The first part of this book is about consent practices, and follows the consent process through the wards and clinics, the medical meetings, and the work of the multi-disciplinary teams in two children's heart surgery units. Examples are also given from the literature about other medical conditions and treatments in hospitals around the world. The second part of the book, while continuing to discuss practical examples, concentrates on less visible issues and theories: families' growing informed awareness, willingness to consent, trust between families and professionals, and debates in medical ethics about consent.

Instead of starting with a theory or history of consent, or a model drawn from law or ethics, I tried to see the families' experiences through their eyes. It soon became clear that some of their concerns are missing from the consent literature,[9] such as how families come to terms with painful realities, how they connect medical decisions with their daily lives, how they cope together during surgery and with whatever the future might bring, and how they give voluntary and proxy consent.

Stephen's family talked about these issues, while fourteen-year-old Stephen was waiting for a heart transplant. Stephen felt too ill and depressed to go to school and stayed alone in his bedroom most of the time. The family began by talking about how they shared medical information.

Stephen: I'm the main person, aren't I? I do know everything that's happened so far. You must, because if you don't know what's going to happen, you think 'What on earth are they doing this for?' If they tell you beforehand, you know what to expect. I reckon they should really ask my parents for permission until I'm responsible for looking after myself.

Father: Yes but we consult you, don't we? If they say they want to do something to you, we always, all three of us have a little chat about it. And maybe we say yes, and perhaps you're not quite in favour, but we always finish up getting an answer which we all agree on.

Stephen: Yes.

Father: Fortunately Stephen can take it, he can understand and get involved, he wants to know all the ins and outs, how everything works. Whereas some people can't take it. They possibly need *not* to be told what's going on.

Stephen: It actually gave me a shock when he said to me 'You probably need to have a heart transplant' . . . All sorts of things were running through my mind. I was thinking, why does it have to happen to me? Would I come through the operation? And what would happen to me after the operation? . . . And, you know . . . [*Stephen sighed.*] I wasn't sure what to think about it . . . Think I'd be all right? Or would it—be a wrong decision to have it? Or . . . ? I was half way. I didn't know what to pick. I would have

it done? Or live the rest of my life how I am now?—and probably get
worse. But I've gradually accepted it. It took me about a week to think it
over and decide for myself what I wanted them to do. I want to have it
done as soon as possible.

Mother: Yes, it's playing on his mind. I've been in tears at times with him
because of what he's going through and I can't help.

Stephen: I just want them to leave me alone until the—operation or
whatever.

Mother: At first I said to him, 'Son, I'm not too keen on it.' And he held my
hand and said, 'Don't worry, I'm going to have—I'm taking the chance.'
But it's not easy to sit waiting and worrying. What will happen to our life?
To everything? You think, and think, and the whole lot builds up in you.

Stephen's family see the operation not just as 'a stitch in time', a brief
technical act. Instead, surgery is like a gateway to his future of better
or worse health, possibly to life or death, or to further surgery. Major
surgery can affect the future of all the family in 'everything', as
Stephen's mother says, down to the smallest details. One example
was that they wanted to finish decorating the house but the paint
fumes made Stephen feel worse. Walking through the stripped hall
was a constant reminder of Stephen waiting for a new life.

Consent is a choice of the lesser of two evils, accepting that the
future, without having the operation, will probably be the worse
option. Such acceptance, especially with high-risk surgery, entails
intense fear of the harm that may be done by the operation, as well as
sadness and mourning that the future without surgery looks so
hopeless. Parents may be more or less aware for years that the child's
life is at risk, but as many said, 'That's something you avoid thinking
about, you live from day to day.' Stephen was shocked when he
realized how serious his illness was. When asked to consent to major
surgery, families are forced to recognize painful realities.

Literature about patient consent[10] tends to imply that doctors
explain the technical facts to patients. Patients then weigh the
potential harms against the benefits of surgery, as they might work
out a mathematical equation. They calculate their answer, whether
to give or withhold their consent. Medical facts may make patients
feel shocked and anxious and this prevents them from thinking out
the best solution clearly. Consent is therefore only valid when given
by patients who are calm and rational.

However, as Stephen suggests, and his mother shows, this is an
unreal picture. Like most of the men I interviewed, Stephen spoke

about thinking, rational choice, being unsure, and making a right or wrong decision. Like most of the women I interviewed, Stephen's mother put into words some of her sadness about the emotional pressure of 'going through' the consent process, which Stephen only hinted at in his unhappy tone of voice. Deciding about risky surgery involves deeply feeling fear, hope, anguish, and trust. Strong, ambivalent feeling also continues well after a decision is made. People take time to make difficult decisions because they have to struggle through complicated feelings as well as thoughts.

Patients and doctors are influenced by confidence or caution, willing commitment to the proposed treatment, or doubt about it. Parents' love and anxiety for their child can impede thought but also enable it, confuse yet enrich their thinking. Without emotions real understanding is impossible. Far from being irrelevant, emotions are a central part of the consent process.

Another concern for families was how much to share information and decisions with one another and with doctors. Families need information, as Stephen said, so that 'you know what to expect', which can greatly decrease fear and uncertainty. Information can be part of therapy because informed patients are found to be less anxious during treatment, and they recover more quickly and with fewer complications afterwards.[11] Information enables members of the family to prepare and support one another. They can share responsibility for final decisions, and 'consult' together, as Stephen's father said, so that they feel that they are moving together towards a chosen rather than an imposed future. Hospital treatment can be the subject of much strife in families, such as for the mother who said of her son, 'He hates me for bringing him back here.' Informed parents are better able to work with, rather than against, their child.

Informed parents, who are convinced that distressing treatment is worth trying, can encourage and persuade their child to co-operate. They are more likely to be able to discuss decisions as a family, and to 'finish up getting an answer which we all agree on'. Parents' information to the child reflects and depends on the quality of clear and convincing medical information given to them. Children also encourage and support their parents, as Stephen did, and often try to protect their parents by hiding their own distress. Information influences the level to which people feel voluntarily committed, able to go through fear and pain, and to cope with the times when patients like Stephen 'want them to leave me alone'.

Without some form of shared, informed commitment, families could endure severe problems before, during, and after treatment. An example was given by an intensive care sister.

This twenty-stone miner came charging into the unit furious with his ex-wife. She gave consent to a shunt operation and then at the last minute to repair on bypass without him knowing. She wasn't clear about the difference and the extra risk with the repair. The child died and now he's blaming her and contesting custody of their other children. He says she's not fit to care for them.

Even with low-risk operations, children die unexpectedly, or need weeks of intensive treatment. It is therefore important for every family to be reasonably warned, about the risks as well as the intended benefits of surgery.

Stephen's father thought that information has to be adapted to how much each person wants and needs to know. 'Some people possibly need *not* to be told.' He later mentioned Stephen's older sister as someone so frightened of medical information, that she might be unable to cope with a heart transplant. Starting to discuss high-risk surgery with patients and their families can be a way of helping them to decide whether they are suitable candidates. It can also give them the time, which Stephen and his mother needed, to change their mind and to come to accept new risks.

At first, decisions about surgery would seem to be based solely on physical realities: the child's condition and the best treatment. Yet the crucial factors are sometimes not physical but social: personal beliefs about the child's best interests. Choice is not always starkly between life and death, but between relative harm and benefit, such as deciding when very high-risk surgery is a reasonable choice because the child's life is so limited by ill health.

Parents spoke to me of their responsibility to share in medical decisions about treatment that might save life, or improve its quality, or perhaps wrongly prolong a miserable existence. For example, Linda's severe heart defects could be palliated but not cured. When Linda was seven her mother said:

The time will come, I think, when we will want to say 'enough is enough'. We are not prepared to put her through endless hopeless ops. We hope that she herself will be old enough to enter a certain amount into discussions of that kind.

Linda's mother qualifies the family's responsibility by saying:

As things stand at present, we have enough confidence in Dr A and his knowledge of Linda, his kindness and consideration to trust his advice and his reading of possible outcomes. He doesn't put children through unnecessary tests or treatments; they have to be essential. We trust him and this is, in my view, essential when thinking along these lines. We are fortunate. We have always felt that he sees Linda as a whole child in a family setting rather than just another interesting heart case.

When Linda's mother talks of the 'whole child', she implies that more than medical criteria are taken into account when deciding Linda's treatment. She also indicates that she sees medical decisions as being shared with the family and not imposed on them by adding:

Linda may feel that anything is worth a try. We will support her if this is the case. Who can tell how anyone will react in any situation until you are actually living in it?

Decisions about major surgery are based partly on subjective estimations of risk and benefit. Diane's parents understood that she had only a slight chance of surviving surgery. Yet they thought that the sooner Diane had her operation, the higher her chance of recovering would be, before her condition became worse.

She can't walk very far. She gets very blue and out of breath and then she'll collapse. And she started having these attacks where the big vein between the heart and the lung was closing up completely. They said if she didn't have the operation it could be fatal. She was having attacks at school and being sent home, so she was ending up in bed every day. And then she had to be pushed around in a push chair. She wants to be out with the other kids you know, so we thought, why not give her the chance.

Estimations of harm and benefit, besides being subjective, change over time, and so need to be seen in context. When Stephen was talking in 1985, heart transplants for adolescents were just beginning to save lives, and the media were full of dramatic stories about them. New techniques offer new choices. Even if eligible patients reject transplant surgery, they still cannot avoid the responsibility of choice, and the potential for joy or remorse which new technology brings. Stephen had the operation four months after the interview, and is now living a full, active life.

Observing families' experiences includes looking at their basic attitudes or theories and comparing these with the theories of consent 'experts'. At least five strongly contradictory theories about children's heart treatment, for example on harm and benefit, emerge.

1. Parents have mixed feelings, hoping for great benefits to their child, yet often being aware of the harms of risky and painful treatment, and of severe difficulties for the whole family due partly to the way hospital treatment is provided.
2. Doctors working in heart surgery units are usually convinced of the benefits of modern medicine and believe their work to be worth while. Yet they have reservations about the suffering involved, and agonize over which levels of risk can be justified.
3. The popular media celebrate 'heroic' heart surgeons and patients, as if heart surgery were simply a success story.
4. Critics of medicine perceive doctors as powerful and dangerous technocrats who deceive patients with unrealistic optimism.[12]
5. Some ethicists say that if only we can think clearly and dispassionately enough, we can weigh the benefits and harms of treatment in equations so logical that everyone will accept them.

Who is right? High-risk treatment of very ill children will always be contentious because in assessing harm and benefit so much depends on personal values. Each of the five views has valid aspects. Yet the complex views which hold opposing principles in tension (hope and doubt, success and failure, decision and uncertainty) rather than trying to split them apart are more perceptive. The closer adults are to caring for these children, the more likely are their theories to fit and illuminate the dilemmas.

Consent is about sharing knowledge and control over decisions. It reflects relations between the medical profession and society, as well as between individual doctors and patients. The public interest in organ transplantation, drug trials, prescribing contraceptives for minors, and the medical response to child abuse concerns how much licence society allows to doctors to decide what they believe to be best for their patients and for society generally. How much should doctors consult the patient or the parents? Informed consent is like a gateway to the future which opens or closes the medical profession's access to freedom of decision and action. It can enable society to regulate the pace of advancing medical knowledge, skill, and authority, advance which is gained through research and experiment that can harm as well as benefit patients.

This book has been written for everyone concerned with proxy consent: patients and parents, doctors and nurses, therapists and social workers, chaplains and lawyers, hospital managers, health authority members, and people concerned with patients' and children's interests. Many people affect the consent process, so that a new, broader approach to consent has practical implications for their work. Informed and voluntary proxy consent depends on the shared understanding of everyone concerned with the patient's care. I hope that this book will contribute towards that shared understanding.

2

Consent in the wards

The next four chapters illustrate the consent process with examples from the Brompton Hospital and the Hospital for Sick Children, Great Ormond Street, here called the Children's Hospital. This chapter starts with the families' experiences in the wards because many babies are admitted there first as emergencies. Less urgent surgery is usually discussed at the out-patient clinics, the subject of the next chapter. Chapter 4 explains the medical meetings when doctors assess each patient before surgery. Chapter 5 looks at the influence on consent of the many members of the hospital team.

Children with heart defects are cared for by paediatric cardiologists who are physicians. When a child needs surgery the care is shared with cardiac surgeons. There were only nine designated children's heart surgery units in England, and none in Wales in the mid-1980s, so that many children travel long distances for their treatment. Both hospitals also admit children from all over the world.

Parents' ability to give proxy consent is affected by the way wards are organized. This in turn is influenced by the attitudes and policies of the hospital staff. Parents need to be at the hospital and to be near their child, to be welcomed and encouraged, if they are to be reasonably informed and involved in decisions. However, barriers limit their access. Some barriers are unavoidable, such as families' relative ignorance of complex medical details. Others can be reduced or avoided, when attitudes and policies which exclude parents change. The hospital setting, the design and routines relate to the quality, amount, and content of discussion preceding consent. The key to involving families is the belief that it is possible, and beneficial to children, to involve parents in child-care and decision-making, and therefore that efforts to do so are worth while.

Access
Salimah's parents talked about visible and invisible barriers that separated them from their baby.

Father: When she was two days old she was suddenly transferred here [the Children's Hospital]. A policeman came to the door at 2 a.m. to tell me. There was no transport. In the end I ran to our local hospital. They told me she had no left side to her heart. It was probably hopeless.

Mother: I don't think they should have said that to us. It wasn't true anyway. They woke me up and said there was something wrong with my daughter. Then they gave me a shot of valium. For the next few days I was living in a world of my own. I didn't understand what had happened to her, or anything. I wish they hadn't done that. I'd like to have come with her. I wish they had a maternity unit here, they have so many little babies.

When I came in to see her, I only had a glimpse. I nearly fainted. I was told I shouldn't have come because I might haemorrhage as I was so upset. I went into a waiting-room and cried, then I went home. I was in a filthy mood, so angry.

Access to the hospital

Many seriously ill patients are referred from their local hospital to a specialist centre. In the few centres treating many patients, high levels of skill and expertise can develop, allowing patients much higher chances of a good recovery. Yet the medical advantages carry serious social disadvantages.

Some new-born babies travel a hundred miles or more to a specialist hospital. Parents' shock is intensified by the news that the baby has already been sent away, or by following a speeding ambulance by car to a little known city. Inner city hospitals often have little or no parking space for visitors. Parents telling me of their discussion with doctors about proposed surgery would say: 'I was too worried about the parking meter/my car being clamped/missing the train home in time to collect my other child/to be able to concentrate.' Their average return journey from home to the children's heart units takes four hours.[1] The travelling is stressful and costly and poor families receive little or no state help. Travel problems can prevent parents from being with their child, and they severely distract the attention of others from medical discussions, thereby restricting their involvement in the consent process.

Many authorities influence the process of consent. Government policy affects the resources available for each patient. Parents can only properly consent if they are present, and for thirty years, British government policy has been to encourage parents to stay in the hospital and to care for their child as much as possible.[2] However, when funding new hospitals, the government does not allow for space for a relative to stay with each child. Hard-pressed inner city councils may not be able to provide social services support, buses, or car parking space. Hospital managers decide whether to provide space for parents to stay, and leaflets informing them about access. Nurse managers support policies which encourage or restrict parents' access. All these authorities affect daily work in the wards and clinics, and they help to open or close gateways in the consent process.

Accommodation

Conscious adult patients have some control over medical interventions because inevitably they are present, and usually able to state their needs. Proxies cannot do this for the patient if they are absent. Accommodation is the second main barrier that excludes parents from the hospital. Many parents repeated to me, 'The single most important thing is that I can stay with my child.' Some nurse managers, even in cramped hospitals, believe that family-centred care is so important that they make space for families to stay, but this does not yet happen everywhere.

Much neonatal surgery is carried out in hospitals with no maternity unit. New mothers usually want to be transferred with their baby, and they need to have meals and rest space quite near the baby's room. By law, a midwife must visit new mothers on each of the first ten days after the birth. A Brompton Hospital sister told me that she spent hours trying to arrange for a community midwife to visit resident mothers, and months negotiating to provide a quiet breastfeeding room, and other amenities. Only those who strongly believe in the value of family-centred care for child patients persist in trying to adapt hospitals to accommodate families.

'Accommodation' includes the amenities that make daily life tolerable—a bed, food, bath/shower, toilets, rest areas, somewhere to wash and dry clothing. Many parents were highly anxious about these, not knowing where they might spend the night and living on snacks because they could not afford canteen food. One in five British children live in families near or below the poverty line; their parents cannot meet ordinary daily expenses, far less the many extra costs of having a child in hospital.[3] A few parents, already under great stress, could not stand the extra, avoidable strains, and went home.

The staff were kind, but some routines contradicted their welcoming words. In the Children's Hospital, the mother of a two-day-old baby said:

The surgeon brought us tea and made sure I was reclining comfortably. He talked to us for a long time and impressed on us that caring for the baby meant caring for the parents too. We felt very grateful . . . We understood that we couldn't go in the pump room so I decided to stay at home.

The pump room was a crowded room for the most intensively nursed patients. Parents would stand in the corridor looking through the window. The next room was very large, but was left empty for months, and then converted into offices. Lack of space gives silent messages that parents are unwelcome or unnecessary.

While usually the mother stayed in a hospital room for parents, fathers stayed in hotels if they could afford it, or else at home. They found separation during the crisis of surgery a great extra strain. 'We need to be together most of all at a time like this. That would help us to cope. Having to be apart makes everything far worse.' Misunderstandings, blame, and guilt easily arose. Joint consent was a luxury some parents couldn't afford, as it was impossible to explain complicated surgery on a coin box telephone in a noisy public area.

Many parents were concerned about the mismatch between excellent medical care and poor social conditions which increased stress when they could least cope with it. They were reluctant to criticize matters which seemed trivial yet which affected them severely.

The medical care is fantastic. They explain every little thing to us. They've saved my lad's life, what more could you want? But I hate the hospital. It's stupid little things missing. There aren't enough bathrooms, and no toilets on this level. We have to go downstairs and I dread that at night. The phones don't work and I'm running up a fortune in reversed charge calls to Norfolk. All sorts of things are missing you take for granted, and it makes you very uncomfortable and anxious.

Local hospitals have formal channels to convey patients' views, through district health authorities and community health councils. Criticisms can be voiced in local newspapers and shown to be constructive, such as when an appeal is launched for funds to improve the hospital car park. Special hospitals like the two described here, admitting patients from a vast area, do not have this dialogue with a local community. Medical excellence is emphasized, but amenities may be below average. This can imply that discomfort is unimportant, or a small price to pay for the patient's recovery. The

Children's Hospital cardiac social worker's post was frozen for many months; a third surgeon was appointed, but with no increase in social support.[4] One father, a film camera man, commented:

All the TV documentaries about this place don't put it into perspective. They just select the quirky things, the expertise and know-how. I feel angry that the level of care people need is devalued. Some of the nurses build bridges, a hand on the shoulder, right words at the right time. Like nurse Stephanie who sat and cried with a mother. You can't measure that.

He praised the care which he thought was given almost despite the authorities. Medical and social care cannot be separated, both are concerned with basic needs.

Adequate accommodation for parents helps them to give adequate support to their child. When parents are part of the paediatric team, they help to give essential nursing care, so benefiting the child, the hospital, and other patients. A consultant with experience of family-centred care in Africa started to have parents staying in his English infectious disease unit.[5] The staff protested that there was no room. However, children were sent home twice as quickly, because they recovered earlier under their parents' care, and parents also learned how to nurse them at home. Half the patients' beds were left empty and the parents stayed in these.

To 'accommodate' literally means to measure or fit with. It involves making space for people and is closely linked to consent. If the hospital team make physical space for families they are likely also to allow them mental space. When they see the benefits of involving parents in practical care, they are likely to involve them also in planning treatment, and to respect psychosocial as well as medical needs when making decisions. Through being practically involved, parents can learn and contribute. The quality and content of discussions between doctors and families during the consent process changes.

Doctors and nurses work very hard to achieve high standards of care in partnership with families. They usually have far too many tasks to fit into the long, intensive hours. Nurses work with few breaks, covering for missing colleagues because of the serious shortage of skilled nurses which puts extra strain on those who remained. They generously give far more than basic care. For example, Nurse Jackie worked from 7 a.m., caring for Naomi who was waiting for her operation. At 3 p.m. the operation was cancelled because there was no nurse for the intensive post-surgery care cot. Jackie offered to work straight on through the late evening shift so that Naomi could have her operation. After Brian died, nurses and parents made a collection for his mother who had no money for the fare home.

Examples of how the staff were not able to do as much as they wanted are not made as criticisms of them. The policies and routines which distressed families, also inconvenienced the staff. When avoidable barriers are reduced, families and staff both benefit. Since there are so many unavoidable stresses in paediatric cardiology, reducing avoidable ones is all the more important for all concerned.

Access to the child

Each hospital had an intensive care unit (ICU) and a ward for children not needing intensive nursing. In the Children's Hospital ICU, there were no formal restrictions, but parents tended to stay in a small sitting-room just outside the unit. There were unofficial and invisible barriers.

Parents had to wear white gowns, although these have been shown to be useless as infection barriers,[6] and are no longer used in many units. Communal gowns seemed likely to encourage rather than reduce cross-infection and worried some parents, who told me, 'They make you feel that you are too germy.' 'They are hot and get in the way when you want to cuddle your baby.' The nurses often seemed too busy and tense to talk. 'You feel frozen out by their attitude in there.' Student nurses were afraid of inviting questions which they could not answer; qualified nurses had a heavy workload of intensive nursing care and of supporting untrained staff. The playworker, in some ways the parents' main helper, also discouraged access. When we first met she told me:

When their child's on the ventilator and doesn't need them, parents stay all the time. When their child really needs them, they're out shopping. They're not allowed to sit in the pump room. There's no space if a nurse has to pounce on the kid straightaway. It's harder to read the machines. The consultants don't really like it. And it's awkward if parents are there and something happens.

In contrast the Brompton ICU had formal barriers restricting parents' access to their child. They had to ring an intercom to ask to enter, and (at the time although less so now) were sent out during medical rounds, X-rays, physiotherapy, and emergencies. 'You seem to spend so much time hanging about in that little waiting-room', was a frequent comment. Yet once they were in the unit, parents felt welcomed and encouraged to stay.

The nursing staff see our child as an individual. They have a very caring attitude. They're very flexible, no matter what you ask. There isn't this cut-off thing—'No I can't help you.' They're very accommodating.

Parents spent far more time in the Brompton ICU. It was spacious and there were no student nurses, so that the team was more relaxed and confident. They worked together in open-plan areas, instead of being isolated in tiny rooms as in the other ICU. The parents found that, far more important than formal, visible barriers, were the invisible attitudes of welcome or non-welcome, especially of the nurses.

Attitudes in intensive care

Parents described the tension which seemed to drive them out of the first ICU.

Of course it's tense in there, that's why it's called intensive care. We can't do anything for her, she's completely in other people's hands and the days are very long. I'd like to stay in there and come out every thirty minutes for a fag for two minutes. But this is the wrong way round. We stay in this waiting-room in no man's land.

Everyday I'm used to *dealing* with problems at work. Here you feel totally inadequate towards your child, helpless, just *waiting* for the next step.

Parents had low expectations of their own ability to help their child. Without encouraging support they were liable to remain in their initial shocked state.

I still haven't come to terms with the awful shock of seeing him in ICU. I feel that it's a dead body, plumbed into everything, immobile. I don't think you can become involved. There's nothing you can do you're just blocking up the way.

I'd just be in the way. Things often go wrong and that would make me panic. I'd rather not be there when they're rushing around. So I go to her for five minutes every hour but I don't want to leave the hospital. But if I sat with her, I'd get hypnotized by those heart beat machines, neurotic about them.

They're very good at explaining. If you don't ask, they'll think you don't want to know. But when you're upset it goes in one ear and—you can't take it in. The pump room's got the most up to date equipment, marvellous machines, but you don't like to go around searching for a chair, so you say, 'Oh, excuse me', and you leave. There's no room for you. That adds to the tension and the trauma.

Attitudes and behaviour interact. When nurses have low expectations of parents, parents have low expectations of themselves, reinforced through their own helplessness. They stay away and so miss opportunities to learn, to help, and to be present when treatment is discussed.

In the Brompton ICU, where there were only trained nurses, parents were more confident. Very few remained so disturbed that they stayed outside. 'We can stay as long as we like, except for the rounds.' 'I'm sure it is very important for him that I'm sitting here, stroking him and going through it with him.' Their confidence was warmly encouraged by the nurses. 'The nurses are very loving and caring.' 'The nurses were excellent in every way, very informative and polite, I was very pleased and impressed with them all.' 'They are wonderful, so busy but they help you all they can.'

The nurses' confidence, in themselves and in the parents, with their support enabled parents to cope with their initial fears. Sitting with 'their' nurse most of the day helped them to learn and to share in giving nursing care.

Sharing child-care

Consent to surgery involves consent to many nursing and medical procedures. Instead of giving blanket consent in advance, parents can help children more effectively by sharing in smaller daily interim decisions, if they can be present. Nurses give much information about details of care, and they are important mediators in helping parents by talking to doctors on their behalf, and in arranging for doctors to talk with parents.

Families are confused about differences between physicians (cardiologists, paediatricians, anaesthetists) and surgeons. In one unit postoperative intensive care was supervised mainly by surgeons, in the other by physicians, and in some hospitals intensivists are beginning to do this. Families need to know who is responsible for which aspects of care and information. This can be outlined in admission leaflets, or on a wall chart with named photographs of the staff.

The practical involvement of parents relates to their invisible involvement in the consent process. Their involvement in the two

ICUs and the two wards varied. From many possible examples, only parents' access to the kitchen and to the child at night, will be discussed. One mother commented:

When I trained as a nurse eleven years ago, the nurses did everything for the children. But now I am here as a mother, there are far fewer nurses and I find the mothers are expected to do almost everything. I think this is right, but we cannot care for the children properly if we are not shown where things are kept, or not allowed into the kitchen, or to stay with them at night.

Kitchens

The Children's Hospital ICU had a notice forbidding parents to use the kitchen as there was 'no room' for them. In contrast, the sister in the ward welcomed parents. She talked to me while sitting on a bean sack with eight-year-old Susan on her knee.

Sister: Sometimes, if the supper trolley comes up and there are crowds of people in the kitchen I say [*mock anguish*] 'Please, everyone out! I can't move.'

Susan: [*In pretended outrage*] You can't say that!

Sister: You have to be jokey and have a good rapport and not make serious rules. But we're small here, we're lucky. . . . The parents love helping. . . . People are so rarely aggressive here, only if they are under great pressure. They accept all sorts of things being done to their child. Perhaps they don't question enough unless you force them to question.

Families appreciated this attitude. A mother said, 'You get this family feeling every time you come back to this ward.'

In the Brompton Hospital parents could not use the ward kitchen (although this changed later). Confident mothers, such as this well-known actress, spoke in childlike terms.

I never know whether I'm supposed to ask a nurse for her feed or go in there and fetch it. Sometimes I slip in and hope no one is looking.

Jason's operation was cancelled three times. The sister said to me, 'His mother's very angry and she won't talk to us.' Jason's mother complained that she could not make a cup of tea, but was willing to talk after I had made her some tea.

I felt so let down. I want it over and done with so we can get back to reality. You're sort of in limbo. It's dragging on and on. He keeps missing meals in case he can go down [for surgery]. They've lost his dummy and he won't sleep without it. He just screams because they leave him alone in here. [The other cots in the room were empty.] His dad and I and the two boys all sleep in one room at home. He doesn't like being on his own. We want to get back home don't we, Jason?

This is a good hospital but it's disorganized. The nurses are very good and all that to the kids, but I wish I could stay here. But they make you pay if you stay, and they'd only send me away [to parents' flats outside the hospital]. What's the point of that? He needs me with him. I'll have spent £80 this week—fares and minicabs. I have to pay a neighbour to look after my daughter. We haven't a phone and if I'm late back she gets panicky, she thinks Jason must be very ill. My husband's taken unpaid leave to be here when Jason goes down, then they cancel it. You're geared up all day for it, then you have to get all geared up again. We're waiting now, but I don't suppose they'll do it today. It'll be difficult to get them back into the little routines at home again when they've been upset.

Hospitals are so stressful that families and professionals expend much energy in managing anxiety.[7] Parents' anxiety may be seen as colouring their attitude towards everything, so that they over-react to unimportant matters such as family disruption. This view is partly true. Under stress, people often react more emotionally than normally. However, this view devalues parents, if it assumes that matters which they think are serious are unimportant, or that they are not really worried directly about them, but are projecting worries about surgery on to smaller matters.

Jason's mother was worried about the specific and, for her, most crucial matter: the welfare of her children. She avoided talking to the nurses because she was angry, not with them, but with major and minor details in the hospital system. She sat all day in a hot, dry ward, exhausted from worry and from trying to pacify Jason and his baby brother. Jason was upset if she went away to the canteen, but she needed an occasional drink to enable her to cope. All the inconveniences expressed two distressing messages: the large hospital machinery was indifferent to the convenience of individual patients and their families; parents were treated as children, expected to be seen but not heard. His mother knew the kind of care Jason needed but she was prevented from providing it. Her responsibility had been taken away, and substituted by hospital care which she thought inadequate.

Jason's mother was implicitly talking about inequality between professionals and parents, coercion and respect, which are central issues in informed consent. If there is such inequality in 'trivial' matters, what kind of equality can parents expect in major matters of deciding treatment? If parents feel that they cannot question a rule banning them from the kitchen, how can they question a surgeon's decision? When parents' dignity is disregarded, it is harder for them to assert any right to be involved in medical discussions. They look and feel inferior, and cannot contribute on equal terms. The social context influences the quality and content of discussions during the consent process.

Night care

The Children's Hospital opened a house for parents to stay. This was greatly appreciated by some parents, yet many parents and children[8] supported by many nurses[9] wanted something much cheaper and simpler—for parents to be able to stay with their children at night. Jamie's mother was told to leave him.

I went back later in the evening and found he was so worked up they had to give him a sedative. He's six months and he's terrible, so clingy. They said they'd call me if he got upset. I thought, there's no reason to let him get upset! As soon as he woke I could have got him to sleep, and there's no way I'll leave him now. By midnight I burst into tears and said, 'Please don't make me leave him.' The nurse said she'd get into trouble if I stayed, but she sat talking with me for two and a half hours explaining all about his operation and all the tubes. I thought it was marvellous. Then she let me stay in his room on a bean sack.

I know it's a fire risk [this was one reason given for not having parents in at night] but Jamie would have been safer with me there to carry him out. I wouldn't have done anything to get that nurse into trouble, but she got a speaking to. And afterwards she said that she told the nursing officer that she goes for the psychological effects on the mother as well as the baby if they are separated. I thought, good for you. What's the point of getting us upset? She said if she had half a chance she'd have mothers staying on the ward.

Senior staff, who were remote from families, resisted pressure for change. A nursing officer told me:

Parents leave the place looking like a pigsty. I've had to throw out a lot of those folding beds we were given for them. I am not having them staying on the ward over night and that is final.

Many children needed a parent to stay within calling distance (as they would do at home). Others were happy if parents stayed somewhere near the hospital. Accommodation officers in both hospitals were worried about inadequacies. One told me that she had drawn up detailed plans.

We need a dormitory for fathers. But it came to nothing. The administrators wanted the rooms for offices. They don't understand the need. Some fathers sleep in cars. Others are paying £36 a night for bed and breakfast, and living on snacks in order to manage. People are terrified of being in London and walking at night from the flats. . . . If the child is very ill they need to stay together. Ten double rooms could take care of the problems. I have to juggle and switch people around. It's a desperate situation. If they knew the despair I see . . . I wish we could be more flexible.

Non-resident parents have extra difficulties because, in being sometimes absent, they are seen by staff as having a less integral part in caring for the child. 'You have to watch out all the time,' said one father, 'or you turn round and find they've done an injection or taken him to X ray.' At one nurses' meeting, it was implied that parents had less right to question medical decisions about a child who was mainly cared for by the hospital staff. Talking of a baby who had lingered for weeks in the unit, the nurses debated whether, in the parents' position, they would have consented to almost certainly fatal surgery. Some said that the baby would have died anyway, and at least knowledge gained from her operation might benefit future children. One nurse said of the parents, 'She was their baby, but who cared for her? We did. She'd never been home. They knew they owed a heck of a lot to the hospital.'

Parents want to stay because even if their children can make requests, they may not be understood or heard. Children become more frightened and bewildered than adult patients. Parents want to ask if an injection is necessary, or if an X-ray can be delayed while it is explained and the child is prepared, or that a child be allowed time to recover from some other upset before an X-ray is taken. Parents explain the child's needs to the staff and the staff's actions to the child.

Parents are also necessary mediators between the immature patient and the potentially overwhelming contact with a range of strangers. They filter and partly control experiences, helping the child to cope.[10] One mother wanted to stay overnight because her eight-year-old was on a drip, and was upset that she could not get to the toilet in time when the nurses did not hear her calling for help. A thirteen-year-old told me how for years she had had to notice her heartbeats to guard against over-exertion. After her operation she listened to all the bleeping heart monitors worrying that any one would stop. Like many children she was frightened at first when moved out of ICU and the full-time care of one nurse to the short-staffed ward, with two night nurses for twenty-four children. She was afraid to go to sleep unless her mother was there because she had started having irregular heart rhythms and was waiting for a pacemaker. The mothers were not being overprotective; they knew how much stress their child could cope with during admission and their main concern was to help to prevent avoidable distress.

Uncertainty about being 'allowed' to stay with their child was one aspect of the way the imbalance of medical to lay knowledge was reinforced by the parents' low status. Junior nurses were unhappy about this. They wanted to work in family-centred children's wards, and were distressed at having to make parents leave. They were not attracted to stay.[11] Half the children's nurses left one unit during 1986 (for many reasons including conditions of work); the other unit was even more short-staffed and at times had to refuse all emergency cases.

Parents now share in caring for their chid in hospital far more than in previous decades. Yet doing tasks is only a step towards sharing in decisions about medical care, or even about parenting care. Voluntariness and unwillingness in proxy consent to surgery are elusive qualities to observe. They are partly indicated by parents' estimates of how much they are respected, involved in making decisions, or excluded. The important but often invisible medical ethics issue of respect for autonomy may be indicated by the visible respect with which individual families are treated and the flexible ways in which parents are able to respond to their child's needs.

Operation routines

Consent to surgery involves consent to a series of events of mixed harm and benefit. If parents are unhappy about their child's treatment they have to decide whether their criticisms are justified and, if so, whether they can or should intervene. From the medical or philosophical view the following details may seem irrelevant to informed consent (since they are so rarely discussed in the consent literature). From the parents' view they are crucially important because proxy consent is about delegating responsibility for care.

At a time when parents most want to act responsibly, many feel at their most weak and vulnerable. They spoke of their sadness, frustration, and anger at being trapped into routines which they thought were partly unnecessary. Consent to surgery involves relinquishing personal control over time, resources, and routines which deeply affect the whole family. Utilitarian and scientific principles of efficiency separate public work and private family life; yet this disconnection is at the root of many families' difficulties.

Parents wanted to trust in the goodwill and efficiency of the staff. Operations were frequently postponed and the parents knew that delays were often complicated for medical reasons. Surgeons planned the operating lists to allow for last-minute changes, and for the length and urgency of operations. Instead of hoping that they could talk on equal terms with the staff, parents tended to sound uncertain and helplessly dependent.

Mother: I don't think we've been treated badly at all, but we came in nine days ago on Sunday expecting the shunt. Then they said they were toying with the idea of doing a catheter on Wednesday. Then it was going to be Friday but some emergencies came in. So on Thursday evening they said it would be next Tuesday. I've seen people come in and go to theatre and we're still sitting here.

I feel we've been put off because it's just a shunt. I don't know whether a shunt is vital. Well I know it's vital to us, but compared to what the others have done, is it important? They seem to keep saying to us 'Tuesday, hopefully', 'Friday hopefully'. I know he isn't desperately ill and urgent, but I mean how long can you go on a 'hopefully'?

I get terrifically geared up for it each time, and then to let the tension go again, to be repeated the next day, which—I'm—I'm finding very difficult. It makes you wonder, how much do they care about him? They are very understanding. The sister, I asked her, 'Am I being unreasonable?' She said, 'No, you're not.'

PA: Unreasonable?

Mother: Well, because I was in despair when they were going to cancel again. They said the only hope was if this little boy had a temperature and the worst of all was he was a private patient. I asked if he was going first because of that. They just shrugged. It makes you very bitter.

Children were starved before or after procedures. One nurse said, 'It's all right for the doctors. They just say, "starve for eight hours". We have to do it.' Rituals before surgery distanced parents from their child. A mother sitting beside the cot in which her baby had been screaming for a long time, said to me, 'I don't think I'm supposed to pick him up, because he's all clean ready for theatre.' Although she felt unable to help him, she also felt unable to leave him for what might be their last time together. Parents avoided asking busy nurses what they were allowed to do.

Means and ends

Consent involves agreement with a proposed end (improved health) and the means towards it (treatment). Having made this commitment, some families seemed almost to be blown off course by the tortuous means. Brian aged eighteen months stayed in the under-fives' room, where children demanded almost constant attention. They struggled to get down on to the floor, the normal play place at that age, but the room was too crowded. It was often noisy with crying, talking, shouting, and the horrible sound of children being 'sucked out' by physiotherapists. My interview tapes from that room had so much background noise that they illustrated the problems of trying to concentrate on informed discussions about surgery.

Brian's mother told me:

They've got to patch up two holes and a couple of valves have got to be enlarged I think. They've cancelled the operation twice and I want to get home. My two other boys are rather clingy. We're not on the phone so I send them postcards. My boyfriend's looking after them. I didn't want them put into care. I'll have to draw some more benefit soon because he hasn't got any money or a job. I don't know what I'll do if we have to stay longer than two weeks. My landlord said he wouldn't notice my friend staying there, in case they stop my benefit. . . . Seeing them laying there asleep, they look so innocent and comfortable. You feel funny inside. The longer you wait, the harder it seems to be. All you can do is sit and hold his hand. You never know what's going to happen next.

Supplementary benefit (SB) could only be drawn at the home post office and if left more than two weeks would be withheld. If single mothers on SB were shown to be cohabiting, SB was withdrawn. If mothers were then without an income or a home, their children were taken into care. In order to keep her children out of care and to be with Brian in hospital, his mother therefore risked losing her income and children, and the hospital delays much increased this risk.

Brian awoke hungry and irritable and having to be starved for the operation which was later cancelled again. With nothing to do he wriggled and worried his mother and then bit her. Already extremely fraught, she bit him back 'to teach you that hurts' and he began to scream.

That evening she was walking around with him because, having been asleep after the pre-med for much of the day, he was now waking up. She said that he screamed if left and she would have to miss supper. She seemed exhausted so I offered to look after Brian and enjoyed holding the warm little boy. Next day, Brian died during his operation. His mother's memories of their last days together were not likely to ease her grief. Consenting to high-risk surgery for their child is arguably one of the most difficult times parents can experience. Much of the strain comes from trying to appear calm in order to reassure the child, feeling helpless and longing to be active. As one father said:

Your whole body is pumping adrenalin around—ready for action to protect your child—and there is nothing to do. You feel so helpless. Yet anything you can do is precious to you, to help you to calm down and stop feeling so useless.

Hospital routines increased tension. Families would travel early on peak fares, but then wait for hours before being seen in wards or clinics. Not knowing when they might be called, they did not know when to take a hungry child to the snack bar, or when to feed a parking meter. Children spent days in hospital, or weeks at home waiting for postponed operations. Sometimes, parents took unpaid leave from work two or three times before the operation was actually carried out. A father missed two weeks of contract work and paid twice to fly over from Ireland. Parents needed the support of friendly staff and clear plans, but some felt isolated and many felt uncertain when the means and ends of surgery were so unpredictable.

Taking leave

Consent involves informing people so that they can make informed choices and remain as far as possible in control over their own life. Just before the child was taken to theatre, there was often an uneasy transition from the parents' care to institutional routines. Diane's parents whispered to me so as not to waken her, 'It's only a five per cent chance of her making it.' She was asleep when the trolley arrived.

Nurse: You won't get any porters, there's a union meeting I'm afraid.
Mother: Can we come with her?
Nurse: Oh well, you can come to the lift but there's no point really because she's asleep.

Her mother kissed Diane and asked her father if he wanted to say goodbye, but there were too many people round the bed. She went a few steps and then suddenly walked away crying. The bed crashed against the doors, waking Diane who stared around her. Taking leave was just one of the events for which parents wanted to be prepared so that they could know what to do. Many said that afterwards they wished that they had known better how to manage this important time.

One mother, who had been a theatre sister, wanted to stay until her twenty-month-old child was unconscious.

Basically it's not done here and different people came with reasons why I shouldn't go [to the anaesthetic room]. They said the gases might induce labour because I'm pregnant. And there is no privacy, I would be able to see into the theatre. And that I shouldn't go into the sterile area. I just stayed with her. She was not upset and she was conscious although they had told me she would be asleep. The consultant anaesthetist came out and said I could go in so I just changed into some overalls and I could actually hold her while she went to sleep. He was very good but I felt the nurses were pretty hostile. I held her till he put the mask on. She cried but—I felt it was a lot less traumatic for her. And I felt a lot better about it, because even if it is only a short wait there, they see so many faces come and go and their perceptions are altered by the drug they've had. So I felt it was just not done to leave her.

I felt better while she was in theatre. I knew I had done everything I could to reduce her fears, and I think in the end she will have suffered less trauma when she comes out of here. The child needs someone familiar until they are asleep and they haven't time to get to know the ward nurses. Anyway I don't think the nurses stay down there long enough. I think some mothers don't realize that the child may have to wait a long time and can get really scared and frightened down there. It is very important to get the child to sleep as peacefully as possible and only someone they know and trust can do that. If I hadn't been able to go I would have felt very angry with the system and that would have undermined my confidence.

Most parents wanted to stay with their child for longer than they were encouraged or allowed to.[12] At the Brompton Hospital, the child could have a parent in the anaesthetic room if families knew to ask in advance. Knowing that other parents went, some assumed that they need not ask and were very distressed when prevented at the last moment from going together. Children now routinely go to the anaesthetic room with a parent at the Brompton Hospital, but not (in 1989) at the Children's Hospital.

Delay

When surgery was delayed, an added anxiety was that this might harm the child. Tamara's mother told me:

They say all her blood is going round the wrong way and it's been roughing up all her tubes for four months. They don't know how much damage it's done, but it gets worse, and eventually . . . they . . . without the operation she'd have a matter of weeks. She's got a one in six chance of surviving the operation—but she's got to have it. Dr A said . . . 'I can't give you, not an *exact* success rate because we've never done it on such a small baby.' They don't know how she'll be later on—because basically it's all down to how much damage they find wrong with her when they open her up, how long she's got to live.

Tamara's parents knew that the operation was urgent in order to prevent further deterioration, and to improve Tamara's short and long-term chances of survival. They also wanted to end the suspense. Surgery was postponed again, a week later. They told me that they were uncertain whether they ought to 'make a fuss', feeling torn between 'being a nuisance' and 'letting Tamara down'. They seemed to be intimidated by impersonal routines, and uncertain about where to turn for help.

The Brompton Hospital ward sister had to carry out, but could seldom influence, the routines. She thought her job was 'just endless hassle', administrative rather than nursing, with little time to talk with families. She was continually being asked to find more bed-space, transport, nurses, and time than were actually available. To defend herself from the disappointment or anger of parents and staff about the inadequate resources, she tended to be abrupt and distant and to stay in her office. Families and nurses missed having someone to support them. Nurses became very unhappy about distressed families, and were frustrated with the barriers between nurses and families. For instance ward nurses told me:

The children get terribly bored and difficult to handle. They need a teacher here. I set up a game of table football but as soon as we started I was sent to clean cupboards.

You never have time to get to know families, you feel cut off from them, because you're always being moved to other patients. But it is nice if you can have a few days in one room. Then the parents really start to talk to you, not just as if you're a nurse, but as if you're their friend.

The Children's Hospital ward was much smaller and more informal, and nurses there worked with a teacher and trained playworker. They were able to offer more support to families, but they were still constrained by rules imposed from outside the ward, such as for parents' accommodation as mentioned earlier.

Cardiac catheterization

Besides surgery, a major procedure for which parents sign a consent form is cardiac catheterization. The catheter, a narrow tube, is inserted through a vein or artery, usually in the groin, and up into the heart. The purpose is to measure pressures in the heart, take blood samples, and inject X-ray opaque dye which shows up the heart and blood vessels on X-ray films. Treatment can also be carried out. A tiny blade or balloon in the catheter tip can cut or tear tissue, to ease or redirect the flow of blood. This method saves the child from having to undergo open-heart surgery.

Catheterizations usually take about an hour or longer and are performed in a darkened laboratory, rather like a small operating theatre. The child stays in hospital for two days. Families are very fully informed using books of photographs made in the wards showing each stage of the catheterization. Children as young as two years old are interested in the books. At the Brompton Hospital, children have a general anaesthetic and so, for them, the procedure is like a surgical operation without the major after-effects.

At the Children's Hospital, children are usually sedated. A nurse stays with each child, sitting at the head of the couch on to which the child is strapped. Many children are very drowsy or asleep; some are aware, and sometimes very frightened. Several parents at this hospital said that catheterization was the event their child most feared. Some parents were convinced that their conscious child needed their support at this time, and asked to be allowed to stay during the procedure. This is allowed very occasionally, and one mother said,

I always prefer to stay with Jeremy during procedures. I find the reality easier to cope with than what I might imagine. Jeremy stayed awake during his last catheter when he was seven, but this time he was out like a light. I don't know whether that was because I was there.

I was absolutely fascinated. I tried to keep out of the way and be inconspicuous. I sat by his head and the nurse pointed out the pressure readings and how they compared with the normal pressures. That bucked me up more than anything, to see that they were so much nearer to normal than I had expected. Maybe she pointed out the numbers because they were so normal, especially in his right ventricle, and she would not have done so if she thought I would have been worried.

Parents were very carefully selected, but I think it would be better to leave parents to choose for themselves. They know whether they can cope. Several said to me, 'Ooh I couldn't go down there', but I was very glad that I was able to go with Jeremy.

Cardiac catheterization is just one example of borderlines between parental and professional responsibility. When the child may remain conscious and need the parent's reassurance, old traditions barring parents' access can begin to be questioned. Changes have slowly evolved over many years. When one ward began to allow mothers to stay overnight, the sister selected the ones whom she thought would cope best. A research study in the ward showed that mothers did not all fit the sister's predictions,[13] and supports Jeremy's mother's point that selection is better made by the parents themselves, encouraged by the nurses.

Consent

The consent form

For parents, signing the form is a crucial symbol of their responsibility for surgical decisions. Some also see it as a chance of insisting on obtaining answers from evasive doctors. Some doctors take the consent form very seriously. For others, signing the form is a chore, often left to a surgical junior, who might know very little about specialized surgery, to do in the evenings when senior doctors are not easily available.

The form as a legal document is worthless in itself, and does not prove that consent is informed. A recent study found forty per cent of patients who had signed a consent form had very little idea of what they had consented to.[14] No court would be satisfied that the form is evidence that consent was informed. Yet it is an essential part of legal evidence if required. So legally, signing the form is an empty formality, unless preceded by reasonable discussion.

Doctors tend to arrive with the form at any time. One parent might be absent, while the other signs, and finds that the busy doctor hurries away before there is time for the discussion they had hoped for. The consent form states that the doctor who also signs the form has explained 'the nature, purpose, and effect' of the operation.

In a not unusual example at the Brompton Hospital, the new house officer (SHO) assured Briony's parents that her operation,[15] a high-risk correction, was very complex, and their child's consultants were among the very few people in the world to understand it thoroughly. In the darkened babies' room there were no spare chairs to enable adults to sit and talk together with dignity, and hardly enough light to read the form. Briony's mother was sitting on her husband's knee. The SHO briefly stood near them, then left them to sign the form, returning later to collect it. He informed me that it was crucial that parents did not lose their faith in surgery, and that sociologists were a dangerous influence, creating mistrust. He seemed to assume that parents needed reassurance about the excellence of the unit and that information would merely arouse anxiety. However, he was in a very difficult position, being reluctant to admit his ignorance because this might undermine the parents' and his own confidence.

The surgical senior registrar (SR) agreed that I might observe the consent signing for Maria, a baby from Portugal. At the time, a new switch operation for transposition of the great arteries was cautiously being accepted as the preferred method in carefully selected cases and was offered in a very few hospitals. Although the switch had a higher early mortality, it was hoped that long-term results would be better than those for the older methods. As in Briony's case, this was controversial surgery with a background of medical uncertainty and choice. That morning a medical meeting had decided that Maria had extra complications and therefore should not have a switch.

We stood in the corridor next to workmen using loud electric drills with people walking past the ladders and a nurse trying to manœuvre a weighing machine around us.

SR: Well, you know her arteries are the wrong way round?
M: Yes.
SR: And the blue blood goes—and the red blood goes—[*waving his hands*]. By putting a joint up here [*waves*] that is what we are going to do. Okay? So if you'll sign this form. My name is Mr——.
F: [*Murmurs to his wife.*]
M: Is it a Mustard's?
SR: Yes.
M: Not a Senning?
SR: No—well there's no difference between the two really.
M: [*Talks with the father.*] She can't have a switch?

SR: Well no, the left side is too . . .

M: And she would have to have had it earlier?

SR: Yes.

M: The surgeon said the risk was higher.

SR: Yes

[*By looks and murmurs the parents convey a sense of the switch being their preferred solution although regrettably not possible, and they sign the form.*]

Some surgeons' faith in the benefits of their work could lead them to behave as if signing the form was an empty and unnecessary formality, and not the best use of their time. Both doctors knew that I was studying informed consent and so presumably considered that their methods were appropriate.

This was in contrast to the care which other doctors took to sit down and explain, and to answer questions fully. Great care was taken to inform many families. Robert's mother described signing the consent form when he was five years old.

Robert was in the play room with his two brothers. Obviously, this had been carefully organized for when the doctor came to talk to us. We sat in the doctors' office, and the senior registrar went through everything that the consultant had told us before. My overwhelming feeling was that we had no choice. He was pretty blue and we didn't feel we were being pushed into it. We'd known since he was born that they planned to operate when he was seven. He'd grown so well that they decided to do it when he was five.

The senior registrar invited us to ask questions, and I asked what would happen if Robert didn't have the operation, and about complications. He explained about chest problems. Part of me was thinking, 'I ought to ask, he's giving me the chance.' But I didn't really want to because I'd been satisfied with what we had been told before, and I'd made up my mind. There was a ninety-five per cent chance of Robert doing well, he was a good candidate for the operation.

My husband said that I ought to sign the form as, being a nurse, I knew more. I didn't feel tremendously guilty. It's got to be done. The consent form seemed almost irrelevant, just part of an enormous process, and I'd already come to the stage where I'd accepted that this was the best course.

This is one of many examples of parents being satisfied that their consent to the operation is reasonably informed and voluntary.

Minor procedures

Written consent is not required for minor procedures. However, to request their consent can help parents to prepare the child, and to know that they may have some control over what happens. In units carrying out many very major procedures, consent to minor ones is sometimes taken for granted.

Maria's senior registrar, after he had spoken to her parents, went to see a baby who had a recurring blister on the surgery wound, and he said, 'We'll just open it up then it'll have a chance to heal up from underneath.' A nurse brought some forceps. Leroy, who was asleep at first, bled on to his father's knee and the nurse kept being sent for more packs of dressings. The baby woke and cried quietly and rather hopelessly, and afterwards stared around with a very scared, wide-eyed look, which a few long-stay babies had. When the surgeon had gone, the father kept saying 'Sorry, sorry,' to the baby, as if distressed that, from the baby's view, he was so closely identified with the procedure, and that he was unable to offer any security, even when the child was asleep in his arms. He said, 'Good thing my wife isn't here—she would have given them a piece of her mind', sounding angry and shaken that this had been done without warning.

Lack of explanation prevented his father from intervening on Leroy's behalf, for example to wake him first, to agree on a suitable place, or to ask for analgesia. The nurses were angrily critical that the wound was opened several times without analgesia, and that their views about necessary pain relief were ignored by the surgeon. This incident was very unusual, but it illustrates a general need. Children benefit from the expert care of several consultants, yet at times each patient also needs one senior doctor, responsible for that individual child's overall, continuing welfare. This would include listening to the nurses and discussing standards of care, but there was no named person to do this.

Echocardiography

Informed consent enables doctors and families to understand one another's intentions, and to work together, rather than at cross purposes. Procedures such as echocardiography may then be carried out more effectively. This is a safe, non-invasive, fairly quick and easy procedure. A few minutes in the out-patient clinic now produces information which formerly might be obtained only by admitting patients for catheterization or surgery. Possibly because echoes are so much easier and safer than other methods, doctors tend to dismiss reservations that, for patients, echoes are mysterious and alarming.[16]

Some doctors carefully prepare families, using the echo time to talk generally with families, to explain the images, and, with the parents, helping the child to lie still and relax. Others work in silence or speak only to their colleagues, leaving the family in mounting suspense. Knowing that the transducer does not hurt like a needle, some doctors overlook the usefulness of reassuring children. The transducer may be pressed firmly and uncomfortably. Tension and expectancy of pain can exacerbate discomfort into perceived pain.[17] Children are expected to lie still for long periods in dark rooms. If the child becomes very upset, doctors try persuasion, distraction, or force, or else they take a break and try again later. An echo video of a four-year-old was presented at a medical meeting with the supposedly humorous comment, 'One attendant at each limb pinning him down because he was a bit wriggly.'

A further medical advantage of echoes is, as one consultant said, 'We can leave fellows to do as many echoes as they like. It's a non-invasive procedure.' Sisters at the Brompton Hospital were aware of problems for the families. They would tell the fellows (doctors on fellowships, usually from abroad) not to do unnecessary practice echoes; not to let the babies become cold; not to take children without informing or asking parents and the ward sister; not to leave parents with the impression that another echo meant that a new problem had been discovered. Fellows were asked to be careful to explain to parents 'that echoes had no dangers or side-effects'.

Besides the constantly changing medical team, many doctors visited from the Institute attached to each hospital. Clinical examination is an important part of cardiac training. Doctors attending courses 'want as much hands-on stuff as possible' said one cardiologist. Children's heart surgery is only provided in teaching hospitals, where patients are expected to act as teaching aids, so that strangers frequently handle the children. Often, when I sat down by a cot to talk to the parents, the child would make a tense movement as if expecting some discomfort. Those old enough to understand relaxed when I said that I was not going to touch them. Doctors did not wear white coats. The children had no way of knowing who might suddenly do something painful to them; many children seemed to wait in constant, tense expectation.

During nurse support meetings, several nurses criticized an incident involving visiting fellows.

They told the father the baby was dying, there was nothing they could do, it was hopeless. He was sitting there crying his eyes out. You only had to look at his face to see grief written all over it. And they came and did another echo for a whole ninety minutes. They wanted a tape of the rare condition. From the father's view, he hadn't seen this before, they might have been hurting the baby. They really dug the probe into her stomach. She was blue and breathless and very exhausted and he must have been thinking they were making her even more exhausted ... He wasn't allowed to hold her until they had finished. Three of us kept saying, 'Can't you be a bit faster?' They said 'We'll only be two more minutes,' but they were half an hour.

The father knew it wouldn't do any good or help his baby. It must have seemed to him like an attack on her, just using her as a teaching aid, an object. Five or six doctors came along and took turns, they were joking and laughing, while the father wept.

Those echocardiographers don't take much notice of us. They treat us as dirt. I wanted to take the plug out of their machine, or smash it up with a hammer. They couldn't see for themselves so they wouldn't listen to us saying how upsetting it must be. They were talking about how rare some of the different parts were. All they care about is their machines.

In this very unusual example, the doctors were not members of the hospital staff. Yet the example illustrates continuing themes: the tensions that could arise between technology and personal care, and between patients as children and as teaching aids; nurses' awareness of the tensions, but their inability to make certain doctors see them; the absence of a senior doctor with the authority to resolve the tensions; the seeming absence of informed consent as a way of regulating minor procedures on child patients.

Permission

Doctors who have to request formal consent are reminded that patients have a right to regulate medical interventions. Patients are often most frightened of 'minor procedures', which cause as much pain, fear, or embarrassment as major procedures performed on anaesthetized patients. Many children are terrified of needles; 'needle phobia' is recognized as a serious psychological problem. EMLA cream (a local anaesthetic) which removes the pain and fear is expensive and to some doctors inconvenient because it needs to be put on one hour before the needle is inserted. It is used by doctors who recognize the severity of children's pain and want to reduce it.

Implied consent to minor procedures, such as the patient lifting an arm for an injection, is considered sufficient for adults, while children's protests are often ignored. Hospitals do not share the *in loco parentis* status of schools, and even that status does not permit teachers to consent to medical procedures on their pupils. It is important to ask for permission for minor procedures, especially if an action might cause distress or anxiety, or will not directly benefit the patient (as with practice echoes). Touching without the patient's consent legally constitutes assault. Discussion beforehand, although holding up busy staff, allows families time to prepare and to reduce the child's fear of sudden, unexpected pain.

Four-year-old Ali arrived from Malaysia with his father who spoke no English, and with two interpreters. Ali seemed terrified while his father wiped away his tears. The men looked worried about his frantic breathing. The consultant examined him gently, and said, 'He's frightened, that's why he's breathing like this. We'd like him calmer.' He explained the operation. The interpreters said they would return later to take the father to his hotel, as private patients' parents could not stay in the hospital. No one seemed to see any advantage in explaining the tests and routines to Ali or his father, or in interpreting Ali's needs to the staff. Talking to the child was not connected with calming him, and explanation was not seen as part of therapy. The SHO said he would 'do the bloods then the echo' an order likely to make Ali more frightened.

If consent had to be requested for minor procedures, then explanation and responding to anxieties would be part of all tests and treatment. Unless junior staff have time, knowledge, help, and an example set by seniors, they may set up barriers to protect themselves by being evasive. In so doing they are reinforcing inequalities between staff and families in knowledge, status, and freedom of choice. This prevents professionals and parents from working together to raise standards of care.

Some of the barriers that prevent families from being informed and involved are briefly described in this and the next chapter, but there were very many more occasions on which the staff carefully explained and consulted with families. The difficulties have been described because they reveal so much about underlying barriers, and understanding these is the first step towards overcoming them where possible.

At its lowest, proxy consent is a legal nicety. At its highest, parents' proxy consent is an expression of family-centred care, in which families and staff share responsibility to suit each patient, because they believe that shared care and decisions benefit children.

Consent in the clinics

The clinic setting, the choice of topics discussed, and each consultant's working methods, all influence consent by affecting the depth and length of discussion with families. The eleven consultant paediatric cardiologists whose clinics I observed emphasized different aspects of their work. Some concentrated on cardiology (highly specialized care of the heart). Others concentrated on paediatrics (child and family-centred care). Some used a family-centred approach for the child's first visit, but a more formal, cardiac approach for later clinics. These different emphases also affect consent. Consultants' use of clinic time reflects their priorities; whether they attend mainly to cardiac expertise or to talking with families, to technical or personal issues. They attended carefully to both aspects of their work, which are partly inseparable, but which also compete for time.

One consultant who spent much time informing families said:

The idea that you can share discussion with parents is nonsense. The imbalance of information is too great. It is a teacher–pupil relationship.

Although parents questioned decisions, and were informed in great detail, they still relied in almost every case on the consultants' knowledge and judgement. One exception was the mother who was advised that her Down's baby should not have corrective surgery, and who 'fought to find a hospital where they would do the operation'. There is space to use only a few examples from hundreds of possible ones, and some of the most difficult cases are described here, in order to consider the extent of medical influence on decisions. They are not representative, and in most cases parents seemed clearly satisfied that the medical decision was the best and only option.

The clinic agenda

'What do parents want from the clinics?' A cardiologist's reply to this question was:

They want to know if their child has something wrong with the heart or not, and if so what the problem is and how we can manage it. The purpose of the clinic is to assess, diagnose, and manage congenital heart disease, or to rule it out. You must give a definitive statement, as far as you have the information to do so. A tertiary referral centre is the end of the line for expertise in technical aspects of making an accurate diagnosis.

Naturally parents agreed that clinical expertise was the most important ingredient of the clinics. Parents in both hospitals spoke of the importance to them of knowing that their child was being treated 'in one of the best centres in the world'. Some parents had waited for days or weeks in uncertainty at other hospitals where doctors had not been able to diagnose the problem.

You worry twenty-four hours a day, you can't think about anything else properly. You can't plan ahead, you've no idea what's going to happen. It was terrific when Dr A knew at once what was wrong, and could tell us the name, and what they were going to do about it, and how long it might take. And it's his certainty and confidence that helps.

Consultants who emphasize cardiology integrate treatment with medical teaching, research, evaluation of treatment, and with adding to medical knowledge. This is best achieved when many cases are reviewed in large teaching clinics. An average consultation would take fourteen minutes,[1] with much time being spent on medical teaching. The agenda is firmly controlled. One consultant said:

It helps if the parents can hold themselves back and give a clear history, give a clear answer to a clear question, in my order not theirs, not to rush in with all their anxieties together, and then at the end the doctor says, 'Any questions?' and they come up with the extras.

Both the cardiac and the paediatric emphases combine clinical expertise with compassion. However, the cardiac approach tends to see anxieties as 'extras', and to centre discussion on precise diagnosis, technical data, and expert decisions. Starting with the medical agenda is efficient for clinical management but less so for informed discussion, if families are preoccupied with trying to hold back their thoughts. Two mothers, a nurse and a biochemist who had attended the clinics for years, said:

I don't think they realize how much you build up the out-patient appointment. You're looking for a great deal of reassurance and information. They're not just there for medical expertise, but for a counselling role as well.

You don't get the attention you need. You can feel quite flattened if you go out and you haven't been able to ask the questions you wanted to. You feel you have let your child down. And if you do ask, they sort of get away with it and dismiss it.

For families, illness is a personal experience, such as a breathless baby's struggle to feed. Their main concerns are often 'minor', visible symptoms and how to cope with them. Doctors tend to concentrate on 'major', invisible problems, heart lesions, haemodynamics, and how to manage them. This can mean that matters very important to the family may be omitted from the medical agenda, or at least not directly addressed. One mother said: 'I feel I've been left alone and in the dark. So many babies here have these feeding problems, yet they seem to treat them as though they were uncommon.'

In contrast, the paediatric emphasis tends to discuss anxieties early during the agenda. Families are then rather more equal partners in discussion. Consultants emphasizing paediatrics (and they included Dutch and American consultants visiting London) encouraged families to talk, and so were in a unique position to collect and distribute practical knowledge and to correct misinformation. For example:

Mother: It's absolute agony feeding him, trying to get it in. He pants so much. Our GP said he *must* have his five ounces.
Consultant: Most babies with heart problems feed poorly. Five ounces is not desperately important.
Mother: [*Seeming very surprised and relieved*] Oh, that's a relief.
Cons.: We may have to accept he's not going to have the five ounces . . . Get in as much as you can. You could try a teat with three holes.

They discuss practical details slowly in response to the parents' concerns. An average session with the consultant most interested in paediatrics would take twenty-three minutes.[2] The consultant explains how the diuretic heart drug would make the baby appear to lose weight. Since the parents are extremely concerned about low weight this warning is likely to save much anxiety.

Much heart treatment is closely related to weight, nausea, anorexia, and resulting family disharmony over the tensions around meals. Three commonly prescribed drugs in the heart units are all listed as having 'gastro-intestinal upset' as one of their known adverse effects.[3] Ventilator tubes make throats sore and affect babies' ability to suck. Feeding is just one of many personal issues affected by disease and treatment. Others include mobility, education, work, income, relationships, and self-image. Families connect cardiac treatment with daily life. Obviously, the need for treatment and its benefits usually exceed the disadvantages, and emphatic warning about possible adverse effects could make anxious patients more likely to be troubled by them. Yet reasonable explanation can help to lessen misunderstandings between children and parents, and reassure them that symptoms produced by drugs do not mean that the child's heart condition is becoming worse.

Consultants cannot give continuing care to hundreds of patients, hold large teaching clinics, and also talk at length with each family. Each activity is important, and each consultant decides on the best ways to use his or her time and skill. With six consultants at the Children's Hospital, there was more medical time, whereas the Brompton Hospital had only two consultants for almost as many children. The final part of this chapter suggests ways of helping families who need more time to talk in the clinics.

The clinic setting

Consent is affected when the clinic setting encourages or discourages open discussion with families. This description is mainly of welcoming aspects of clinics which help families to feel at ease. (By implication the opposite features tend to discourage conversation.) The Children's Hospital tends to hold the more welcoming clinics, although much depends on each consultant's manner. The decor is informal, with pictures, mobiles, and, in every room, boxes of quiet, well-chosen toys maintained by the two playworkers. The consultant sits talking with families in a close group away from the desk.[4] There are few if any observers, and the door is closed.

Children are undressed, and remain on the couch, as briefly as possible. Small children sit or lie on their parent's knees to be examined. The couch is in a corner, with a curtain so that the child need not feel too exposed. (In some clinics doctors stood round three sides of the couch under bright lights, not seeming to notice the fear and embarrassment shown by all ages of children.)

Children sit on adult-size chairs, and are included in the conversation. (If children sit on small chairs, adults tend to talk above them.)

The children also speak, laugh, and protest more,[5] and doctors respond with interest and reassurance. The child's daily life is treated as a topic of interest in itself, as well as a source of medical information. For example, a consultant greeted five-year-old Katy with:

Cons.: Where's my Christmas card? [*They talk about Katy's lively Christmas.*] Can I listen to you?
Katy: No.
Father: But we came all this way. We got up at 5.30, in the dark!
Cons.: We'll start with the pulses. Do you remember about them?
Katy: Yes. [*Gently resists at first*]
Cons.: Now I'm only going to press your tummy.
Katy: Uurgh, it's cold.
Cons.: Shhhh. The baby before you was good. You'll have to be quiet.
Katy: Uurgh, it *does* hurt, really. [*She hovers between laughing and crying.*]
Cons.: Do you remember about taking giant breaths? . . .
Father: We've had no more problems about nausea now that she's on new drugs. . . . The school's very pleased, she's more independent now, they say she's a different girl.
Katy: [*Sounding frightened*] I'm not a different girl.
Cons.: Well, not exactly.
Mother: No, it's words people use. [*She explains. Katy whispers.*] Can she have crisps, with salt?
Cons.: Yes. [*Katy cries with excitement.*]

This approach encourages children to describe their state of health, and any problems which might be relieved, such as nausea. The question about crisps which could be seen as trivial was perhaps central to Katy's understanding of herself as fully recovered after major surgery.

In clinics which emphasize cardiology, a large volume of clinical work is achieved through very concentrated use of time. Many more patients are seen in each session, and for this to be possible they are often seen in overlapping pairs in two examination areas served by a central desk. Time spent teaching the four or more observing doctors helps families to learn about the heart condition and to think about their questions, although some families find the medical talk of their own and other cases confusing and alarming. Doctors tend to ask closed questions.

Cons.: How old is he now?
Father: Er, over four.

Cons.: Can you slip his top off? [*Checks notes*] Yes four and a half. And how do you find him?
Father: Er, he's much better.
Cons.: He goes to school?
Father: Yes.
Cons.: Can he manage a full day at school?
Father: Yes. He goes half-day.
Cons.: That's because of his age?
Father: Yes, he's starting full day in September.
Cons.: Right. Does he get many chest infections? [*To child*] Hullo, stand up. [*Starts to examine child*]

Specific questions, such as whether a child can physically manage a full day at school, imply that certain answers are irrelevant or incorrect, which does not encourage families to speak freely. Some also find formal clinics intimidating, and seem unable to explain their needs, even in minor ways. For example, the one chair, in a narrow room at the head of the examination couch, was fully used, hung with clothes and bags, and the only place a parent could sit to wait, to comfort the child, and to face the group of doctors. During two consecutive clinics, parents of ten patients in turn stood through the consultation, away from the couch, holding the clothes, behind the doctors and therefore blocked off from the child and the medical conversations. A gauge which measures blood pressure had been left on the chair. None of the staff seemed to notice the box, or the parents' changed position, and the families appeared not to have the confidence to move it or to ask for permission to do so.

Descriptions of the clinics cannot convey the way people relate intuitively. Kindness and sympathy which every consultant showed can only be observed and recorded subjectively and 'unscientifically', in accounts which risk sentimental, 'mushy thinking'.[6] Yet attempts to be objective fall into the opposite trap of what Paul Halmos calls 'mechano analysis'. This imagines that only matters which can be explicitly demonstrated are relevant. Mysterious, complex experiences are then fragmented, split into parts by the detached approach described in chapter one.

Halmos thinks that reverential language is needed to convey opaque, total experiences of rapport or trust, a language balancing objectivity and subjectivity, logic and sympathy. In trying to avoid mushy thinking, I may give too harsh an impression, implying that impersonal medical discussion expressed deliberate indifference.

This would deny doctors' intentions to benefit which were shown through their healing work as well as in looks and tones of sympathy.

Sharing information

Clinicians and families face many difficulties. Standard information is not given in systematic stages because cases differ, and the consent process is fragmented. Different facets of the case are discussed over time. No one can ensure that families understand and recall each stage, so doctors tend to rely on them to ask for information. Yet parents may not know what to ask. A mother who had been a nurse said:

I don't think you know the key questions at first. I think you start picking up little bits of information from each clinic, and reading books and talking to other parents. You suddenly realize how things start falling into place. You begin to build up a pattern about your own child, and then you can sort of start filling in the gaps or reinforce things when you go back to the clinic. You begin to understand what the doctor is saying. It does help if you can take home a diagram or something written about the defect to help you to sort out what they were saying.

Dealing with masses of information in a limited time means that inevitably much remains submerged like icebergs, showing only in brief allusions. One medical method is to summarize the issues, pausing between each one so that parents can ask questions if they choose to. Joseph Rodin, aged three, has several serious heart defects.[7] Recently he had collapsed from a lack of oxygen, suffered severe brain damage, and had a palliative shunt operation. Mrs Rodin asked how the defects might be corrected.

Cons.: It's an enormously complicated process to put a patch in to close those holes. It is so difficult that one sometimes wonders whether a shunt as he has had, and another one on the other side at a later date if necessary, might not be a better option than total correction. And one's not obliged to do that in view of the—um . . .
Mother: Does corrective surgery sort it out—if it's successful?
Cons.: Well it sorts out his heart, if his heart is his main problem.
Mother: Mm. If it's successful; usually is it?
Cons.: Well—you may not get *perfect* anatomical results. You often don't, even when the child survives because with one big common valve, you have to make two out of it . . .
Mother: Yes?

Cons.: [*Explains about making new valves, then adds*] It's still not a normal valve . . . The problem is that sometimes the valve leaks a bit then you have to start trying to prevent the leak and there may not be enough actual valve to give you a *perfect* result. You may get a very good result, maybe . . . Against all that background one wonders—I mean one can go on for thirty or forty years having shunts if they are good and work.

Mrs Rodin then asked about life expectancy, and the doctor replied with several qualifications that with shunts, 'his life expectancy isn't badly affected. . . . It's not going to be much worse because we don't . . .'. Again he paused as if ready to continue if asked to. Mrs Rodin moved on to questions about Joseph's daily care. Underlying questions include: How will surgery decisions affect the length and quality of Joseph's life? What is an acceptable mortality and morbidity risk now and in the future? Each issue involves allusions to numerous facts and opinions. For example, 'if his heart is his main problem' hints at a comparison between the disadvantages of Joseph's heart defects, and of his brain damage and Down's syndrome.

There are several possible reasons for issues not being explored in the busy clinic. This was only one of many opportunities for Joseph's mother to talk with doctors. Many parents were concerned with coping with the present, taking one day at a time, fearing bad news and talk of the future, and so on. When the consultant replied about life span, 'It's not going to be so much worse because we don't . . .', instead of asking 'Much worse than what?' Mrs Rodin immediately returned to the present symptoms. Parents wanted a well child with as little treatment as possible; they consented to surgery when the child was clearly ill or when doctors convinced them emphatically that surgery was necessary, but they were unlikely to request it otherwise.

Another reason which enables yet limits discussion is 'obligations', as if adults in the units felt they had a duty to raise certain issues in fairness to the child but not necessarily to develop them. They ticked off a list of topics as a way of fulfilling obligations, if only to be able to dismiss the topic because no response could be taken as understanding and agreement. For example, the consultant paused during several remarks: 'one's not obliged to do that in view of . . .'; life expectancy would not be 'much worse because we don't . . .'; but he was not asked to finish them. Whereas when he said, 'you have to make two valves . . .', Mrs Rodin prompted 'Yes?' and he continued to explain. Many conversations are channelled by these cues and checks to filter out undue elaboration. The process is complicated in the clinics if parents hold back questions in order to avoid looking ignorant or seeming to take too much time.

The consultant waited each time for Joseph's mother to raise topics. In replying he reassured her about the condition and thereby warned her against surgery: a sudden attack was unlikely, the shunt was working well, and so on. He did not mention precise ages of life expectancy. High risk is implied ('even when the child survives') but not specified. The operation is presented as difficult yet not impossible, and the surgeon's high aims and perfectionism are stressed.

Another factor limiting the discussion may be intuition. Mrs Rodin had told me earlier,

> I dreaded coming down to a moral decision of whether to treat a child because of a [mental] handicap. I felt if a decision had to be made I would leave it to him [the consultant]. . . . We never ask about what *might* happen—we thought when the time came they'd tell us the possibilities. . . . The consultants both told us that knowing the future was a matter of seeing visit by visit.

The consultant seemed to see Mrs Rodin's reluctance and left her to raise the issues as she chose.

In this clinic of fourteen patients Shanta, aged five, also had Joseph's heart problems and other complications, but not Down's syndrome.[8] Before Shanta came into the room, the consultant told the other doctors, 'We had a lot of discussion [at the medical meeting]; it will be very difficult surgery.' When the family arrived he told them,

> *Cons.*: I think we should put her name down for a repeated catheter test—to look very hard at er—what we should do . . . The options are: easy—do the shunt on the other side, low risk, easy to do, of course that doesn't correct her heart. Or we have to think about, um, a bigger corrective operation, sort of open-heart surgery, which is a big operation, mm . . . which would obviously have more associated risk. . . . On the other hand I think we need to know exactly what her heart is like now, so that we can then discuss with the—what we think is her best bet. [*He continued talking about the need for more accurate information, implying although not specifying risk and at the same time reassuring the parents about Shanta's present condition.*]
>
> *Father*: What does the open-heart consist of? What would you do?
>
> *Cons.*: . . . she has a big hole in the middle with a common valve—with a

hole above it and below it. So the surgeon puts two patches, one above and one below like that [*demonstrates with a gesture*] to block off the holes. We would then hope at that time that the, er, valve that was there works properly on both sides, because you've got a common valve and you make two out of them. Well perhaps we'd—and then the area that was narrowed would have to be opened up and probably a gusset put in to let it out—to make it bigger so that the blood can go through to the lungs. So it's essentially—and then you take down the shunt she's already had. That's easy, you just tie it off. But it's—tricky, a big operation . . . We'd have to be certain it was the right thing to do. [*He explains that she may need another shunt instead of corrective surgery. The catheter is*] to see if it looks technically er—to be reasonable.

[*He starts teaching other doctors, indirectly warning the family that risk was very high in comparison with other cases, by saying*] This little girl is very complex, like the child we saw earlier but even more complex because [*and he lists the complications. Eventually he turns back to the parents to say they would do a repeat catheter*] and when we *know* the facts sit down with you and talk through what's the best thing to do.

Mother: Do you know when you'll do the catheter?

[*After talking about the timing the family leave.*]

The parents are asked to agree to investigations, and to be open-minded about later decisions. Twice the explanations end in a short pause, as if the doctor began rapidly to explain medical concepts and then sensed a gap between what he was describing and the parents' level of medical understanding. As if this seemed impossible to bridge, he gave up the attempt and moved on to the next comment.

There was not time in this long clinic to teach parents through a chain of questions and answers, to connect new ideas to ones already understood, and to clarify with drawings. The consultant thought that continuity of care, personally seeing as many of his patients as possible, was important, and the families valued the continuity and the expertise. Other consultants made time by arranging for junior doctors to see many of their patients.

Doctors can convey a sense either of sharing responsibility with families and acknowledging their part in giving consent, or of shouldering the whole decision. Shanta's doctor encourages the family to trust medical expertise. Risk remains an abstract, technical concept, a challenge to medical skill, when the subject of risk (the child's life and health) is not mentioned. By definition, 'risk' is about uncertainty and incomplete control. However, doctors prefer to speak of precise certainties, of knowing 'exactly', and of confident, competent management. 'Easy' is said twice, 'tricky' hardly suggests possibly fatal difficulty, and 'her best bet' just hints at the limits of medical skill and knowledge.

Shanta and her small brother were shouting and banging toys. Small children interrupted and older ones overheard conversations, which increased the adults' difficulties. Parents were reluctant to inform their children fully of serious risks because this entailed talking about how very ill the child was. Some avoided talking much about hoped-for benefits ('You'll be able to grow/play football/run with your friends') in case this could not be achieved and the child felt more disappointed and betrayed.

Kelly is one of many examples of deciding when the child's life is so restricted or deteriorating that it is worth attempting to improve health through risking possibly fatal surgery. Before Kelly, aged eleven, came into the room, the doctors talked of the severe problems in assessing and managing her complicated heart defects and the resulting lung disease.[9] A year earlier, the medical meeting had recommended surgery, but the consultant said, 'It seemed wrong to do it on a well child so I left it.' They examined Kelly.

Cons.: My impression is that she's slowing down a bit but she's still leading a fairly good life.

Mother: It does stop her doing things.

Cons.: What things?

Kelly: Run—I get puffed when I walk uphill. . . . I sometimes play games outside.

Cons.: Not football? [*Jokes about football.*]

The situation is this. [*He explains the techniques of the operation and that it would be best to wait until Kelly is adult size.*] It may be better to defer surgery, unless we're pushed into it for good clinical reasons, bearing in mind the quality of life and bearing in mind the risks. We sort of came to a conclusion in a rather muddled way last time to . . . If she has friends, and a good social life and it doesn't interfere with education—the question is should we get it over now? [*Kelly's mother looks worried.*]

Understanding the desire to get it over and done with, but wanting to choose the optimal time . . . We're going to look at her data again. . . . I will drop you a line indicating the sorts of risks involved but—we want to be sure we're doing it at the right time for the right reasons.

Mother: I wouldn't want to have it done unnecessarily, but she's becoming increasingly affected.

Cons.: Yes, she's been remarkably well for a long time. Unless you think her limitations are too great, I don't see any harm in waiting.

Mother: She does get breathless, even getting out of bed.

Cons.: She'll grow quite a lot in the next year or two, that's the advantage in waiting. . . .

Mother: [*to Kelly*] How do you think it's affecting you? . . . [*Pause, but Kelly doesn't answer.*] Don't know? She's too used to it.

Cons.: Do you get breathless?

Mother: I think she gets perhaps frustrated sometimes. She stomps around.

Cons.: Don't we all? . . . All right, miss, are you in a great rush for your operation? [*Kelly looks embarrassed.*]

Mother: She was very disappointed when it was cancelled last year.

Cons.: Okay. [*He leaves the room.*]

The medical decision is based on clinical data and on clear, objective rules. 'We've got to measure up the risks and weigh them up, the risks against the benefits,' said one consultant. When I asked whether you could measure and compare such matters he answered, 'You've got to, somebody's got to make decisions.' Data such as pressures in the heart and lungs reveal answers which can relieve part of the burden of making medical decisions by allowing them to be less an arbitrary, individual response.

The family assess Kelly's daily life, but need to describe this in terms which are acceptable in the clinic. These terms are physical symptoms, in which doctors are the experts. Kelly's frustration is the kind of non-specific data which scientific assessment tries to avoid. Another doctor present said, 'She is tense, psychologically the wait is not good.' The child, lying undressed on the couch, becomes a barrier to communication as she seems to be unable to assert her views or to reinforce her mother's views firmly, and her silence is interpreted as assent. When families seem likely to request very risky treatment, some doctors set a brisk optimistic tone, remark on the child's (comparative) wellness, and emphasize the need to make decisions 'for the right reasons'.

Measures of illness vary, such as:

actual physical lung damage;

medical assessment of lung disease as partially examined through investigations;

patients' own feelings of health or incapacity.

Objective measures are complicated by the subjective experience of ill health. Some patients resist illness and struggle to remain active, others readily succumb; their reactions are likely to alter the progress of the disease.[10] A further complication is children's limited ability to admit to illness, to describe it, and to measure its seriousness. Whereas orthopaedic patients feel pain, or see the twisted limb, cardiac patients have vaguer symptoms and depend on doctors to interpret them.

How accurately do medical assessments of lung disease relate to the patient's present quality of life? Or therefore predict the future for this patient and, by analogy, for others? Which is the more salient measure or prediction, the patient's experience or the medical assessment? Cardiologists are devising increasingly sophisticated laboratory measures of haemodynamics and cardiac function on which to base clinical decisions. Yet other medical specialties are moving the opposite way, towards growing awareness of the effects of patient's subjective responses and daily life on the course of diseases such as cancer.

There are many complicated arguments for and against surgery for Kelly. Waiting until she is nearer adult size is one, although a year earlier some doctors advised against waiting any longer. The medical discussion after Kelly left indicated that a primary reason against surgery is the very high risk. If lower risk surgery could help her it would probably be offered. Instead, a secondary reason against surgery is stressed (that she is relatively well) as if it is a primary one, the main basis for decisions. This approach has two effects on informed consent.

First, families' opinion of their child's ill health, conflicts with the medical view that affirms relatively good health. 'Relatively' could mean better than most children with this serious defect, or than similar cases who have had unsuccessful surgery. Yet when the basis for assessing relative health is unclear, parents are less able to form and to state their assessment. So the consultant says to Kelly's mother 'unless you think her limitations are too great', and to another mother 'if you are worried come back'. Yet he seems to leave them uncertain about what is 'too great', or what ought to cause worry. Then they are unclear about when to ask for medical help and how best to represent their child in discussions about surgery.

Second, emphasizing the child's relative health, although it offers the very important therapeutic influence of hope, shifts discussion away from the families' main concerns, and discourages them from asking for non-surgical help. A father complained that his life was impossible as his wife cried whenever their son undressed because he was so thin. Knowing that patients rarely survived surgery for the child's defect, the consultant assured the parents that the boy was doing remarkably well and was merely skinny. If low weight could be acknowledged as a problem, a dietician might be involved. Such matters were supposed to be arranged by local paediatricians and GPs. Yet problems were not always referred back to them. Sometimes doctors seemed to try to protect families from full knowledge by redefining anxiety, changing 'very thin' to 'skinny'. Other doctors encouraged families to talk about their daily problems, and if need be referred them to the social worker, or other professionals.

Values are not stated explicitly, although they pervade the discussions. For example, corrective surgery is advised for Shanta, but not in Joseph's slightly less technically complex case. The doctors disagree on the risks of delaying Kelly's operation. The medical phrases have moral significance. Parents like Mrs Rodin want consultants to make moral decisions. Others want a greater share in making decisions, but have difficulty in putting their views if discussion is restricted mainly to questions of medical expertise.

Meeting families' needs

Hidden misunderstandings occur when families expect cardiologists to help them with a wide range of problems associated with the child's heart condition. Cardiologists tend to confine their work to investigating and diagnosing clinical conditions, and to treating these with drugs or referral for surgery. There are three ways of offering the more comprehensive service which many families expect: the medical network, the paediatric approach, and the clinic team.

The medical network

Paediatric cardiologists hold joint clinics with paediatricians in the local referring hospitals. This has many medical and social advantages. Families need not travel far to regular clinics. Local paediatric teams are closely involved in giving care. They learn how to diagnose and manage congenital heart disease, and when to refer children in good time to the specialist unit. 'Babies no longer arrive here moribund because the local paediatricians know more about cardiology now,' said one cardiologist. Children can convalesce in their local hospital if need be, so reducing the stressful time in London. They benefit from continuing care locally and centrally. The consultants who emphasize cardiology spend much time in joint clinics at the referring hospitals.

Parents are encouraged to talk about 'non-cardiac' matters with their paediatrician or GP. They have time to discuss detailed care with paediatricians who know a great deal about the daily care of chronically ill children. One disadvantage is if matters are defined as 'non-cardiac' and left to the paediatrician which families would prefer to be treated by the cardiologist as an integral part of cardiac care. However, the paediatrician can help to make the connection when necessary. The different kinds of medical expertise offer families a strong three-tier network.

The paediatric approach

Some paediatric cardiologists give particular emphasis to talking with families, as illustrated by the following few details from one long consultation. Before the family came in, the consultant explained to two observing doctors that John had recently been admitted for investigations, and a case conference had discussed the results.[11] A Fontan operation had been attempted three years earlier.

But it failed and we had to do a shunt instead. He was very, very sick and nearly died on many occasions. He's pretty good, now he's seven. He can do most days at school. I think unfortunately we should try again. Obviously there is an emotional problem on our part, as we nearly killed him three years ago. But he is getting very limited and blue. We'll see what his parents say. I want to talk without John. Will you take him for an ECG?

The family came in and they all talked about John enjoying life but getting very tired at school.

Cons.: Would it be nice if you could do more?
Mother: Would you like to do more?
Father: More running? More football?

John doesn't answer. The consultant asks him to take his sister to 'meet Eric in the ECG room', and they leave with the two doctors.

Mother: Are you reasonably pleased with him?
Cons.: We spent ages trying to go through everything. Naturally we had a large attack of cold feet. [*He explains the medical discussion and catheter report at length*.] We've clearly learnt a lot in the last three years, including with John. His shunt is very nice and his arteries have grown. But he's

starting to slow down a little because the shunt tends to get smaller. I think we should plan a Fontan.
Father: Could you do another shunt? The Fontan is obviously a big risk.

They talked in detail about the risks of different options, John's father saying several times 'We've got no choice really? No other way?'

Mother: Just to know there was a good chance would be nice.
Cons.: Four out of five kids come through.
Father: Last time it was 40/60 wasn't it?
Cons.: Mmm. Shall I tell him?
Father: No, we will.

At last the consultant said, 'Write your questions down when you get home; phone or write to me.' John returned and gave the consultant a Christmas card he had made. The consultant said, 'I think we can plan to make you better and less breathless.' John died during his operation and his parents thanked the consultant for his honesty and concern.

The clinic team

A third way to achieve detailed discussion with families is to involve the whole team of professionals. The many people working in the clinics strongly affect the consent process. Many of the out-patient nurses, technicians, and therapists had chosen, and trained, to work with children. A few said that they preferred adult patients, and disliked the 'hassle' with children. The importance of ensuring that all the staff know how to treat child patients was shown when some families were too fraught to attend properly by the time they arrived in the consultation room. 'He was screaming his heart out at the X-ray and ECG,' said the mother of a three-year-old, 'I can't get over what is happening to this little young man.' The mother of an eight-year-old veteran said, 'She screamed a little. When the technician said, "They all do", I thought, if only you could explain. It would only take a few seconds, but they just make them scream.' 'It sounds like a murder,' said a consultant of the noise in the weighing room. When I asked the nurse why a child was crying she answered, 'I've just weighed him. He's been in recently—got a big red scar. I got a child yesterday, just to take a tiny stitch out and he yelled the place down—blasted my ears out.' Nurses and technicians can inform and reassure, or cause great distress. That much of this distress is unnecessary is shown by the skilled staff who manage to prevent it.[12]

When consultants are fully occupied with assessment, diagnosis, planning treatment, and teaching, although the end of all their work is social benefit, little time is left to address social concerns directly. A cardio-thoracic children's clinical nurse specialist can help families and clinicians by ensuring that all aspects of the clinic complement the high medical standards.

These are some of the tasks which would greatly relieve pressure, and encourage informed discussion during consultations. The specialist nurse could:

talk with families before and after consultations to help them, if necessary, to unravel their concerns and misunderstandings;

ask junior doctors or consultants to talk further with families who are still uncertain;

co-ordinate the clinic team ensuring that families see the social worker, speech therapist, dietician, psychologist, and other professionals as required;

discuss children's daily care, such as feeding problems;

help parents to share with one another their specialized, hard-won knowledge of children with heart disease;

arrange for children to be cared for when parents need to talk without their child overhearing or interrupting;

ensure that all clinic staff understand how to treat child patients;

encourage a welcoming, relaxed atmosphere in the clinic.

In response to complaints from patients about the clinics, such as the very long waiting periods, one of the hospitals commissioned two enquiries. The report of one enquiry, written by a paediatric nurse, recommended that a clinical nurse be appointed. One of her main tasks would be 'to educate staff to become more aware of the emotional needs of child patients', in order to ensure that the clinic would not be 'a negative and traumatic experience'. Many of the children would need lifelong medical care; 'fear in childhood' could lead dangerously to 'avoidance in adulthood'.

As in the wards, there are barriers in the clinics which restrict discussion between clinicians and families. Both visible barriers (such as nurses mishandling the child) and invisible ones (such as conflicting expectations) start in the separation of technical efficiency from social and emotional concern. A clinical nurse could draw differing aspects of the clinic together to everyone's benefit, and for greater efficiency.

Not all essential information for consent can possibly be covered in clinics, and this stage can seem too early to discuss consent. However, after a child has been admitted for surgery, suddenly it can seem too late to demur. Families need much information before admission to help them to consider decisions and to prepare for surgery. Gaps in information are not routinely filled in after admission, and the clinic is the only chance some families have to talk with a consultant before surgery. However, out-patient clinics are only one stage in decision-making. One of their main purposes is to collect data for discussion at the medical case conferences described in the next chapter.

4

Medical decisions: the medical background to consent

Children's heart surgery offers clear illustrations of the consent process, partly because teams of clinicians discuss each case. The first part of this chapter considers an example of the effects of this team management on the families' part in decisions. The second part reviews ways in which doctors reach decisions to which parents are asked to consent.

Limitations of the parents' influence on decisions are illustrated in the rare cases when they disagree with medical recommendations, as in the following example of dissent in the Children's Hospital.

Dissent

David Hughes was two weeks old. His parents were standing by his cot tube-feeding him. They thought that he became more breathless when he had a large feed every four hours, but he had to have this to fit the nursing rotas. Mr Hughes told me that the consultant had said David

has an ASD and a mitral valve problem. His valve might need replacing but he said he would not choose this for any child of his.[1] We feel that we are in a dilemma. David is breathing very fast but if this clears up he may not need surgery. We don't know if his diarrhoea is making him worse and more breathless.

The following description is of just one stage in a long series of discussions between the doctors and parents. Two registrars arrived. Mrs Hughes told them she was worried that David had mistakenly been given formula milk instead of her own expressed milk. The doctors said that this had probably caused David's diarrhoea. David's parents became more upset. The registrar said, 'Fluid loss from the diarrhoea isn't a problem. Without it she [sic] would have to be on diuretics and formula is doing the trick instead.' While his parents considered David's whole state of health related to his nursing care, the doctors talked about how his cardiac condition related to his fluid balance. They did not reply to the parents' concern that nursing methods might increase the need for surgery.

Registrar: I'm almost a hundred per cent convinced the problem is not the valve itself but growth of tissue above it. That could be cut away with little risk and no need to repeat the surgery. . . . We see more of these cases than anywhere else. I've reviewed all the literature and looked at all our videos on this condition.

Father: Dr A (consultant) said ten years ago all children with this died. I think he said something about a lot of children with mitral valve replacements die, or at least they've never done one on anyone so young. And biennial valve replacements will be necessary.

Reg.: No, it's nothing like what you think. It doesn't mean ops every six months, of course we wouldn't consider anything like that. It means a replacement after two or three years, then another later but perhaps not more than three operations. But of course, we can't tell now, it depends how fast she grows. We put in the biggest valve possible [*and he continued with technical details*]. We can't be certain until the surgeon looks at the open heart. Doctors only decide to do what is sensible and in the child's best interests. They wouldn't consider anything that was too much for the child. You just concentrate on the baby and leave the decisions to us, we know the best thing to decide.

In concentrating on technical details, the registrar emphasizes his medical knowledge, thereby implying his wisdom to determine the child's interests. It enables him to shift the argument from *whether* surgery might be done to *how* it might be done. The parents do not mention that David is a 'he', or that 'biennial' means every second, not every half, year and therefore is not so different from the registrar's prediction of the near future. They say they want David's condition to be treated unless he needs a valve replacement, in which case they want the surgeon to stop, in mid-operation if necessary, and close the heart without carrying out any treatment. Knowing this could be fatal, the registrar looks amazed.

But you can't do that. You have to leave the decision to the surgeon. . . . And anyway the decision is made by all of us in committee, all the experts together, we decide what's best, up there [in the conference room].

Consultants tended to speak less directly, and may have wanted to avoid making parents feel clearly coerced. Yet the meeting could be presented as a formidable power by junior doctors. After the registrars had gone, the parents looked red-faced and angry. They argued, his father wanting to pick up David, his mother saying that this made him more upset. Mrs Hughes told me that she had had heart surgery as a baby with a seventy per cent mortality risk, and had spent much of her childhood in a wheelchair.

Mother: When I was five, I only attended four half-days at school all my first term.

PA: So you want to save David from that sort of life?

Mother: Oh no, it wasn't for me, it was for my mother. I was only five so I wasn't aware of what was happening. *I* just don't want that sort of life. I want to go back to work. How can I if he's ill like that?

Father: [*Turning away angrily*] Oh, I'm having nothing to do with that sort of talk.

David's mother, knowing the pressures of chronic illness, doubts whether she can or should cope with them. (I did not ask Mr Hughes what he might consider doing.) Parents' concern about breathlessness, diarrhoea, and their child's agitation, is likely to affect their evaluation of what makes his life tolerable. So their conclusions may differ from clinical decisions which discount these factors.

David's parents were anxious that the consent form was vague. It stated:

I hereby consent to the submission of the above child
to investigation by _____
and operative treatment for _____
the purpose and nature of which have been explained to me by Dr/Mr

_____

I also consent to such further treatment or alternative measures as may be found necessary to the investigation or during the course of operation afterwards, together with the administration of general, local or other anaesthetic for any of these purposes.

The form is partly designed to protect health authorities from litigation and to leave surgeons freedom of decision.

A cardiologist's view of dissent

I asked David's consultant for his views. He immediately sat down to talk for half an hour. I thought he was conscientious and well-intentioned. Like other consultants he tended to concentrate on the topics which he selected and, as he said, 'to help' by giving positive and definitive answers. He therefore tended to avoid what he called 'difficult, straight' questions on matters where he felt doubtful. He saw choice as enormously complicated by medical details which tend to submerge the moral issues. He emphasized medical authority and knowledge, but was uncertain about who holds final authority, the medical team or the individual surgeon.

He was frank about medical limitations, but in a general abstract way unrelated to particular patients. I asked him if he thought parents could ask the surgeon to stop, if necessary in mid-operation. He replied, 'Not really. Essentially, I mean', and he began a long account of David's condition and the nature of valve problems. He spoke slowly and clearly, with much repetition, emphasis, and in the manner other doctors had of describing uncertainty with definitive precision. For example:

One of the areas one looks at is the left-sided valve, the mitral valve, and in David's case his mitral valve or the *area* of his mitral valve is clearly abnormal. Now, the exact nature of what the abnormality is at the valve is very hard to determine. [*He ended with:*] Very often the diagnosis of the precise abnormality is made by the surgeon on the operating table.

It's a question of considering the optimum timing for intervention— almost the later the better. *If* the child has mitral valve stenosis, then the options are really to do a mitral valve replacement if possible. The youngest we have done here is at one month and he is very, very well. He's clearly not—ideal, haemodynamically, there's obvious obstruction still, but the child is well. . . . I didn't say I wouldn't have it done for my child, but that I would think very carefully about it and be not at all sure because it did mean a series of operations. . . .

They're very difficult parents, er, very nice, highly informed. I was amazed at how rational they were under this crisis but it was very difficult. They kept asking such straight questions. I think I want to answer questions that will help them to understand. But when they ask these difficult questions, I don't know, and I have to say, 'well, maybe'. I don't think that helps. They are highly intelligent parents and know what to expect.

After he had spoken more about the difficulty of diagnosis before surgery, I asked again whether parents could ask surgeons not to replace a valve. The consultant emphasized the need for careful medical discussion, ending:

Cons.: If there's a valvular problem we will do our best to attempt to replace the valve.
PA: Mm. And do you . . .

Cons.: And that discussion should come up. . . . We have problems [*and he described 'last hope' surgery in neonates and went on to mastectomies, which he thought were 'identical' in that the patient consented both to a biopsy or a mastectomy depending on the surgeon's decision*].

If you felt it was technically feasible and a reasonable thing to do, even if it had a very uncertain long-term future, I think you'd find it very hard not to do. . . . One aims, with the hope of not having a child who's going to spend most of their childhood sick. . . . One would think very seriously about whether this was a, a viable option. . . . But no one can tell what the long-term effects are of many of the operations we do. It may fall to pieces, and you can't guarantee where the child will come in a range of success, even whether the child will be better after surgery. I don't believe in the word 'cure' for heart surgery [*and he described future risks*].

Senior registrar: [*Who had come in a few minutes earlier*] I wouldn't agree to a mitral valve replacement if it were my child.

Cons.: A lot of operations are on that grey scale. [*He listed surgery he would accept for his own child, but did not mention any operation he would reject, although he said:*] But I'm not sure of some of the more complex things we do, how I'd react as a parent. . . . Dr C who follows up our cases into adolescence always talks about 'early triumphs and late disasters'. I think it's very important to see neonatal treatment in that context. We think the things we do are marvellous now, but whether they're going to be marvellous in ten or twenty years' time is another matter.

Doctors would often begin by talking confidently about their work and slowly would become more pessimistic, suggesting the problems for them of making connections between clinical work and its effects on families.

A surgeon's view

The tension between medical and parental knowledge and responsibility to the child, together with medical uncertainty was further explained to me by a surgeon. (It is difficult to describe the mixture of commitment, energy, and concern, mixed with humour and self-criticism with which the cardiac teams worked. One indication is a small plaque in the surgeon's office saying, 'We do precision guess work here.') When I asked a question, as with David's cardiologist, the surgeon at once sat down and talked fully. He explained that sometimes the only way to know whether a valve could be repaired was to start cutting it.

If it starts to leak catastrophically, usually you can't put it back where it was. You may find that the only way to get the child off the table [to survive the operation] is to replace the valve.

I asked how he would advise parents. He replied that after the medical meeting he would have a long talk to see how definite the parents still were when the difficulties had been very carefully assessed and explained.

And then you would perhaps only go in on the understanding that you may have to replace the valve. I think it comes down to: would you do it to your own child? I go home and look at my kids and I think about it a lot.

Parents talked specifically about the child's discomfort or disability. Doctors tended to talk abstractly about surgery as a 'reasonable' or 'viable' option. This approach can lead to assessing surgery for technical feasibility, whether a new valve can actually be fitted, instead of whether the valve will harm or benefit the child. The surgeon just quoted thought that the difference between people's relations with, say, a bank manager and with a doctor was fear—of harm and death. He wanted to try to redress this imbalance through sharing medical knowledge in a reassuring way. So his information was influenced by his own reservations yet enthusiasm. He was 'very much in favour of transplantation' despite extra problems for growing children with the long-term use of toxic drugs.

Transplantation will become so routine we won't be questioning the ethics of it. . . . So the stress will be less, because the kids will be great afterwards. If you like, we've already done over four hundred heart transplants here, because we use homograft aortic valves taken from a cadaver donor. I mean those kids are running around normal. I'm not yet sure of the risks because we're just reviewing the results but the risks seem to be very low for homografts. You have a very high risk if you put in dacron or plastic or metal. . . . It is difficult when you bring the age down. The potential benefit becomes more complex, short-term risk versus long-term benefit.

As they talked, both doctors became more hesitant about assessing the benefit of their work. The surgeon continued:

But who am I to judge the value of what I do? That's up to public opinion and the media, that's reality, and the politicians we elect to make value judgements about what is worth funding.

In my whole life, I'm going to save less children than die every five minutes in Ethiopia, and . . . these have all got twisted hearts. I'm doing this because I love the kick I get when the children get better, because it's technically satisfying. But its value in a world sense is very questionable. I generate handicap—to a mild degree and it's better than dying, but it is still a handicap. It's a cost to society. . . . There is no doubt that open-heart surgery is not as safe as we think it is.

Benefit is also measured in the experience of the child and family. At some level, technical and social medicine have to combine.

Medical meetings

Cardiologists and cardiac surgeons divide the medical and surgical work between them in overlapping ways. They are concerned with risky, varied, unusual, and complex cases, and with a large body of knowledge continually being increased and assessed. Some decisions concern how cautious or radical approaches to treatment should be. All this encourages team-work. As one doctor said: 'It is difficult if you make decisions and the child dies. It's easier if it's made by a group of us at the meeting.' The meetings[2] have several purposes: to review each patient's data; to decide if surgery is advisable and if so when and of what kind; to classify unusual cases or cases that are part of a trend to be identified and counted; to learn and teach about the defects, treatments, and how to present cases, analyse data, and make decisions; to record every diagnosis for computer records used for reviews and research. The meetings are also concerned with the general advance of medical knowledge, and help to reaffirm the purpose and value of the work in each unit. In both hospitals, patients are discussed before surgery at a medical meeting, mainly by consultant cardiologists and surgeons.

The Children's Hospital

At the centre of medical discussion is the tension between technical and social values. A surgeon described this tension for the JCC (joint cardiac conference).

The management of the child combines technical and social aspects. At times these aspects have to be combined like two pathways meeting. But at some stage, each has to be considered separately. At the JCC you must have complete objectivity, and then go on to the final discussion with the parents. Deciding how much of the social to take into account when making medical decisions—well that is a very important issue which needs deep thought. I think we do talk about that a lot in the JCC.

Patients were 'JCCed' at leisurely midday meetings held three times a week and attended by several surgeons. Often there were long silences while everyone thought about a problem. The doctors worked closely together sitting around a table. They did not need to explain everything fully, but would imply an answer with a glance or a nod, or murmur quietly. Many doctors said they valued this close, friendly team-work. A surgeon said:

We never reach a decision on our own. It's almost unheard of for us to make a spontaneous decision of radical treatment. In each case surgery is discussed at least three times in a major way. . . . It's pretty unusual for a wrong decision to slip through. . . . In my experience the JCC is unique. It's what made me stay here. I felt that the decisions which were being reached about the patients were being made on as logical, as informed, and as caring a basis as possible in the British system.

After discussion, a consultant cardiologist and a surgeon wrote the decision on the child's JCC form, both signed the form and the cardiologist undertook to write to inform the parents. 'The form records the nubbins of the information so that everyone knows what has been agreed,' said one surgeon.

Clinics emphasizing the paediatric approach were held mainly in this hospital. Although families were encouraged to talk in the clinic, their part in decision-making was limited by the JCC. These clinics tended to concentrate on collecting data for the JCC, rather than on making decisions with parents. Also, surgeons strongly influenced JCC decisions, but they were less likely to have met the families by this stage. When families were informed by cardiologists in clinics about the likely treatment, this was often qualified with, 'when I have talked with my colleagues, we'll let you know what we decide'.

After the JCC a letter, sometimes including the percentage mortality risk of planned surgery, was sent to the parents. They had definite written news from a named consultant to contact if there was uncertainty or delay. Yet this system was in some ways impersonal. A letter was necessary if decisions were not discussed with families in clinics. To parents, it might seem easier to negotiate during a clinic discussion than to question a formal, recorded committee statement. The six cardiologists shared some cases so that formal records were important.

The Brompton Hospital

The clinics were less child-centred in this hospital, but cardiologists who knew the families had a stronger influence at medical meetings. They outnumbered the surgeons. There was often critical argument, rather than the friendly discussion of the JCC. The surgeons were interested in deciding on the best operation. Cardiologists wanted to review all the options including medical (non-surgical) treatment. In closer contact with families, cardiologists were perhaps more aware of what risk would mean to them and could 'sense' meanings indirectly through being with families, as well as directly by talking with them. Decisions were not formally recorded and signed as at the JCC, leaving cardiologists free to discuss and revise decisions with families more flexibly.

The meetings started at 8 a.m. each Monday and were formal, concentrated, and attended by rows of observers. Cases were reviewed in quick succession. The registrar who presented the cases noted the decisions and arranged the next stage, such as a letter to the surgeon asking for the child to be put on his list. The registrar would have been on duty since Friday evening, and would be working through until about 1 p.m. on Monday presenting cases at the meeting and then on the big ward round. 'People work incredibly hard and carefully' to remember, record, and follow up the decisions, one doctor told me. They had to concentrate intently on each case, yet at the same time be ready to switch attention quickly to other cases.

There were only two consultant cardiologists, treating nearly as many children as attended the other unit. They held many more joint clinics and worked more closely with local paediatricians. Besides tending to hold more decisive clinics, they gave continuing care to their own patients. They thought that X-rays and ECGs were 'essential' preparation before most consultations (instead of being taken afterwards if needed as in the first hospital). One said that with these data, he often knew the diagnosis before seeing the child and so could use examining and discussion time with the families more efficiently. He thought that each case should be managed primarily by the child's own consultant, not by a committee. The meeting was a useful discussion forum, but not necessarily the final arbiter.

Involving families in decisions

Robert's mother, a nurse, explained the pros and cons of the Children's Hospital JCC routine, the differences between continuous care from a known doctor and shared care among a team, the value of doctors knowing the child and family, and of moderate, 'questioning' medical practice.

Dr B said, 'We all get together and discuss these cases and then we'll let you know.' And I thought how super, it was uplifting. We were filled with such confidence in their ability to do the right thing and make the best decisions. It was amazing when Robert was first admitted, several high-powered-looking doctors descended on him and told us all they were doing. I felt a sense of privilege really. We were overawed.

But the doctors don't all see it from the parents' point of view. I'd prefer to have a clear decision at the consultation but if you don't see your consultant you get a sensation that the other doctors can't make decisions. Continuity is terribly important. Doctors *must* do their homework. My friend told one doctor that her child had had a valve taken out and he said, 'Oh no, he never had that done.' She felt terribly upset because she knew she was right. We saw different doctors in the clinics and they told us conflicting decisions. We wrote to Dr B and he wrote a nice letter back saying it was a mistake. But lots of people don't know they can write. It's such an advantage being white and middle class and articulate. It's not what you know, it's who you know.

'And how you are known', Robert's mother might have added, how well doctors understand the family's experience. She continued to talk about the relationship between the doctor and the family.

Now we always manage to see Dr B. He's confident in an intelligent, questioning sort of way, he's honest. You're treated as if you are part of the process, not just a number. He sees the child as a member of the family; it horrifies me that there are people who don't function like that. I think sometimes Dr B is aware when that is going on but there is not much he can do about it.

Centring decision-making into the JCC shifts it away from the family. Their views can be represented only very briefly and impersonally, if at all, by the cardiologist who has met them. In out-patient clinics, anxiety or relief are conveyed vividly although not always in words. The atmosphere of the medical meetings, concentrating on technical knowledge, is not conducive to discussing personal details, or intuitive awareness,[3] however important the cardiologist who knows the family might consider these to be in the clinical decisions.

Technical and social values

It is questionable how far wise surgery decisions are based on scientific detachment or also on involvement with the family. The danger is that mechanical notions of what is technically feasible will obscure the costs to the family; that 'risk' will be defined as prediction of probable achievement instead of assessment of possible harm to the child. During the early stages of scientific medicine, Richard Titmuss warned that:

Scientific medicine has let into clinical medicine a new spirit of criticism and questioning. . . . The danger is, however, that . . . a new authoritarianism will replace the old one. For the greater the expectations we place on the doctor the more may we strengthen his need to maintain his role, and while attempting to satisfy others, to satisfy himself. . . . There is a danger of medicine becoming a technology. . . . The task of the future is to make medicine more 'social' in its application without losing in the process the benefits of science and specialized knowledge.[4]

This suggests that decisions need to be informed by the experience of being with the family, not just by a report of them. Doctors seemed uncertain how to combine detachment and involvement in informing parents or asking for their opinions. A cardiologist told me, 'We write to parents to tell them of the JCC decision and invite them to discuss it at the next out-patients.' Yet a surgeon told me, 'More or less, parents accept our decision by our team at the JCC.' However, discussing one child at the JCC he said:

Surgeon: Palliation has a better survival rate than repairs, but long term . . . It is very, very . . .
Registrar: I saw one very, very well child on Tuesday, palliated.
Surgeon: Yes, . . . yes . . . if . . . I'd be slightly more inclined . . . if it was my child. . . . Talk to the parents. We have a ninety per cent mortality, look . . . um.
Cardiologist: She won't survive. She's very breathless.
Surgeon: It's not urgent. Leave the parents time to talk.
Senior reg.: They're very dependent on what we say. They'll follow what we tell them.

A registrar came in to say that a child had just died during her operation, and talked about another patient who might not survive. This illustrates the pressure on surgeons to keep at some distance from families when they are so directly involved in fatalities.

Another surgeon, whom parents found very kind and supportive, talked to me about the authority of the JCC and the extent of parents' freedom to respond to JCC decisions, also about the difficulty of making technical decisions when feeling personally involved.

Surgeon: Because of the very technical nature of the job, and the fact that most of the decisions we have to make are very tough in terms of life and death—quality of life, the social side of it does tend to get pushed into the background. . . . The emotional side of it does tend to get displaced, and I think it has to, to produce clarity of decision about the haemodynamics to some extent. Because you've got to concentrate completely on these problems for short periods of time, to get the decision right. Some are very unpalatable, with a high risk. Nobody wants to go back and operate on Nicholas again, but we've got to. It's his only chance of survival.

That doesn't mean to say that is 'the decision'. That means that is what we have advised as a team. We then go and discuss it with the parents. So we need a venue for that kind of clear policy. But we don't carry it forward without a potential for modifying it with the views of the parents. And if his parents said, 'We've had enough, no more', I don't think any of us would think they'd made an unwise decision. Personally I would say to them, 'If it was my child I would have another go. Let's try once more.'

PA: Do you think that might put intolerable pressure on parents? They might feel they could not refuse?

Surgeon: No, no. I think by that stage they know full well what they are doing. It's not intolerable, it's a position of great relief.

PA: But what if you do sense, maybe it's gone too far?

Surgeon: Some doctors are more open to that suggestion than others, and some find it easier to do than others. It would be naïve of me to say that every doctor was capable of handling that kind of situation. I don't think it can be easily taught. It's part of the personality, so if the decisions that we reach, have to be made away from that kind of . . . The clinical decisions, I think, must be made coldly. Not coldly, that is without any emotion. They must be made on the basis of medical evidence. What is correct given the data that you have available. If there's more data, or the parents say 'No', or you feel you want to influence the parents in another way, then I think the decision you have reached is wrong. You've got a whole new problem. And then you adapt that decision on the basis of other factors, you take it back to the JCC.

PA: Do you find that you have to select what you consider to be the main arguments, you've put them in a certain balance, so inevitably you're slanting your information?

Surgeon: I'm not frightened of slanting my information one way or the other because we've already made a decision in the JCC what's best for the child.

The surgeon considers the questions: What are the appropriate data for medical decisions? How much should social information be combined with technical issues? How personal or impersonal should the doctors' approach to cases be? And how far are patients objectively informed or subjectively influenced?

One definition of voluntary consent is that people taking part in medical research 'should be able to exercise free power of choice, without the intervention of any element of force, fraud, deceit, duress, overreaching, or other ulterior form of constraint or coercion'.[5] This definition can apply to patients if, although coerced by the illness, they do not feel coerced by the opinions of hospital staff. However, patients' knowledge is based on the medical diagnosis and prognosis, which cannot be wholly objective and impartial, especially in complex, high-risk cases. There is rarely a clear, single truth, and knowledge and hope cannot be separated totally.

The surgeon continued to talk about balancing detachment with involvement.

There are ethical questions, value judgements that I feel I must not make, unless pushed into a corner to make them. I help parents. I help their beliefs and opinions. But I'm here to do a job, to make that child better in the best context for the family. I'm not always in a position to have all the data which enables me to make that decision. I've got to sense it.

He seemed to consider that it was more ethical to offer surgery than to withhold it. If he needed to persuade parents of a mortally ill child that no surgery could help, 'which I realize is contentious in every possible way' he would keep talking about risks and problems until:

eventually they'll say to you, 'Is it worth going on?' and that's when you start debating with the parents themselves, and some consensus will emerge.

Emphasizing detachment and that their decisions are determined by scientific rules helps to relieve the clinicians' burden of personal choice and involvement. Yet it may lead them to exclude issues which are crucial to families.

Themes in the medical meetings

Recurrent themes in the medical meetings, as in the clinics, include making a series of rapid decisions; separating medical from social concerns; measuring morbidity either clinically or through patients' experiences; attempting precise predictions; allocating limited resources.

Two themes dominated the meetings: chronic illness and risk versus benefit. To quote an average meeting of fourteen cases in the Brompton Hospital: three seemed likely to recover well; in two cases there was some doubt about the type of surgery to offer; eight children had had months or years of chronic illness which could be alleviated but not cured (a baby of seven months had always lived in hospital and another baby died shortly after the meeting); one fatal condition would not be treated. Meetings represented the work-load of the unit, but not the success rate; sick children were repeatedly reviewed, but cured cases seldom were.

Chronic illness led on to the other main theme, risk. Doctors balanced high mortality and morbidity risks of surgery against risks of postponing surgery until it was too late, and against harms of chronic illness and severe incapacity. This is the connecting point between medical knowledge of technical risk and social knowledge of the child's daily life and the family's values.

Medical trust in objective scientific assessment can conflict with trust in the families' views. Social matters acceptable in the GP surgery may be avoided in highly technical medicine. Yet many, if not most, of the children had defects which (so far) cannot wholly be cured. Some had years of illness. Their families were not looking only for 'the heroism of cure', but also for the 'vulnerability of care'[6] of doctors helping them to cope practically and psychologically with chronic heart disease.

Patients present dilemmas for all concerned, dilemmas of knowledge and responsibility, choices between: scientific versus subjective knowledge; medical versus personal or parental authority; clinical versus personal assessment of health; and so on. Whereas doctors specializing in highly technical medicine tend to separate the pairs and to exclude the non-medical side, families try to unite them: to share responsibility; to combine different values and types of knowledge; to connect medical treatment with the patient's daily experience.

Since there is no general solution, such as to when surgical risk is too high, a decision must be made in each case. Medical decisions demand too much time and energy, unless doctors restrict themselves to reasonably objective and manageable criteria, while continually making hard decisions for years on end. Connecting technical and social values is therefore a problem for doctors, yet separating them can be a problem for families.

The tendency of doctors and families to work in opposite directions is central to their interpretation of informed consent. Consent may be seen either as acceptance of a medical proposal, or else as working towards agreement within technical and social tensions. If families dissent, in the first view of consent, doctors are liable to offer more explanation and reassurance. In the second view, doctors may consider families' reservations with them, and possibly modify the medical decision. At some level technical and social aspects meet, as the surgeon said, like two pathways. The degree to which they converge affects the quality of consent.

This chapter has considered just one example of doctors presenting a difficult medical decision to parents. David did not have an operation; he was often unwell during early childhood. His example is unusual and not representative. Yet it does illustrate general trends underlying medical thinking in the units I observed.[7] The next chapter considers how the rest of the caring team respond to medical decisions, and how their response influences proxy consent.

5

Professional team-work

Scientific medicine ventures into new areas of knowledge and skill. These ventures depend on the informed commitment not only of patients but also of the professionals caring for them. This chapter considers how professional team-work affects the consent process.[1] The first section shows the stresses of medical uncertainty and the nurses' responses. The next part describes the differing approaches of nurses and doctors when informing families. The medical mosaic describes how different grades of doctors contribute various information. This is followed by a section on professionals who offer psychological and social support. The final section considers ways of co-ordinating the professional team-work.

Medical uncertainty

In some cases it was very difficult to reach a consensus. One example was Richard who was born with a form of truncus which could rarely be treated successfully. Two years earlier his brother had died of the same defect. An intensive care sister told me that Richard's mother

really loves that baby. It's as if she's in a world of her own. She stayed up all Wednesday night cuddling him. Then the operation was cancelled. If only the dreadful effects on parents were taken into account. She had to wait over the whole weekend. . . .

We didn't expect him to come back from theatre and when he did the parents were jubilant. We were so pleased, but after a day or so, it became clear that the mitral valve was regurgitating. The surgeon came round today and said he's going to die. The parents are still so happy. How can we explain it to them?

Eleven days later Richard's parents were still hopeful. During a ward round the doctors spoke in a subdued way.

Cons.: He looks a bad colour. All the systems are failing. He won't survive. He'll just deteriorate.

SR: Well the neurological system seems [*he explains hopefully*].

SHO: Is it a question that he might recover neurologically?

Cons.: It's a question that we cannot be a hundred per cent certain that he will not recover.

Sister: The parents want us to do everything we possibly can, as they did last time.

They talk sadly about Richard's parents having no other children and being unable to have any more. The doctors question the ethics of going on or of ending treatment and say there is no clear answer except to an 'armchair philosopher', someone with no practical responsibility.

A doctor who read a draft of this book said that it was misleading, because it did not show how doctors agonize over medical decisions. Doctors seldom said, 'I feel very sad, or very guilty', as nurses frequently did at their meetings. There is little quotable material about doctors' experiences, apart from the care and time they took over discussing the decisions. Clearly the burden of decisions is far heavier for the senior doctors. As one nurse said, 'We moan about the doctors' decisions sometimes, but I'm glad I don't have to make them; I couldn't.' Clinicians have to live with the consequences of their decisions, when they repeatedly review the children they cannot restore to health, 'our mistakes' as one consultant said. They also live with the continual pressure to make such decisions. A social worker said:

I don't think you can choose a more devastating line of work than paediatric cardiology, always dealing with loss, and death, and despair, and mutilation of babies. If you don't quite get it right they die. You can't even take a year off. Planning scientific research is a way of avoiding pain, and guilt, and anger, and your impotence, and frustration at not being able to cure all your patients.

The doctors continued to discuss Richard.

Cons.: I think he'll just deteriorate.

SR: Well, maybe [*he describes encouraging signs*].

Cons.: Mm. I think we should be very, very pessimistic with the parents. You should talk to them again, and I'll talk to them, over the next day or so. I think we should not just go on and on.

SR: I don't think the parents will accept active withdrawal of treatment.

Cons.: Oh no, no. . . . But if he arrests? Do we resuscitate? [*Several doctors shook their heads but it was not clear whether they were giving an opinion or agreeing with a senior doctor. They moved to another patient. Richard's nurse had been called away and now came back.*]

Sister: I don't quite know what they've decided. I think Dr A [the consultant] is more pessimistic than the others.

Ward clerk: I've got these very, very nervous parents [*ringing the intercom to ask to come back in after the medical round. She fetched Richard's parents and as usual they washed their hands, sat down and stared at him intently. The nurse made and recorded the observations.*]

Nurse: We're clearing out the system every half-hour now. We were doing it every hour but now we're doing it more to see that it is really cleared out. And apart from that he's—good.

Nurses' responses to uncertainty

Conclusions varied when they were based partly on subjective assessments of complex information. When doctors were uncertain, nurses could not convey a clear message, of hope or pessimism. If she had heard the consultant, the nurse might have hinted that having to do more 'clearing out' was a danger sign. Possibly the parents gained, or clung to, an impression that more activity meant more determination to win. Warning of pessimism is quite different from altering the course of treatment into terminal care, when hope of recovery is definitely relinquished. While treatment continues, it may be as necessary to the staff at the bedside as to the parents to keep up comfort and to say, 'He's—good.'

During delays, waiting for surgery or recovery, nurses worked within a controlled suspense, maintaining orderly routine, yet aware of parents' need for clear detail set against clinical uncertainty. Modern nursing methods, such as the Nursing Process, value clear plans. Yet much cardiac care is about managing uncertainty. A sister said to me:

In a terminal unit it's clear what's going to happen, you prepare patients for death and you can talk openly. But here, we are working in uncertainty and that's very hard. You can't say, 'Cuddle your baby because he's going to die tomorrow', but you can't be jolly and cheerful either. We need an expert to come to tell us what to say.

Some parents are very difficult, they go through such terrible highs and such dreadful lows. They seem to live from day to day and not be able to look ahead.

Families interpret medical information as good or bad news, but some parents described to me their extreme uncertainty, almost as a refuge against despair or vain hope. I asked the sister about this response.

PA: Some parents say the only way they can cope is to take each day at a time. They thought that after the first operation, everything would be fine. It was such a shock when it wasn't fine, that even if they were told now that all would be well, they wouldn't dare to believe it for fear of being disappointed.

Sister: Yes, I suppose each time, they thought that would be the end, and it was only another beginning of something else. But I still feel that if we could give people a plan to stick to, that would help them to formulate their own life in the hospital.

When nurses were supporting the family through distressing treatment, they needed to be convinced that they were part of a united team serving the patient's best interests. So the nurses needed to go through their own form of willing consent to treatment. At times, they had reservations, such as the senior nurse who said, 'I wish I did not have to give some of the IV drugs, the side-effects are so nasty.' Sometimes nurses had doubts about the trust they were expected to encourage in the parents. At a nurse support meeting[2] one nurse said:

I think parents don't understand risk. Dr B told these parents that Fontans had a risk of ten per cent. I asked one of the surgeons and he said, ninety-five per cent success rate. I'm sure it's much lower, about fifty. The last few children have all died. I think they operate because of scientific interest, not always because it is the best thing for the child.

If a few children died after the same kind of operation, it was hard for the nurses to take an impersonal or optimistic view.

At a unit meeting, nurses and doctors discussed an investigative operation on Roger's larynx. He was hoarse after weeks on a ventilator, and three operations. Some nurses thought this would increase his hoarseness.

SHO: We all discussed it; we knew it was traumatic and some of us didn't want it done, but we wanted to fully document and understand the neurological problems. We did spend time talking to his mother, she did seem to understand and I don't think she was upset. It seemed fair enough to do it while he was here, rather than have to readmit him.
SR: But his voice was getting better so why do it?
SHO: I wasn't aware it was.
SR: The parents thought it was.

Sister: It's not just what the parents feel, it's the effect on the child.

SHO: Where we went wrong, we didn't explain to the nurses as well as to his mother, so that they could back us up.

Sister: We couldn't see why. He could breathe well.

SR: Yes, we need to think about the issue of informing nurses.

Nurses' beliefs affected the families. A sister said to me:

I know the problem, we fragment things. The doctors say, 'Put in another line.' The nurses say to the parents, 'Isn't it sad we have to put another line in.' Nurses don't back up the doctors. There is a gap between them. So senior nurses were saying, 'Why the heck is Roger having this investigation?' It filtered down to the juniors and then the parents get worried. We should be free to disagree and tell the doctors what we honestly think, but doctors and senior nurses shouldn't say that to the parents.

Nurse support meetings were held by a nurse teacher and the social worker. At these, nurses would express anger and doubt. Yet it was as if venting their negative reactions helped them to cope, and then they would remember successes, everyone's determination to try to save life, and pleasure in unexpected recoveries. Key themes of the nurses' meetings were about: coping with distress; preparing families for possible loss; providing information and care; and the nurses' own sense of inadequacy. These were also times for nurses to work out together more clearly what they thought had, and should have, happened, and to encourage one another.

Medical and nursing meetings shared parallel contrasts between medical and nursing journals. Medical journals concentrate on disease and technical treatment detached from personal circumstances. Nursing journals concentrate on 'anecdotes', personal aspects of disease and the nursing response, on the words, actions, and feelings of the people experiencing illness and giving care. The nurses talked about how families could be helped to work towards informed, committed choices. Doctors shared these concerns individually, when I spoke with them, but rarely talked of them at medical meetings and they rarely told the story of the human events as the nurses did, for example, of eleven-year-old Nicholas.

Sister: They had got him off bypass then the next call came saying he'd just died. We were all on tenterhooks. I was in charge. Everyone came and asked, even some parents. I said, 'He's still in theatre', though I knew. We are a small close unit here. Nick had been in here for three months. He'd had three major operations.

Nursery nurse: It was too new for us. We couldn't say the actual words. It was easier to say, 'He's still in theatre.' We'd be more honest later. You have to consider the people you are talking to. Anyway, we hadn't found his parents yet, to tell them first.

Sister: But I think the others knew.

Social worker: It's partly your shock, partly to protect yourselves.

The nurses needed to ensure that parents understood risk, partly because nurses usually take the impact of giving information after unsuccessful surgery. Even if doctors gave the actual news, while nurses waited for the doctor to arrive, remaining silent could be as complicated as speaking. 'When you ask parents to wait, in that voice, they know at once. They can tell from your face.'

Nurses frequently discussed how to compromise between unfeeling detachment and being so involved that they 'broke down', how to use feelings positively, as one nurse said, 'in being a strong, calm support'. Here 'strong' suggests not physical or intellectual strength, but emotional strength. The meeting continued by discussing how 'to nurse' feelings, one's own and other people's, and how to teach new nurses to give bad news.

Nurse: Even if you are warned, it is worse than you expect. You feel totally insensible, it's not you at all. . . . You have to nurse it and cope in your own way.

Sister: You can't explain. Talking is so different from going through it. You want to run sometimes. If I didn't have a break next week I'd be having a nervous breakdown. But there are more good times than bad times, thanks, goodbyes, recoveries.

For a few weeks after Nicholas's death, the nurses' meetings debated whether surgery had been the best choice for him, whether 'eighty-per-cent risk is different from days and days of fighting in intensive care'. They were concerned that Nicholas had not been consulted. His parents had been advised 'to go off for a walk and think about their decision'. 'He was rushed to theatre early on Sunday morning, shouting "I don't want to die, Mummy." His mother, and the nurses will never forget that.' The nurses' discussions illustrated the importance of informing and trying to convince everyone closely affected by medical decisions.

A central question was how the staff could discuss all the medical risks and options freely, without losing the confidence of families and some staff members. One answer was to have parents present on the general ward medical rounds, but to exclude them from intensive care unit rounds, although this did not resolve all the problems.

Nursing and medical information

Reaching clear agreement is hampered on many levels by: uncertainty about which treatments to prescribe; change in the patient's condition; changing staff rotas; and the lack of an appointed person who ensures that everyone closely concerned is informed. Nurses talked about the value of giving practical co-ordinated information as much as was possible.

Sister: Leroy's mother just comes in and says, 'Oh, is he still ventilated?' And we knew right from the operation that he would be ventilated for five days at least [because of his condition and problems from previous surgery].

PA: Did you tell her he might be on for five days?

Sister: Well, I can't remember telling her, because I assumed she'd know. That is the sort of thing I think should be mentioned at consent. Like, 'Your son's going to be sick for a long time after the operation. He'll probably need to be on the ventilator for a week, two weeks because he has got these problems.' That's a doctor's job. I don't know what the doctors say.

A lot of the nurses get very, very upset when parents are ignorant of the child's condition. They feel the medical staff don't give them enough time and they explain everything in such high-falutin' language. But I catch myself whizzing over medical terms that I'm so used to. And sometimes parents will just tell you a lot of nonsense. Once I thought a registrar hadn't explained anything properly, from what the parents said. It was very high-risk surgery and I was so angry I went down to see him and it turned out he had told them. They just hadn't understood.

It is easier for nurses to talk in a unit where they don't exclude parents from the [medical] rounds because then there isn't the feeling: Should we tell them? The atmosphere is very different. You're not frightened to tell parents what's going on, if everything is done in front of parents, and they are actively encouraged to be there. . . . The parents need different levels of information from different people but it isn't being co-ordinated.

Later, I asked the senior registrar what he might tell Leroy's parents about the likely postoperative course. He explained how, in Leroy's condition,[3] 'their pulmonary arteries can clamp down while they are on the ventilator and reduce the cardiac output considerably'. Leroy's paralysed left diaphragm 'in itself will definitely predispose to collapse of the left lower lobe [of the lung]'.

This doctor spent much time talking with parents. His long explanation to me of Leroy's condition and treatment does not represent a typical explanation to parents, because there was not one. Explanations varied with the time, and place, the people concerned, and, most of all, the questions parents asked. Yet this interview is typical (from what I observed and heard from staff and parents) in four characteristics.

First is the emphasis on physiology, on causes and effects of prolonged ventilation on the body systems, from the perspective of medical management.

Second is the serious way many doctors take the explanation, assuming not only that it is possible for lay people to understand medical concepts but that it is important that they do so.

Third is a willingness to admit medical limitations related to unwanted effects of surgery and to the patient's very serious defects, as long as these are handled carefully. The senior registrar thinks that it is vital that experienced doctors explain a 'complex or political' case carefully. 'If you have to redo an operation, parents are going to wonder, did they do the right thing signing the form. I've got no doubts that obviously the surgeon did exactly the right thing, and it is necessary to make this clear to parents.'

Fourth is uncertainty about how information-giving should be shared. Patients such as Leroy, referred from another paediatric cardiac centre and having several operations, are seen by many doctors who give varied information. 'Ideally doctors at the surgical unit should go through everything . . . but we just don't have as much time to speak to parents as we should.'

Medical information involves hopes and uncertain predictions. These are conveyed through attitudes, looks, tones of voice, confidence or pessimism (in one's own ability as well as the patient's condition), and through willingness or diffidence in sharing information. The senior registrar told me:

For example, with Adam, we've gone over all the problems on the ward round. We all know what the others think of him. There are—are some medical uncertainties why he is not well, but—overall we know this is an extremely difficult condition to treat. Many patients don't survive, whatever you do. So even from the beginning a certain amount of pessimism is realistic and a good thing to present the parents with.

We don't know what they are thinking, what they've been told before. I think they quite rightly want to hear it again, in terms of the problems there are now, an unbiased up-to-the-minute view. [*He would try to sense how prepared parents were to be pessimistic.*] Because you're trying to be honest with them. What's important is to know how quickly you can be that honest. . . . It depends on how rapidly you can turn their attention to that degree of pessimism. So if the outlook is extremely pessimistic then you can sense that it comes as no surprise to them when you start saying he's not doing well.

Knowledge is here seen as awareness, personally given and gradually accepted. Parents are offered the chance to question and adjust their understanding, so that information is exchanged and 'sensed'. It is not standardized when each doctor develops a personal style, has different levels of knowledge, and the many details of the case may frequently change.

Information about surgery can be divided broadly into the medical view and the family view. Whereas the sister spoke of Leroy's parents' need to be warned about visible experiences, such as length of ventilation, the medical view tends to concentrate on invisible inner physiology. For example:

PA: What would you say to Leroy's parents about the postoperative course?
SR: I don't think I'd point out anything in particular, um, that there's a much higher risk than any other patient because then they'll say 'Why?' and then you'd get fairly technical, talking about pulmonary crises, things like that.

In contrast, the family are mainly concerned with whatever they might see, hear, or feel. When told, 'the risk is ten per cent', parents would ask, 'What does that mean? Is that a serious risk?' When told about a lesion, they wanted to know 'what it meant' in practical terms of the child's welfare, discomfort, recovery, and so on. In Leroy's case of repeated surgery, predicting timing was particularly difficult. So that although the sister thought that doctors should warn about timing, nurses may be better able to give families this kind of information. Sitting beside the cot all day, they are more likely to be aware of what families want to know.

Many parents wanted to know how they could help their child, to base their consent on practical as well as theoretical information. Doctors' concentration on medical management of symptoms, and nurses' assumption that parents have been fully informed, can mean that the practical information is omitted. Divisions of care further reduce opportunities to inform families. Parents were shown the

Brompton ICU, which is remote from the ward, the evening before the operation, which many thought was too late to help them to prepare their child. In the Children's Hospital, very detailed practical preparation was given to parents and children well in advance, and children were shown the ICU and books about the stages of recovery after surgery.

The medical mosaic

Each doctor provides different kinds of information to families. The most junior doctors, senior house officers (SHOs), vary in how much they say. Some said they were cautious about talking in case they said something 'wrong or stupid'.

We can explain simple things like a hole, but not complicated conditions, and operation risks or the prognosis. That's not our job. We're not cardiologists and anyway we don't need to explain, the parents will have been informed very fully in out-patients.

SHOs manage the patients' daily treatment and inform families about the general medical care.

On the next grade, the registrar described the long time needed to learn cardiology. (He echoed Hippocrates' view that 'life is short and art long; opportunity is fleeting, experiment perilous and judgement difficult'.) A staff meeting with a psychiatrist was talking of Gwenda who had just died of endocarditis, infection in her heart.

Reg.: Shortly after the operation she had to be taken back to theatre. She was bleeding a lot where the conduit was connected to the heart. Maybe the infection was introduced then.

Psych.: So why didn't they do their stitches tight?

Reg.: Well the heart isn't pumping at the time. You can't tell until you've restarted the heart. Sometimes there's a clot or a stitch, or tissue gives way. Lots of problems can arise.

Psych.: Would the family be prepared that it might not work?

Reg.: . . . Cardiologists might talk—very carefully in the clinic. . . . In the clinic I'll speak in terms of mortality but not in terms of long-term complications such as, 'He might sustain brain complications and even be mentally retarded.' It's difficult to know if you should spill all the beans.

Sister: In the States you must.

Reg.: There are so many risks, it's enormous. Some risks never occurred to us. Maybe the consultants knew, but we juniors didn't, and that's only one of hundreds of possible problems.

As already shown, consultants are very involved with diagnosis and information in the clinics. Senior registrars, the grade before consultants, are also a main source of specialized cardiac information. They work closely with the families, nurses, and medical teams, and are therefore aware of the need to co-ordinate information, and support families and staff. They spend long hours talking with nurses and parents on the wards or by telephone before admission. 'A lot of them do phone; this proves there is an obvious need for information.' One senior registrar said that she thought that such extremely demanding work could only be continued for a few years, after which she would need a consultant post which has different responsibilities and less intensive work with patients and nurses in the wards.

Meetings of nurses and junior doctors frequently discussed what should be told, who should tell, and at which stage. They were aware of many difficulties. An SHO said at the meeting just quoted:

When I first came I thought the rounds were awful. You can hear the quiver in fathers' voices when they try to talk, they're so intimidated by that big crowd, but there's no other time they can catch a consultant. After a few weeks I got used to it. I suppose doctors doing it for years don't see how hard it is for parents.

A nurse added that when a consultant was asked to speak to two parents during a round,

he talked very nicely, and the parents got so much less tense and were very pleased and afterwards I heard the consultant say to the sister that it was very useful. But *why* don't they do it with the others? Why does the nurse have to ask?

There was concern not only about whether to tell certain news, but how to present it.

SHO: I can't believe what's said on ward rounds. Such as, 'Williams syndrome—do you know the incidence of mental retardation is seventy per cent?' The parents looked aghast and were ignored but they looked as if they had never heard of it before. Then the next child—'The chances of surviving the operation are thirty per cent.' Christ, if it was my child I'd go mad.

SW: And the boy they said was only the second case in the world with that anatomy. His mother was ready to fall apart anyway.

Reg.: That does happen a lot, we do rather take it for granted.

Talking with families competed with other activities. Consultants regarded the long ward rounds as important for teaching and for making clinical decisions, leaving little time for other matters. As families are encouraged to become more informed and involved, inevitably they hear disturbing news. There is not always time to adjust between discussion among doctors and medical discussion with families, so that people are sometimes unintentionally hurt. One alternative would be to exclude parents more, but older child patients would then overhear medical talk without having their parents' support and explanations.

One doctor summed up the discussion: 'Parents seem to get told in dribs and drabs through the tertiary referral. Some parents are difficult to tell things to, and some doctors are better at telling.' Much effort is put into giving medical information. Yet so many people are involved that the effect is like a mosaic in which the parts do not all tessellate. They are not all clearly defined, they overlap and leave gaps. There is uncertainty about who said what, when, and where, and who should provide each part. Families receive a detailed picture sometimes in ways which confuse rather than inform.

In return, families cannot ensure that all the staff directly concerned know their views and needs. Messages change as people retain, reject, pass on, or reinterpret various details. Ways of clarifying the mosaic are considered later under 'team-work'.

Social and psychological support

Each member of the unit team could influence the consent process, by helping to ease the fit between medical and social aspects of care. Secretaries, ward clerks, and playworkers received and reported much medical and social information about the children, sharing this between the family and the staff. Although all the staff could offer (or withhold) psychosocial support, this section mainly considers the staff who specialize in this work.

In the Children's Hospital, the social worker's post was frozen during most of this study. A psychologist attended a weekly meeting with a few staff but rarely worked directly with families. In the Brompton Hospital there were a few meetings with a research psychiatrist. Apart from this, support was mainly offered by the clinical nurse teacher and the social worker. This section is therefore not broadly based, but considers examples of support which was needed or offered and how this could influence consent.

Social workers offer two main kinds of help: practical, and

psychological which one described as 'help in sorting out the family's confused feelings towards the child, who through no fault of its own creates so many problems for the family'. An example of their help was given by a single mother in the Children's Hospital, whose intelligent eight-year-old daughter Gilly, after a long cardiac arrest a week earlier, suddenly had a mental age of about eighteen months. Gilly's mother had not known where to find money for the following day's fare to hospital. After seeing the social worker she said, 'I feel human again. The first thing, she offered me a fag and we had a really good chat in her room and she's found £80 for me.' Social support helped parents to be physically present, and psychologically prepared to cope with medical discussions.

The Brompton social worker held support groups for parents to help them to cope with stress. Through sharing their anxieties, and realizing their common feelings they came to feel slightly less isolated and inadequate.[4] The phrase 'sit down and talk' was often used to denote talking about serious news. It suggests allowing time and sitting face to face on an equal level. This could only happen if there were spare chairs and quiet space, so the social worker raised funds to furnish a room for quiet interviews, and relaxation.

Some parents prefer to cope on their own. 'We dread tea and sympathy,' said one father, 'We'd rather go and make our own coffee and cry on our own.' Other parents are grateful for the support of the staff, and often share supportive relationships with other families. 'One of the best things that come out of staying here, is being so close to some of the other parents. You go through so much together', was a typical comment. Both groups manage in the way they prefer. However, some parents are very isolated, seeming to receive no support from other parents, the staff, or from their own family.[5] Those in greatest need of help seem too crippled by anxiety to be able to ask for it, and the social workers, who could not answer all the requests for help, had no time to go around offering more.

Caring for parents

The units are intended to correct hearts, not to run a family support service. They cannot wrap people in cotton wool, vainly attempting to prevent all distress. That would be wasteful, futile, and demeaning to parents. The other extreme, to deny all psychosocial support, would be equally misguided, as if patients could simply be physically repaired like broken machines. A practical compromise is to offer the support which families need in order to care for the child as nearly as possible as they would do at home. This involves listening to the families' views on necessary support, and on unnecessary interference, respecting and working with them, encouraging their independence, and making decisions with them.

Adequate care for child patients includes supporting parents for the following reasons:

to help families to cope with the severe extra psychological and financial problems posed by the child's illness;
to alleviate the stress resulting from ways in which treatment is provided (such as in specialist centres far from patients' homes);
to help parents to be in a fit state to be able to care for their child;
to prevent the child being harmed if parents become severely depressed.

Psychological effects of information

Just as powerful drugs bring benefits but also harmful side-effects, medical information can be a mixed blessing. It presents families with painful knowledge and dilemmas, and can be a source of family turmoil. A social worker said of one family:

It's very important that this decision is discussed fully with both parents. It may relieve a lot of their enormous worries. Last time Mrs White had to consent without Mr White being there and he was very angry. He's in a bad state now so it is essential, it's *vital*, that he is fully aware of what the next operation is going to be like so that Mrs White is protected in case something goes wrong.

My intention is not to imply that information ought to be withheld, but to show how it needs to be given with care, respect, and support. It may be argued that in disturbed families, parents will quarrel over any excuse, and hospital staff should therefore have nothing to do with family rows about the consent form. However, prolonged family tension is likely to be closely associated with the child's heart disease. The whole topic of consent is very sensitive both in its direct meaning (committing the child into danger) and as a symbol (the consent form assumes united parental responsibility for the child which may not be the case). For the child's sake, care over the potentially contentious matter of consent may be seen as partly the hospital's responsibility. Giving proxy consent to high-risk surgery, or to withholding life-saving treatment can involve the sense of guilt or blame even in united families, because it is deeply disturbing for any parent.

The following example illustrates how social work counselling can complement medical information. Kenneth Howard had spent almost all his sixteen months in hospitals. He still only weighed his birthweight. The consultant said: 'He is a very sick, floppy little baby. Very great pressure was put on us by the parents to operate. We put on a band, now what can we do? There is no hope in operating. You need to really sit down with them for an hour to talk about this.' The staff agreed that the most compassionate decision for Kenneth was to reduce the drugs and send him back to the referring hospital to die. The social worker was asked to help to prepare Kenneth's father (his mother had left the family) to accept that there was no hope. She told me that she thought:

Doctors tend to leave things open, they are not conclusive and clear when it is bad news. Maybe they feel they have to keep alive some hope, but their dilemma is that they can only offer something if they're convinced it'll work and if it's the appropriate thing—not to be wishy-washy. . . .

John, the SHO, came in with me and he was very good, gently putting forward in a slow way what they'd hoped to do, what possibly could have been, but now Kenny wasn't growing it was cruel to give him surgery that wouldn't cure him, and drugs that wouldn't help, but gave him a rash. For about five minutes Mr Howard insisted the rash was due to the baby being allergic to the sheets. He couldn't accept the idea of bad medicine. . . . He was trying to keep up some kind of faith.

We went on, John saying, 'But Kenny isn't growing', Mr Howard saying, 'Look, he's getting longer', and John saying, 'He's not growing.' I said, 'It's very difficult for you to accept that Kenny's not doing as well as you want.' And that broke the escalation of their argument. It was good, the social worker and doctor working together. I interpreted the doctor's facts and John did his good talk about the prognosis being poor. He only later used the word 'die', and then Mr Howard went in for real denial, saying, 'Yes, he'll have surgery later and he'll get better and be running around.' John: 'No he won't.' Me: 'You really need to hang on to that hope that he'll get better.' Mr Howard: 'Yes. You don't know definitely he'll die. Who knows that?' as if he felt quite impotent. You need to have some element of control in the destiny of *your* child. When a doctor says, 'He'll die', a bit of you wants to say, 'No. no. He's mine.' Then at the end, John spelt out, 'Kenny is going to die.' Mr Howard said, 'Yes, I've known for a year—but he's going to live.' It ended with nothing settled.

This example indicates the time and skill required to help some parents to reach some form of voluntary consent.

Doctors as gatekeepers between patients and paramedical workers open gates by referring patients for psychosocial care, discussing patients on fairly equal terms with non-medical staff, listening to their views, and taking these into account. Non-medical staff thought that their work was more effective and patients benefited when medical and social care were combined in this way. 'I feel interested and committed, almost dragged into his team. My insights are used,' said a social worker of one such consultant. Other consultants were less interested in psychosocial problems. The social worker said,

Their science training tells them that you can't let emotion get in the way if you want to think logically and rationally. So they risk forgetting the human element and thinking that feelings are not valid. But if you irrationally try to deny pain and anxiety they can disturb you more than if you acknowledge them.

A psychologist at the Children's Hospital said:

They don't often make referrals I feel there must be so many children and parents in distress I don't hear of. I'm sure there are particular psychiatric problems with cardiology. I think they don't see any need for anything except the medical. They're so geared up to drama—to intensive care and emergencies, they haven't an interest in the more human side. And they have to some extent to ignore it in order to cope and to be able to go on working there.

A cardiologist commented,

It's not that we are not interested, but that psychological aspects are only one part of all the aspects of treatment we have to consider. Whereas for a psychologist, psychological care is the only aspect. We asked a haematologist to look at one of our patients. All the data he needed were in the notes but he said that he was amazed that the haematological details were so briefly recorded. Yet we can't possibly attend to everything fully and we have to decide what are the priorities. We are already overstretched.

It is not that we do not care, or we are not aware, or are not trying hard enough. You have to care to go on working here. But the doctors who stay have to be, not tough because we do get distressed, but emotionally resilient. It is very wearing, physically, emotionally, and socially to go on working here. We need the government to fund far more supporting services for the patients and the staff.

Compared with many papers on psychological aspects of cancer, there are few on the psychology of congenital heart disease. The social worker said, 'If doctors keep ignoring psychosocial information from the nurses, the nurses can't value it and keep passing it on, so decisions can't be made with the full facts.' Psychosocial needs may then be overlooked in individual patients, and on related general levels of medical practice, research, publications, and training. As Max Weber pointed out, rationality does not inhere in things, it is attributed to them. We only value things if we can notice and attend to them.

One reason for avoiding non-medical issues was doctors' wish not to intrude unnecessarily. An SHO talked of this with the social worker at the Brompton Hospital when discussing ten-year-old Alan Morley.

SHO: I don't want to be nosey and interfere. I wouldn't want people prying into my private life. But I feel we've put this family under such pressure. They are strange, but they might have gone jogging happily along if we hadn't interfered. But we've kept Alan in here for so long. And there's the suspense of not being able to tell them what was wrong and what we could do. The GP says Mr Morley has threatened to kill Alan. . . . I feel responsible and that I ought to do something, as long as I can help, not just interefere.

SW: I think Alan is a very upset child and we are not doing our job if we send him home in a worse state. The mothers complain that the children get so bored and depressed here. They're left on their beds and they're lonely. They need a teacher and a play therapist. At least we ought to initiate some family therapy which they can follow up at home, though it will take a very long time. . . . Here, children bring in problems and take them home again. That whole aspect is totally missed. We need short-term support here, to help to prevent long-term problems. And to make the other staff, doctors and nurses—to raise their consciousness about children's warped fantasies. . . .

SHO: At my last job we reluctantly sent a child back to a violent home . . . and a few weeks later he was dead. I felt responsible then, and I feel very anxious about Alan.

The SHO's words illustrate doctors' wish to select only clear information which they can use for effective, beneficial intervention.

One method for doctors to cope with patients' distress was to use impersonal language. The following example shows the power of words to create different responses, and how the social worker tried to bridge the language barrier between the medical and the parents' response. The social worker heard a medical report that eleven-year-old Gwenda was very ill, given in rather formal terms about cardiac function. Later, she looked white and shaking, and told me:

I've just met Mrs Davis. She came into my room and burst into such terrible sobs. They just want to go home. She knows Gwenda is dying, that she is very, very ill. It's awful. If she were my child I would opt for surgery. I couldn't bear to go on with this. It's so dreadful to see. I hadn't gathered this from the doctors.

The social worker interpreted her part in the consent process as reporting the family's views to the doctors who were considering surgery. Later, the surgeon decided that the mortality risk of operating would be 'one hundred per cent'. Gwenda insisted that she wanted to go home and eventually a nurse and an ambulance were found to take her back to Wales. She arrived home just before she died, and afterwards her mother said, 'We feel as if she is here with us.'

  Law cases usually concern parents refusing treatment for their child. A more common problem is parents feeling unable to refuse treatment which turns out to be ineffective or harmful. They are pressured by the dangers of leaving their child's serious condition untreated, and because no one can be certain that the treatment will not help. Doctors and nurses who are sceptical about treatment plans are reluctant to speak if others are still optimistic. Some doctors think that to send a child back to the referring hospital to die admits defeat. They prefer to attempt almost certainly fatal surgery, or resuscitation on children who arrest. Of course their efforts save lives, but they also mean that many children die suddenly without their parents being present. The greatest, but hidden, cost of medical progress is carried by the children whose treatment fails, and by their bereaved families. One way to reduce their suffering is to agree in time that the child is dying. Then parents like Gwenda's can gain some comfort from knowing that they fulfilled their child's last wish. One mother said, 'The comforting thing about him dying was that I was allowed to let him die how I wanted, which was in my arms, in bed together with no wires.' The risk of giving up too soon conflicts with the risk of persisting for too long. There are seldom clear answers but there is a great need for more honest and careful discussion in these difficult cases.

  Parents used the social worker as their advocate. One mother told me that she was angry about her son's treatment, but she wanted to preserve good relations with the doctors. She said: 'I told the social worker exactly how furious I was and I think she has had a word with them. Things are certainly better.' Link workers who interpret for Asian mothers in hospital find that they inevitably become two-way advocates; explaining to the staff how routines distress women and working for improvements in care, while also explaining to the mothers reasons for necessary practices.[6] Similarly, non-medical workers act as interpreters and advocates between the medical and the family world. Sometimes doctors assume that interpretation need be only one way: to explain medical details to the family. Psycho-social workers saw their work as two-way and thought a vital part was to help doctors to listen to patients. The social worker said:

Information gets lost. It's told to people but it's not passed on. No one puts it all together, so decisions can't be made with the full facts in mind. Some doctors are very formal, they inhibit things. They are full of things to tell and they won't listen—or only to information they decide to ask for, strictly in the given way they determine.

Yet she appreciated that people's accounts could be many layered. 'It's all splitting and projection. For example, we put good things into doctors, and think they are kind and powerful. And then parents get angry because doctors aren't omnipotent. But how much should we reasonably expect from them?'

When consultants held a joint session with a family, this could be very beneficial. The social worker described an interview with Alan Morley's father.

Alan's father started by saying why couldn't Alan have a brain scan if we didn't know what was wrong with him. Dr A laid it all out superbly, precisely, in beautiful clear language. He described exactly what was wrong and what could be done, and how there is only one other hospital in the world where this could be diagnosed and treated. He spoke with great authority but he was very calm and relaxed. He wasn't authoritarian, but Mr Morley had no way of manipulating him. Dr A made it clear precisely where we stood with treatment, and we all felt calmer and more confident.

A few ways in which connections between medical and psycho-social issues are managed have been outlined. Non-medical staff play an important part in the achievement of informed and voluntary consent. They can help families to understand medical decisions, and the staff to understand the families' views, more clearly.

Team-work

There are three ways of co-ordinating professionals' varied contributions to the consent process: team meetings, a named person, and rethinking hospital hierarchies.

Team meetings

Much of the Brompton Hospital senior registrar's work concerned 'sitting down and trying to get to grips with the situation' with families and staff. He thought that staff meetings were important for exchanging ideas and adjusting attitudes. He arranged a meeting for all the staff caring for an Indian child, two-year-old Nimmi, who could not be weaned off the ventilator for weeks after surgery. Of the extra pressures on overseas families of private patients there were the language barriers and the high daily charge for hospital care. 'Many are not rich families,' one sister said. 'They mortgage their house to come here. If their child dies, they go back with no child and no home.' The social worker told me:

The meeting was useful because it became apparent that all of us had received bits of information from the parents that went unheeded. One nurse said they would be devastated if treatment were stopped but none of us knew that. We need to meet as a team to carry responsibility. It would make decision-making and anxiety less difficult.

The senior registrar said:

I've no doubt that sort of meeting should be held every week, to clear the air . . . But the strains on our time are all so great. . . . I think the purpose of the meeting was to convince everybody working with her that we needed to be active and aggressive in treating her, because there was still reasonable potential for her to become an active normal child. . . . You've got to change with changes in the patient. But so many people looking after her were disaffected, disenchanted—bored—depressed . . . They felt they were being cruel . . . persisting with the treatment, if she was going to die anyway.

I think any patient like that should be discussed so that everybody can be encouraged to remain optimistic to a reasonable degree. It was important to get the nurses to understand why we were persisting and try and increase their enthusiasm and their own optimism, and therefore be able to cope not only with their own feelings but with the parents . . . If the nurse isn't convinced it's hard for them to be convincing. I think everybody needs a pep talk from time to time . . . even though the patient is very depressing.

'Managing a case' includes co-ordinating the patient's treatment and also the morale of the family and the caring team, as well as explaining decisions or necessary indecision to those closely involved in the child's care.

A named person

The patients, especially long-stay ones, need one person to be in overall charge of the continuing care, so that, as one mother said, treatment is part of a whole plan and not 'grasping at straws'. In-patient care is shared among the consultants, and as one doctor said:

It's difficult for them all the time to share exactly the same views. It's a good way to run a ward but . . . there may be some confusion from time to time . . . among all the staff about what the total plan or outlook for the patient is.

With some patients, there are weekly changes if one consultant favours surgery or a hopeful prognosis, and another does not. Medical team-work depends on loyalty to colleagues and deference to whichever consultant is on duty. The consultants have to respect one another's decisions as 'perfectly reasonable' even if they would have decided otherwise. Sharing the care increases the skill and knowledge available to each patient, and also offers consultants a manageable case-load. Yet the care sometimes seems to families impersonal and fragmented. After Darren had stayed in hospital for five weeks 'with a complicated and rare condition', the sister said:

I think his mother must be so fed up and depressed, pushed from pillar to post in this place, never a proper answer, no one seems to know. I'd be livid if I were her. She's been very good. No one else would put up with it. She doesn't talk because she is angry. She doesn't want to upset us.

One solution is when the child's own consultant is readily available to talk with junior staff and parents, and then with other consultants to resolve such problems.

Another solution is when each patient has a qualified primary nurse.[7] The primary nurse listens to the family, and ensures that medical staff also listen and respond to them. Paediatric nurses teach parents who want to learn skilled nursing techniques, so helping to increase their knowledge and confidence. Nurses can bridge gaps in knowledge and status between doctors and families, so that there may be more equal sharing of decisions and care. However, this is only possible when hospital traditions change.

Rethinking hierarchies

In traditional hospitals, doctors are at the top, nurses and other health workers in the middle, and patients at the bottom in terms of knowledge, autonomy, and control over resources. There are also clear vertical orders of seniority within and between the professions.

Yet informed consent is a horizontal, democratic approach, with doctors supposedly on equal if not deferential terms with patients or their parents. Introducing the new equality of consent between doctors and patients challenges traditional hierarchies; it is like new wine in old bottles.

Consent is seldom a contract between individuals, but one between the patient and family and the hospital team. The quality of consent depends on how all the relevant staff contribute information, extend and clarify it, correct misunderstandings, and help patients to absorb and come to terms with difficult news. To do this they have to be adequately informed. To maintain reasonable confidentiality, information is only shared among the staff most directly concerned with the patient, although this may be as many as seventy people, and certain information must be restricted to a few individuals.

The quality of patients' voluntary consent is influenced by the caring team's commitment to the chosen treatment. Patients quickly detect doubt or disagreement among the staff and this affects their own willing consent. Fear and doubt are inevitable aspects of risky treatment but the consent process can be a means of helping patients to decide that the potential benefits of the agreed plan of care are greater than the risks. This sometimes difficult process depends on the support of many hospital staff in helping patients to work through their reservations. Patients may give vital information to junior staff, or discuss with them anxieties which can only be resolved when referred on to senior doctors or nurses.

It is therefore important, not only that information flows down the hierarchy, but also that it can easily be passed up to senior staff when necessary. Members of the hospital staff speak more freely to one another when they are reasonably equal in status, when consultants listen patiently to other staff. This is not to suggest that junior staff take over medical management. Yet, as consultants increasingly share decisions with patients, rather than imposing decisions on them, there are repercussions for how much consultants discuss decisions with all their colleagues. The extra time required for discussing consent with patients can then be shared by the team, rather than the consultant having to carry this responsibility alone. Patient consent is related to changes in hospitals from autocratic to more democratic forms of medical leadership.

The professional team

There are many parallels between the modern cardiac team and the sailor adventurers five hundred years ago, charting unknown territory, hoping for great gain at high risk. Both depend on the loyalty of everyone involved in the venture. This used to be ensured partly through fear. The loyalty of the modern hospital team depends on each person being sufficiently informed and respected. When their doubts are discussed fairly, this can increase the confidence and efficiency of the unit.

Maintaining reasonable unanimity is difficult, especially among a very large, frequently changing team. Like Renaissance ships, hospitals can be uncomfortable work places, with limited space and resources. Perhaps the greatest challenge to unity is that both ventures (medical and nautical) explore the edges of a new world. Desire for the benefits of the new world of scientific medicine blends with fear that it is alien and dangerous. Nostalgia for the old world of personal medical care conflicts with awareness of its limitations.

Patients' commitment to treatment was influenced by the way each nurse and doctor explained procedures. Parents would describe how potent non-verbal messages could be. 'You could tell by that glimmer in her eye.' Such messages, vividly conveying underlying attitudes, influenced parents' beliefs in the harm or benefit of treatment. This is why the *esprit de corps* of the cardiac team, their doubt and commitment, their aims and self-criticism in not achieving a perfection which they knew was impossible, have been briefly considered. Selected quotations cannot convey these complex attitudes, which need to be seen in their whole context. Nurses' meetings were angry and gloomy. Yet this was their way of releasing tension in order to be able to continue with work they believed to be very worth while.

Only a few basic patterns in professional influences on the consent process have been considered here. They suggest that the staff teams face four main problems. First is the intractable nature of some physical defects, with the present limitations in treatment and the resulting stress on everyone involved in trying to push back the limits. Second is the challenge of a large group of individuals, with

differing aims and needs, trying to work in harmony. Third i
hospital routine, often essential and beneficial, but sometimes caus
ing unnecessary distress. Fourth are the inevitable personal limita
tions, such as of time and knowledge. All four problems complicate
efforts to keep everyone directly involved with the patient reasonably
informed and unanimously committed.

Informed consent: awareness

The next four chapters are about issues which affect all the stages of proxy consent that have been considered so far: information, voluntariness, trust, and issues debated in medical ethics.

Hundreds of papers have been written on informed consent, and I shall not attempt to summarize all the main themes.[1] Instead, this chapter looks mainly at the purpose and meaning of informed proxy consent and how this affects parents and children. Consent is more than being passively informed. It is also about becoming actively aware, learning through thinking and feeling. Informed proxy consent involves exchanging and evaluating information in order to make the best or least harmful decision for the child, and whenever possible with the child. The way in which details are explained can be almost as important as the actual details.

Three years after the event, Mrs Brown recalled when, one day after his birth, her son Mark was taken into a special care baby unit.

MB: Somebody whisked him off and they said they thought there was a heart murmur. After about half an hour somebody appeared and said they thought there was something else more serious wrong with him. They were taking X-rays, and he would be put in one of those things—an oxygen box. Then a doctor came and said there was something wrong with his heart and they would be sending him off to this hospital. It was just devastating. I think I was probably a little bit numb because having had a Caesarean you weren't totally aware of what's going on, it was just very confusing. Then a nurse came and said she wanted to check the religion.

PA: Did she say why?

MB: No.

PA: What did you think?

MB: I thought he was going to die. I was on a drip and they wheeled me along to special care and the priest came and baptized him and—then an ambulance came and took him away. A paediatrician came and tried to explain what they thought was wrong but I just didn't absorb it at that stage. It was all too much. I was just shattered. You think it's never going to happen to you.

During an emergency, even if there is time to inform the family, they may be too shocked to absorb the details. If a baby is sent to a specialist hospital without the parents, the referring staff may not know what to tell them, while they are waiting to learn not only the treatment plans but even the diagnosis. Many barriers, physical and mental, limit how much families can be informed and involved, as Mark's mother said.

In these cases, informed consent could be dismissed as an impossible ideal. This need not be so, but before seeing whether informed consent can be achieved in complicated cases like Mark's, I will say why it matters, and what it involves. Four advantages of informed consent are that it can: satisfy patients' wish to be informed; help them to accept and understand their treatment; help them to resist unwanted interventions; and respect their right of self-determination.

The benefits of informed consent

Satisfying the wish to be informed

Large British and American studies confirm that most patients want to be informed about their condition and treatment, and complain that they are not given enough information.[2] Many parents felt an extra obligation to become informed before giving consent on their child's behalf, such as the lawyer father who compared giving consent to his own recent back surgery with the greater responsibility of consenting to his son's heart surgery.

Aiding adjustment

Information aids therapeutic adjustment to illness and treatment. Even very young children perceive admission to hospital and painful treatment as punishment or wanton cruelty, unless they are frequently reminded of how each procedure is intended to help them.[3] Reassuring information helps to allay their rational fears and their fantasies, but children quickly sense the emotional messages more than the verbal ones, and detect underlying doubts. It is therefore essential that the informing adults are themselves convinced about the information they give. Parents translate medical information into terms which their child is most likely to understand; they can encourage children to ask questions and can sort out misunderstandings, as long as they have been adequately informed, and their doubts have been answered.

Louise Wallace's research demonstrates that 'informed consent can be . . . a therapeutic process, involving emotional preparation, a sense of control and helping the patient to have realistic expectations of the staff and hence perhaps less disappointment after the operation'. Informed patients are less anxious during treatment and recover more easily afterwards.[4] Information may not increase actual anxiety, but encourages patients to talk more about their latent anxiety, so enabling them to seek help and to dispel unnecessary fears. Fred Clough studied girls in an orthopaedic ward.[5] He found that meanings which patients construct about their illness and treatment vitally affect their perceptions of treatment. Children reacted with hostility and appeared to have more pain if they thought their treatment was unnecessary; they reacted with appreciation and easier recovery if they believed it to be necessary. Michael Kelley's research shows that patients' informed acceptance of treatment is a necessary, beneficial part of their adjustment to ileostomy. Damaging, bitter regret was felt by those who remained unconvinced of the need for surgery long after having an ileostomy.[6] Bernie Siegel, a surgeon, believes that patients' informed understanding of their illness and treatment is a vital part of their energy which helps them to overcome cancer.[7] A Norwegian educational therapist explains the effects of bone marrow transplants on the blood cells, to three- and four-year-old children with leukaemia, through a fairy story about a boy called Ola. The story helps the children during preparation and treatment. After her transplant one very ill girl with her mouth full of ulcers whispered 'Ola', asking to hear the story again, as if it encouraged her to bear the agonizing treatment.[8]

Informed patients who understand the meaning and purpose of treatment are more likely to co-operate; they will know for example when and why to take prescribed drugs. Parents too need to be informed when they share in giving treatment and in persuading the child to co-operate. Children like Mark Brown, with serious congenital defects, need months or years of medical care shared between the paediatric team and the family. It is therefore worth establishing habits of sharing information and decisions between them as early as possible.

Defending against unwanted interventions

Informed consent helps to defend patients against unwanted medical interventions. It enables patients or their parents to decide when they believe medical explanations to be inadequate or unconvincing, and when they wish to refuse proposed treatment. Doctors in the heart units were usually very willing to inform families. However, if doctors withhold information, they also hold on to the major share in making medical and personal decisions for patients. Helen Harrison summarized over seventy examples of harmful practices in American neonatal treatment. She concluded that parents ought to be informed.

In order to protect our children from abusive over-treatment [or] discriminatory under-treatment . . . parents can take steps to enter the decision-making process . . . by fully informing ourselves and others about the complex ethical problems created by neonatal medicine. [This would include] rethinking policies, no matter how well-intended, that promote withholding information from parents or that effectively deny parents access to divergent medical opinions.[9]

Informed consent involves exchanging medical and personal information. Patrick's case shows the value of this exchange. Patrick, aged ten, was unable to stand up straight because of his cerebral palsy, but he could run in an ungainly way, and enjoyed playing football. Patrick's orthopaedic surgeon operated to straighten his legs. Although to the surgeon the operation was a success because Patrick looked more normal, to Patrick it was a disaster because he could no longer run.

One cardiologist told me, 'There is a slightly higher risk for this operation when we operate on younger babies, but we prefer to do that. We believe that it is easier for parents to lose a younger baby.' Not all parents shared this view. Some wanted to have their child with them for as long as possible. 'We thank the surgeon for giving us those few precious extra months with her', said one couple when their baby died after her second operation. When Maxine, aged one week, had heart surgery her mother said,

I can't imagine her ever being any more precious to me than she is now. I can hardly bear feeling so close to her as it is. As soon as I wake up in the morning, I can't wait until I see her again. It's worse than being in love.

The father of another small baby said,

It seems obvious to say that the sooner they die, the better. I've thought that myself sometimes, but I'm not sure it's true. I think it's an impossible question to answer. People feel differently and you can only take each case as it comes. You need the best opinion from the medical view but doctors shouldn't make up people's minds for them.

When informed consent is taken seriously, and the central risks and benefits of surgery are discussed openly, then both doctors and families can inform one another about which interventions are advisable and when.

Respecting rights and interests

The commonest argument in favour of informed consent is that it is a token of respect for the rights of autonomous patients.[10] Arguments about rights and autonomy present problems for young children (as considered later), and I have used the language of children's interests rather than their rights.

Parents are uncertain whether to base proxy decisions on what they believe to be the child's best interests, or on what they imagine the baby might want now, or later. As one mother said, 'I'm so worried that when she's older she'll blame me for what I decided, I wish I knew what she really wants.' Professionals and parents may deliberately misinform one another, or the child, in attempts to impose their beliefs about the best option. Some parents put their own welfare, or that of the whole family, before the child's, as when they refuse to take a handicapped baby home. Others choose options that will injure the child physically, such as Jehovah's Witnesses who refuse life-saving blood transfusions. Some mothers invent symptoms so that their healthy child has many dangerous investigations including surgery, apparently because the mother enjoys all the dramatic medical and nursing attention.[11] This rare form of child abuse links with physical and sexual abuse of children, in which the mature, nurturing side of the parent is repressed or split off from the immature, destructive side, temporarily or permanently.[12]

Yet there are several reasons for not automatically excluding abusive and negligent parents from sharing in medical decisions about their child. Almost all parents show rage and violence, however rarely, and 'abuse' covers such a wide spectrum that in a broad definition almost everyone is guilty. Where is the dividing line between good-enough and inadequate parents?[13] Parents who harm their child are not necessarily incapable of loving concern, especially when the child is threatened by dangers from outside the family. Possibly 90 per cent of child abuse occurs, or at least begins, because parents believe that punishment is good for the child and they intend well.[14]

After accidents parents tend to feel extremely guilty, even if they are not to blame. Burnt and injured children are torn between anger that their seemingly all-powerful parents could allow the accident, and longing for their parents' presence. The psychological damage may be as severe as the physical damage, and harder to heal. The confidence of both child and parent in the parent's ability to care is further damaged if they are separated, and is only restored if parents are involved in helping to heal the child.[15] Children of good-enough parents appear to survive separation with more resilience than children of inadequate parents, who tend to be intensely distressed at being sent away from home.[16] Where there is a chance of the child living safely in future with one or both parents, this is probably increased if they are involved in the child's continuing care, and are helped to become better parents.[17] This happens in wards where the nurses nurture parents as well as children, and do not judge or reject them. One sister explained how even young babies who have severe burns 'hate their body. We have to help them to learn to love their disfigured body.' Similarly, parents who hate themselves for not preventing the damage, have to learn to reaccept themselves before they can be good-enough parents.

These arguments are not made to support parents' rights, but to protect children's interests. Excluding abusive parents protects children from potential harm. Yet it also denies them the potential benefits of including the parents' unique knowledge of their child's needs in the medical discussion.

Proxy consent is criticized as meaningless because children do not authorize their proxy;[18] if they could do so, they would be too competent to need one. A different meaning of proxy is not an authorized person but someone who stands in the place of another (as at elaborate feudal betrothal ceremonies where proxies stood in for the absent infant fiancés). One important element in proxy consent is that parents standing in for their child can take the view of someone receiving the proposed health care, from the perspective of the individual child, family, and home. This view may be very different from that of people who provide the treatment in the hospital or surgery. Some doctors believe that as the most informed members in a debate about a patient, they can act as proxies for the child. Yet it is not possible to combine the opposite positions of a provider and a receiver of professional treatment, and the essence of proxy consent is this potentially creative opposition.

Decisions for children should be guided by beliefs about the child's best interests, but many beliefs are uncertain, contentious, and rapidly change fashion.[19] Doctors and parents make fatal mistakes, and proxy consent does not provide complete protection or ideal solutions. Yet it offers the next best thing: the opportunity for everyone concerned to question and scrutinize decisions, and to examine alternatives, so raising the child's chances of receiving reasonably safe and effective treatment.

Definitions of informed consent

What should patients and parents be told?

Informed consent is most clearly defined in guidelines on consent to medical research, not to treatment. The Nuremberg Code[20] requires that 'there should be made known' to each research subject:

'the nature, duration and purpose' of the intervention;
'the method and means by which it is to be conducted;
all inconveniences and hazards reasonably to be expected;
the effects upon his health or person which may possibly come';
and the 'liberty' to withdraw 'if he has reached the physical or mental
    state where continuation of the experiment seems to him to be
    impossible'.

Guidelines in 1986 recommended that in order to be able to withdraw their child if necessary: 'where possible parents should be encouraged to be present' during procedures.[21]

The Declaration of Helsinki[22] adds that potential subjects should be informed of:

'anticipated benefits';
and their 'liberty' to refuse to take part.

These guidelines on research are only slowly being applied in medical treatment. The double standard has been criticized by some doctors.[23] Two vital extra kinds of information in consent to treatment are:

the alternative available treatments;
the prognosis of different treatments and of non-treatment.

Apart from ethical guidelines agreed by medical associations, the other main guidance on consent is given by the law, mainly case law, evolved through the courts in response to particular disputes. The law is not clear or comprehensive, and is complicated by vague words such as 'reasonable'. American case law on medical treatment defines a 'reasonable' amount of information as what a *prudent patient* would want to know in order to make an informed choice.[2] American and Canadian law hold the doctor responsible for answering the patient's questions. The surgeon should also, 'without being questioned, disclose to him the nature of the proposed operation, its gravity, any material risks and any special or unusual risks attendant upon the performance of the operation'.[25]

British law still allows 'professional judgement in the context of the doctor's relationship with a particular patient'[26] to determine what a *reasonable doctor* would decide to tell.[27] In 1984 a judge ruled that the doctrine of informed consent was 'no part of English law' since most patients 'preferred to put themselves unreservedly in the hands of their doctors'.[28] However, opinions are slowly changing and Lord Scarman warned that unless the medical profession 'put its house in order' and ensured that patients were reasonably informed reforms may be enforced through the courts.[29]

The lawyer Ian Kennedy distinguishes between the standard of the *reasonable doctor* which he thinks is too conservative, and the *particular patient in each case* which he thinks is too unjustly variable and subjective.[30] Kennedy favours the *prudent patient*'s definition of being reasonably informed, but this compromise would be defined by 'the Courts' which means conservative judges who see few child patients. This debate shows the difficulty of deciding how fully patients should be warned about the risks of treatment, and of defining standards that are fair to all patients and doctors.

Risks are complicated to estimate. If a new operation has been performed on very few, and perhaps very sick, patients, percentage mortality rates for average cases will not be known. If patients survive for a few weeks after surgery, the cause of death, and therefore where to place the patient in the surgery statistics, may be uncertain. Success rates for the same operation vary between different hospitals and surgeons, and they change over time. Recent figures may look very promising, but they cannot include the longer term effects.

Morbidity rates (any ill health or ill effects) are even more complicated than mortality rates. A single effect may cover a wide spectrum of symptoms and severity, which do not all fall into neat, agreed categories of 'moderate' or 'severe'. The range of opinion was indicated when I asked various staff, 'What is the risk of neurological damage from cardiac bypass surgery?' (without specifying whether this meant temporary or permanent harms). A surgeon, looking for long-term overall success rates, assumed that only serious, lasting damage need be considered. He thought the risk was half to one per cent. A physician gave an estimate of two to five per cent, 'but it might be something very slight, maybe just affecting movement in the little finger'. A sister, aware of the effect on families of even minor and temporary symptoms, estimated 'maybe up to ten per cent'.

Another physician considered that in law[31] families should be informed of harms with more than two per cent chance of occurring. This could mean that in the surgeon's view, warnings about neurological damage are not legally necessary. The sister, considering support for families through often temporary distress, thought that some warning was beneficial. How fully patients are informed varies not only with individual definitions of how serious or how likely to occur the risk may be,[32] but also with individual motives—to prepare patients or to prevent litigation.

A general legal standard can increase the problem of confusing patients so that the primary, most important issues to them are lost in masses of secondary details. Families may not be warned that treatment is likely to be long, painful, and hazardous, possibly leaving the patient permanently damaged and everyone with bitter regrets. One surgeon (not cardiac) commented on a child who had spent all of his two-year life in hospital undergoing over twenty operations for his seven congenital defects. He said the boy had 'outstanding parents. Most people would have cracked, their marriage would have broken up, they would have abandoned their child.'[33] Prolonged treatment cannot always be foreseen, but when it is likely, parents need to have time to discuss and think about these possibilities before being asked to consent to them.

The American bioethicists Ruth Faden and Tom Beauchamp propose a standard of *sufficient or reasonable information* which could keep the main issues clear.[34] They stress the importance of doctors' skills in personal communication as well as impersonal legal standards. Their standard combines Kennedy's three possible standards. They recommend that doctors inform by making core disclosures based on *what patients usually want to know* and also *what the doctor thinks they should know*. This includes facts and recommendations with reasons for any advice that is offered. Core

disclosures help patients to realize what further questions they nee
to ask, and therefore opens up discussion and shared understandin
in which *patients can discuss their individual concerns*. Discussion
neither too narrowly limited to patients' questions, nor too broadl
spread over all possible details.

Who can give consent?

Adult patients are responsible for consent to their own treatmen
and even if they are too ill to consent, no one else can do this for ther
in English law.[35] Proxy consent can only be given on behalf c
children under the age of consent. Some American and Australia
states accept proxy consent by guardians on behalf of adults who ar
judged unable to make decisions.[36] There is concern in Britain abou
these adults who at present are excluded from any kind of conser
process.

On *proxy consent to medical research*, the 1983 revision of th
Declaration of Helsinki states:

when the [research] subject is a minor, permission from the responsibl
relative replaces that of the subject in accordance with national legislatio
Whenever the minor child is in fact able to give consent, the minor's conser
must be obtained in addition to the consent of the minor's legal guardian.[3]

The 'must' is important as 'voluntary and informed consent
mandatory to turn what would otherwise be a trespass [or] assau
into a legally sanctioned act'.[38] It has also been recommended tha
the child's assent should be sought from the age of seven upward
and the child's consent from the age of fourteen upwards.[39] Assent
agreement, and consent is informed and voluntary commitment. Th
American guidelines add that children aged fourteen should b
presumed to be competent to give informed consent to medic
research, and children under fourteen should not be presumed to b
incompetent.[40]

A strict reading of English law appears to prevent parents fro
consenting to medical research which is non-therapeutic (of no direc
benefit to the child). However, medical guidelines which allo
non-therapeutic research of 'no greater than minimal risk'[41] have n
been challenged, and would probably be supported in the court
American and British guidelines advise that 'therapeutic researc
(which involves treatment that may benefit the child) may be pe
mitted if the hoped-for benefit is greater than the potential harm.[42]

Proxy consent to medical treatment seems to be quite restricted in the United States. The essence of consent is free choice, including the option to refuse. American legislation 'to mandate treatment for all infants considered potentially viable' gives parents 'the right to consent to medical care for their dependent children, but not the co-equal right to refuse care deemed medically necessary'.[43] This would seem to deprive parents of both rights; if you cannot say 'no', 'yes' has little meaning. In effect, it seems difficult to refuse treatment for American children, and the age of majority in some states is eighteen years.

English common law is vague about the age of consent to medical treatment, ranging from eighteen down to sixteen for girls and fourteen for boys,[44] whereas Scottish common law defines the age as twelve for a girl and fourteen for a boy.[45] An English Act in 1969 stated:

the consent of a minor who has attained the age of 16 to any surgical, medical or dental treatment . . . shall be as effective as it would be if he were of full age; and [if the minor has given] an effective consent to any treatment it shall not be necessary to obtain any consent for it from his parents or guardians.[46]

In hospitals this is usually taken to mean that a parent must sign the consent form for children under sixteen. Local authorities have 'parental' rights to give consent for children under certain care orders. The social services committee delegates a social worker to sign the form. For children in 'voluntary' care, the parents' consent should be requested, especially for major treatment. If the parents cannot be traced, the authority should probably take a formal 'parental rights resolution' before consenting to major treatment, or in extreme cases make the child a ward of court. If children are wards of court, all significant medical steps must have the consent of the court and a court order would be signed by the judge or registrar. Consent for very minor treatment may be given by whoever has been granted care and control of the child by the court.[47]

No Western European country grants children automatic rights of consent below the age of sixteen, although several allow children of any age to be given contraception without parental consent,[48] so respecting their case as confidential.[49] In Western Australia a law is being considered making thirteen years the age of competence to consent to medical treatment, and a Canadian law in

1972 allowed minors aged over fourteen to consent to medical treatment.[50]

The 1969 English law stated sixteen as the age above which patients can automatically give consent. It did not say that children below that age cannot give consent, and the law is increasingly concerned not with age but with each child's competence to consent. This relates to 'the child's maturity and understanding and the nature [*seriousness and complexity*] of the consent which is requested'.[51] The Gillick debate in the mid-1980s reflected social change since Victorian times when children were regarded almost as their father's property. Today, parents have rights over their child only in so far as this enables them 'to discharge the duty of maintenance, protection and education until he reaches such an age as to be able to look after himself and make his own decisions'.[52] Doctors are now in law expected to request children's consent 'when the child achieves a sufficient understanding and intelligence to enable him or her to understand fully what is proposed', and 'sufficient discretion to enable him or her to make a wise choice in his or her own interests'.[53]

Informed consent for adults means their right to make any choice however seemingly misjudged, but consent for children must be informed and also wise.[54] Parents who want to reject medical treatment for their child may be taken to court,[55] although in many cases the parents and paediatric team agree together when it is best for the child that treatment be withheld or withdrawn.[56]

The Gillick ruling[57] suggests a duty on doctors to determine when the child is competent to give informed consent. Five aspects of competence to consent (in psychiatric patients) have been identified as the patient's ability:

to give free voluntary consent;
to have all the relevant information;
to be competent to give consent;
to understand the information;
to make a decision which the doctor will respect.[58]

All five criteria are subjective. They pose difficulties for patients who are confused by the hospital setting, or by medical information that is explained in very complicated terms, who refuse treatment because they think it could be worse than the disease, or who disagree with medical opinion. Dissent may itself be regarded as a sign of mental incompetence. This double bind traps those who are diagnosed as insane. Both their agreement or their disagreement with medical opinion can be interpreted as confirming the diagnosis.

Elaborate tests of children's competence by experts have been recommended.[59] Yet these are unlikely to be widely used. They are inevitably subjective, tend to expect children to show greater competence than the average adult patient would, consume time and resources, and discriminate against children who fail the test.

The lawyer Sheila McLean proposes a simpler alternative: to examine the competence of the decision instead of the person.[60] Citing Scottish law which holds children as young as five to be morally responsible (for their misdeeds), she suggests that children could be assumed to be moral agents, able to make sensible decisions in their own interests. The onus then rests on adults to inform children and to justify their decisions if they disagree with the child. When children make obviously ignorant, short-sighted, or harmful choices, further discussion is needed, to help them to make informed decisions, and to understand when and why treatment is essential for their well-being. Minor decisions, and ones that can be delayed or changed later might be left to the child's discretion. Children can consent to (and therefore refuse) increasingly major decisions as they mature. After eleven-year-old Nicky chose to have major, corrective surgery, her mother said,

If it's a life or death decision, you've got to help them to make it. But if they've just got bat ears and they say, 'I don't care what I look like', well, it's up to them whether they have the operation.

Some school-age children will be too immature, frightened, or ill to share in decisions. Yet these occasions could be the exception rather than the rule, the adults first having to justify not involving the child. Children's freedom to consent could expose them to pressures and harms that proxy consent is intended to shield them from. The idea of proxy consent as a process and debate, not just a decision, is useful here. Starting with the child, the debate moves outwards, if necessary, through the protective concentric circles of the parents, the health-care professionals, and the law.

The first assumption is to trust the child, whose choice is viewed not as 'correct' but for how it makes sense in the child's own terms. Many younger children want their parents to decide for them.[61] When children's choices seem potentially harmful, and when they cannot speak for themselves, the next assumption could be to trust the parents to decide the matter with or for the child. If the parents' decision is contentious, it can be debated between the family and the consultant, if necessary involving the hospital team, leading to wider critical discussion. When the 'right' decision is in serious doubt, there cannot be a 'wrong' decision,[62] just one that attempts to be least harmful, and this could be left to the child and parents. When all the adults disagree with the child, it is not yet clear what the legal response might be in Britain.[63] When all the professionals disagree with the parents, the child can be made a ward of court.[64]

The experience of informed consent

Laws and guidelines on consent tend to imply that medical information can be neatly defined and passed like a packet to rational patients. The reality may be far more vague and complicated. The second part of this chapter is about the practical difficulties facing the staff and families trying to achieve informed consent.

Beyond rationality

Only people who are competent and rational are supposed to be able to give informed consent. Research studies on consent assess how correctly patients can comprehend, retain, recall, and recount medical data, to see how precisely the patients' understanding mirrors the doctors'. However, patients' recall of medical details months later does not necessarily show how informed their consent was. Many parents told me 'You need to forget.' Consent has more to do with grasping the essential principles at the time than with later recall.

Empirical studies arrive at different conclusions depending on whether well or sick people are questioned, and at what stage or intensity of illness. Older studies tend to stress problems of informed consent, more recent studies reveal advantages.[65] This change may be due to changing theories and methods of the researchers, or to doctors' and patients' rising expectations and expertise as consent comes to be an accepted part of medical practice.

Critics of patient consent argue that information harms patients by confusing them. It increases anxiety and therefore reduces rationality. They assert that many patients cannot understand medical details, or would rather not know them, or are frightened into refusing beneficial treatment. Patients are supposed to benefit from relying on superior medical reasoning until their health and their own reasoning powers are fully restored. Caring doctors are presented as shielding patients from distressing news and choices. Medical paternalism is believed to promote a positive psychological and medical outcome. Patients prefer 'a childlike dependency [with] intense feelings . . . that the physician is powerful and reminiscent of . . . a kindly, loving parent', whereas patients treated in an 'egalitarian manner' might feel abandoned, and would 'retain a critical, evaluative attitude'.[66]

Anxiety is assumed to be negative. An American neonatologist argued that parents' 'over-anxiety' in response to 'too much information' could harm their sick baby by causing them to stop visiting the hospital.[67] A report on parents' 'coping strategies' in an American intensive care unit assumed that parental anxiety should be suppressed by parents' 'internal mastering' of anxiety 'to maintain effective equilibrium'.[68] The nurse authors in their questionnaire offered parents passive options, such as, 'being allowed to stay', or 'being provided with hope' (a question which is meaningless out of context). Semi-passive options included 'trying not to let myself get too emotional'.

Those in favour of patient consent reply that patients want more information; that being left in ignorance can be worse than being informed; and that patients are able to understand, to cope calmly, and to use medical details to make positive decisions. In this debate,[69] both sides tend to assume that people can only think clearly if they stop feeling; that anxiety is negative and should be avoided.

Yet feelings are part of rational understanding in informed consent. Parents who are not anxious about their seriously ill child, would seem ignorant or callous. A positive view of anxiety, as a warning and source of motivation, in the 'coping strategies' report would offer parents active options and a greater share in caring for the child. Significantly, parents in the report said they found most helpful 'being permitted to stay with my child as much as possible', whereas 'going home to rest' was found to be 'the least helpful'.[70]

Understanding proxy consent involves understanding the place of awareness. Alvin Gouldner, the sociologist, explains awareness by recognizing two forms of knowledge.[71]

First, knowledge as objective information:
is understood solely at an intellectual level;
remains the same whether it is stored in a file, a computer, or a
    human mind;

is consistent regardless of who is reporting or receiving it;
is a definitive, objective packet of date, unaffected by the subjective
   understandings of the people using it;
can be assessed as correct or incorrect.

Second, knowledge as awareness:
works at mental, physical, and emotional levels of understanding;
unfolds in a process of ever more complex depths of understanding;
discovers and misses different facets depending on who is reporting
   and receiving the information;
experiences knowledge as partly subjective because as it is absorbed
   it becomes part of the person;
realizes that different versions of reality can be valid and appropriate, and that there is not always a single correct version;
reveals personal meanings in information as good or bad news;
transforms our understanding, even our whole lives.

Ideas are not seen as eternally fixed and apart from us, but they
change in meaning as we absorb them and come to terms with
experiences. Laws and guidelines on consent tend to discuss knowledge as information, whereas parents giving proxy consent tend to
experience knowledge as awareness. Mark's mother, quoted earlier,
understood some things clearly, and recalled them vividly years later.
She was 'shattered' *because* she understood that her son was likely to
die.

   Scientific objectivity mistrusts and tries to exclude the 'treacherous' self from thinking, assuming that 'a bloodless and disembodied
mind' works best.[72] Yet we learn through growing self-awareness,
which is often described in images about the 'impact' of good or bad
news which invades and 'shatters' the self. When someone 'takes in'
and 'absorbs' news until it becomes part of herself, she has to reorder
her inner space, her hopes and values, as if to make room for the new
knowledge by rearranging former knowledge in relation to new
understanding. The images of space and impact are only metaphors
for the abstract process of gaining knowledge. Yet they graphically
express how we learn through physical and mental awareness.

   The psychoanalyst Wilfred Bion shows how we tend to 'take
in' important news first as a physical reaction. When a baby is
distressed,

the earliest forms of communication take place without any mediation by
verbal or nonverbal symbols. In a direct and often raw compelling way the

baby conveys its feelings to the mother. If the baby is alarmed or distressed, what he does about this is to arouse alarm or distress in the mother. He causes the mother to experience in her own feelings what he cannot yet bear to keep inside himself.[73]

Just as the baby becomes aware through sensation, the mother learns of the baby's state, not through symbol (mental interpretation) but through direct feeling. This could be labelled intuition or empathy except that neither word conveys the pre-thought 'gut' feeling which precedes and gives substance to thought.

Parents made aware of great risk, and doctors and nurses awakening their awareness have to 'bear the pain of thinking'. It is much more than an intellectual problem. One way of coping is to deny the pain, another is to respond to feeling. If the baby is to learn to cope, and 'to develop sensation into feeling and thought', the caring adult has to act 'as the container for painful states of being'. This is essential 'for development within the self of one's own capacity to bear the pain of thinking'.[74]

And the mother has to cope with these feelings of alarm and distress in *herself*, before she is able to respond appropriately and give relief to the baby. The mother who is not too immersed in her own difficulties replies to the baby's behaviour [cries, smiles] as though she believes that such behaviour is a meaningful communication which requires to be understood and responded to. Her response is probably an essential prerequisite enabling the baby gradually to build up some form of realisation of his own that behaviour is meaningful and communicative.

Many of the staff regarded parents' consent as a partly emotional process. A sister spoke of two parents who, she felt, did not seem to realize the potential dangers of their baby's proposed operation. She said that someone would have to talk to the parents again to try to get them to understand. When I asked why, if surgery was the baby's only hope, she did not leave the parents in relatively comfortable unawareness, the sister said:

Because if the worst comes to the worst and the child dies they'd have had no preparation and the shock would be even greater afterwards. I think they can be informed about the technical side of surgery and still not understand the implications of it.

The sister described the emotional states she would expect to see, in order that she could be convinced that parents understood.

In parents just told, say, that there is a risk of their child dying—I would expect them to be tearful. If parents seemed fairly light and jolly and didn't even register any shock, even that blank shock where tears aren't enough, if there's no reaction, I'd wonder if they'd taken it in.

In reacting to news with shock, rage, or tears, it is as if the subconscious and the body powerfully grasp the implications of, say, loss or danger, well before the mind is able to think through the meaning. When serious news involves inward upheaval, thinking clearly involves feeling deeply and learning from feelings. Even numbness can be part of growing awareness, slowing this to a manageable pace and centring attention on the crucial issues.

An emergency can be a stage of heightened awareness, when families gain unique knowledge through their very distress, as an essential part of truly informed decisions. When Amy was two days old she was rushed with her parents to the Children's Hospital. Amy's father told me, 'We couldn't bear to look at her. . . . She was struggling for breath, obviously in some discomfort and screaming.' Amy's parents were told that only one of them could stay overnight, and in a room far from the baby, so they decided that they would leave Amy and go home. Later a surgeon arrived with the consent form. Amy's father said,

I gave permission and didn't give it a second thought till afterwards. There was very little soul-searching. It was essential, once they'd explained it to me. Afterwards, I imagined the gory details and felt more uncomfortable. You think about your child and the knife afterwards, but at the time you're happy to agree.

It happened at a difficult stage when you [*looking at his wife*] had gone to the dining-room in tears and I had just gone up to tell them we wouldn't stay. And they explained with a model of the heart. They asked me where you were. I said you were upset and told them to carry on. The surgeon said did I know about the working of the heart. I said, 'Yes', hoping I'd remember O level biology. I was conscious of wanting to be with you so I didn't ask as many questions as I'd normally do.

Taking time during an emergency to explain with a model showed concern that parents be informed as fully as possible. The approach emphasizes reason, expecting parents to set aside anxieties and concentrate on technicalities. Yet Amy's father suggests that he did not absorb or 'give a second thought to' the technical knowledge, like 'O level biology', until later when he had 'qualms'. Qualms could be seen as unnecessary sentiment, or else as responsible empathy.

Fathers rarely admitted their own distress, but said they were anxious for their child and the mother's unhappiness. Recently shocked by the distress of his daughter and his wife, Amy's father felt a heightened understanding which many parents mentioned. They were less able to think about medical information when worried about being separated, at a time when they most needed to be together. This sense of family unity can be seen as part of a protective instinct necessary for the child's welfare. If parents are respected and their concerns heard, if hospitals are reorganized to reduce avoidable stress (such as separation), parents are better able to cope with unavoidable stress and with technical explanations.

In working so closely with very sick children and their families, nurses were directly aware of the importance of feelings, and of their own need 'to respond appropriately and give relief'. One of countless instances given by nurses of their feeling reaction was given at a unit team meeting. A sister described the last-minute rush when a porter suddenly arrives to take a child to the operating theatre.

Sometimes it all seems to go wrong. The child's crying, the parents are crying and I feel like crying. I wish I could call the theatre and ask them to wait half an hour so that I had time to calm everyone down.

Nurses spoke of not knowing how to cope with their own, and the families' distress.[75] They could only do so within hospital systems which help and do not hinder the work of giving relief. They wanted to ensure that families understood risk clearly and intensely, and could not offer false comfort by denying danger. Yet they needed to offer some comfort in order to help families to work through their initial shock and come to terms with information. The sister, quoted earlier saying that she would look for emotional signs of rational understanding, described how she would respond with a mixture of sympathy, comfort, and information.

They should be able to be tearful. If necessary, to feel private. I would find a screen, because I feel that is a healthy reaction to anxiety. I hope no one would stop them. I might even take the baby away if it's crying. Just a few feet away so that the mother can cry without having to be concerned about the baby.

If they were upset after a doctor had spoken to them, I'd stay with them. I'd find out why they were upset. If there was a significant risk, I'd emphasize to them it's a risk they're going to have to take if they want their child treated. I'd say, as the baby's not thriving and will not do well (we always use euphemistic terms) without an operation, and the operation is the only means to give him a normal life, so that is their only option. They always agree. It helps them to have a second person saying it. . . .

If their child is brain damaged or if he dies in theatre, parents feel guilty afterwards. So it's even more important to emphasize to them that the baby needed the operation. It was their only option. All parents agree that if it's the child's only chance, however small, they'll take it.

The sister works within the contradiction of trying to increase informed awareness, yet to help parents not to be overwhelmed by it. She incidentally shows the pressures of illness and information on the parents' decisions.

Pain

Knowledge as information or awareness has very different effects on the way people perceive and respond to events, as shown by differing responses to pain. The following example from the *Lancet* has no connection with the two cardiac units. It illustrates the debate about pain relief, in this case during surgery on premature babies to close the ductus arteriosus, a blood vessel near the heart which normally closes soon after birth.[76] The researchers were 'surprised to find that major [surgical] procedures were performed commonly with minimal or even no anaesthesia' on premature infants.[77] Nearly half the paediatric anaesthetists who replied to a British survey in 1987 did not use pain relieving supplements in anaesthetics on new-born babies,[78] and 'it is clear that some newborn babies still receive no anaesthetic' during surgery in Britain, and the United States.[79] One reason is that too much anaesthesia can be lethal, and is particularly complicated in heart and lung patients, since these organs are so directly affected by anaesthesia.

In the *Lancet* study, sixteen babies were given conventional drugs: curare a paralysing agent, and nitrous oxide which induces unconsciousness and some degree of anaesthesia—loss of sensation. Eight babies were also given extra pain relief, fentanyl, and eight were not.

The study found big differences between the two groups in the babies' hormonal and metabolic changes. 'The findings indicate that . . . this massive stress response' of premature babies to surgery may be 'abolished' by fentanyl analgesia. Fentanyl also 'may be associated with an improved postoperative outcome', preventing complications and a 'clinically unstable course' observed in the non-fentanyl babies.[80]

The authors defined pain in detached scientific terms as a cerebral and biochemical response.

It is widely believed that . . . newborn babies are not capable of perceiving or localising pain and that they may not be capable of interpreting pain since they do not have a memory of previous painful experiences. [*Examples are given of apparent responses to pain in premature infants.*] Clearly, the perception, measurement, and management of painful experiences in the premature infant are very important topics for further exploration. We would suggest that the degree of analgesia, particularly in paralysed and ventilated infants, can be assessed reliably only by measurement of the biochemical and endocrine markers of stress.[81]

Doctors remain detached in order to be able to plan the best treatment clearly and to avoid harmful over-use of drugs. Yet too much detachment can also be harmful, such as when it insists on objective proof of pain. I asked a junior anaesthetist if she thought the *Lancet* study was ethical and she replied, 'Yes. *We* know the idea that babies can't feel pain is codswallop. But the only way you'll convince some doctors is by this kind of scientific study.' The premiss that new-born babies do not feel pain illustrates the bias in supposedly neutral science. There is far more evidence to demonstrate that babies do feel pain, but this evidence derives mainly not from science but from awareness.

Letters from doctors commenting on the *Lancet* report discussed other ways of perceiving pain, such as through common sense. One writer questioned the nature of parents' informed consent for surgery when 'analgesia is withheld', and asked how an ethics committee could permit such a study into

the wholly unacceptable tenet . . . that preterm babies are not able to perceive pain. . . . I believe this [awareness of babies' pain] to be only common sense and do not believe it is ethical to do this type of study to try to prove it.[82]

Another letter defined pain as partly an emotional experience recognized through empathy.

Doctors caring for children are often unaware of the fact [of sensitive pain reactions] in newborn and premature babies. These are easily recognized, even without complex laboratory methods, and they are difficult to interpret in terms other than distress, anger, unease, or, simply, pain. Any experienced nurse or competent mother would have been able to describe reliably how babies react to a heel stab or a venipuncture—not to mention, a thoracotomy [*opening up the chest for surgery*]—when not paralysed. . . . Surgeons, who declare infants insensitive to pain . . . do so contrary to everyday experience and scientific knowledge.[83]

Pain is difficult to treat as well as to assess. 'A lot of the problem is discomfort', an anaesthetist in one of the heart units told me. 'A ventilator tube is like having two fingers stuck down your throat but no drugs can relieve that sensation.' Another anaesthetist said, 'Pain is so uncertain. We can't be sure how much babies are feeling. How much is in the mind. It's difficult here. Some people mainly have the goal in mind.' Safety and ultimate cure are the goals. When the treatment of very serious conditions has to involve much discomfort, deciding how far the hoped-for goal justifies the painful means is complicated. A clinical nurse teacher said that the ventilator

must be awfully painful. It makes you want to cough with that bent tube in. You're held down, so powerless and dependent and defenceless. Suction is awful although there is relief afterwards, but it's a nightmare for the little ones when you can't explain. The gag and cough reflexes are very powerful unless you are very anaesthetized.

The nurse teacher went on to say that calming babies by gently stroking and talking to them, can give effective pain relief, reducing the need for drugs.

Sometimes a baby will be going berserk and he will need the tender touch. Sam was going loopy, sending his blood pressure sky high. He was angry with us fiddling and sticking tubes down his throat—acceptably angry. He had so much secretion, he kept needing suction. The more suction he had the more agitated he became and the more he secreted. It was a vicious circle. His nose is sore and every time he moves the [ventilator] tube goes in and out which makes it worse for him.

You have to be able to tell the difference between what he was doing and a child who is thrashing about and irritable because he's had brain damage, to tell whether he's becoming ill or having temper tantrums. He seems to be the sort of baby who is quite active and vigorous and won't put up with what he doesn't like. And you can calm him down a lot by talking to him and stroking him. He needed nursing and then you might be able to get away without paralysing him.

If doctors saw an inexperienced nurse, not able to handle the situation, who said, 'Help, you've got to sedate him, got to paralyse him, I can't cope', they'd go along with the nurse. But you need to stop and see what is happening and whether you can settle the baby down. Doctors are better if they've had babies themselves.

Nursing involves feeling with patients in order to assess need and to provide appropriate care. Teaching nurses involves working closely with them so that they learn, as this nurse teacher said, 'not just the technical things' but how to interact with patients and how patients subtly respond.

Experienced and confident nurses, by calming the family, enable parents and less experienced nurses to help the child to cope with pain and anxiety. If this calm response was missing, parents felt extreme anxiety, aware of the child's need but helpless to answer it, as described by two mothers in the Children's Hospital, which had many student nurses.

We get worried leaving them with students. Some are good, some very poor, unconfident. You're frightened if the nurse isn't confident. You don't want to go to bed. They practically forcibly evicted me—well, not that, but it's, 'Oh, are you still here?' I don't want to leave her. It boils down to standards of nursing. If you've got confidence, you can go and have lunch, but not if you're worried. And you're worried all the time.

Some of the student nurses were very anxious about having responsibilities when they did not feel adequately trained and supported. Senior nurses were aware of their stress but could not alter the basic problem of the scarcity of trained nurses. Many experienced nurses were leaving the two units, and this put greater stress on all the remaining nurses as well as the families. They all missed the experienced nurses' technical skills, as well as their reassuring support.

Mark's mother talked after his operation when he was three years old.

The ventilator didn't look comfortable for him. It pulled his face out of shape. . . . He was sleeping on and off all the time, but he got very agitated when the pain killer wore off. He tried to cry with no sound[84] but there were tears. It was obvious he was in pain, he was thrashing about. They put some more omnopon in the drip in his neck. It seemed to work quite fast—in about two minutes, but they seemed long minutes. . . .

We were told before the operation that they could tell even before he woke up that a child would be in pain, but they waited until a child showed pain. I wasn't happy about that. I often said, 'He's in pain', and they did something. It makes you wonder what would have happened if I hadn't been there. He did get very upset every time I was asked to leave, and if it kept your child in a

happy frame of mind I would have thought it would be more beneficial to
stay in with him.

Parents spoke of the child's pain as an experience which they partly
shared, such as when time seemed to move slowly, 'they seemed long
minutes'.

Hospital nurses can only give pain relief which is prescribed by a
doctor. The staff were concerned that this safeguard leads to delays
while nurses decide whether to call a doctor, and how much extra
relief to ask for. In turn, knowing the risks, doctors are anxious not
to prescribe more than seems absolutely necessary, but they have no
scientific means of deciding what is the appropriate amount. If
parents in the non-intensive ward said that their child was in pain,
nurses would sometimes ask them to wait until the next drug round.
A senior registrar asked a consultant, 'Can we put this baby on to
opiates? He has severe angina and nothing has worked for the last
twenty-four hours.' Opiates would hasten the baby's expected death
so that it was appropriate to allow time for the decision, but
twenty-four hours was a long time to be without pain relief which
'worked'. This was a very rare example, but the examples are given
to show the general pressures on doctors and nurses to avoid
over-use of analgesics, as happens in every hospital. Anaesthetists
agree that much research is needed 'before uncontrolled pain ceases
to be a major cause of human suffering in our time'.[85] A cardiologist
told the parents of a baby waiting for surgery, 'You'll suffer more
than she will. A lot of care goes into seeing that the children here do
not suffer.' Yet as levels of safety and of the patients' actual need for
drugs cannot be measured precisely, it is difficult to balance caution
with comfort.

The debate on pain illustrates how informed consent is set in a
spectrum of forms of knowledge. At one extreme some doctors insist
on the detached integrity of scientific analysis as the only basis for
knowledge. At the other extreme are child patients experiencing
pain, with some adults intensely aware of this. In between, professionals like those in the two heart units combine common-sense
awareness with scientific assessment of pain levels in order to provide
adequate yet safe relief.

When adult patients are taught to administer their own postoperative pain relief, they adopt a very different pattern from the
'usual' pattern of prescriptions. Yet overall they take a lower dosage,

especially if this is combined with 'subjective' pain control. For example, patients keep a descriptive pain chart, talk about personal fear of pain, learn how to relax, and know that adequate relief will be given when they need it.[86] American parents and nurses are adapting these approaches to the care of sick babies, and questioning inadequate pain relief practices. The American Association for Critical Care Nurses publishes a list of questions for parents to ask about the risks of giving and of withholding analgesics before consenting to surgery.[87] British nurses find that, for example, children with cancer are more likely to take all their drugs when these are administered by the parents, and that even young children benefit from 'being in charge' of their own intravenous line.[88] Pain relief is best achieved when professionals, patients, and parents share their different knowledge.[89]

Continuing consent

Consent to surgery involves consent to many details, such as pain and its relief, which are understood through both scientific data and feeling awareness of the child's needs. Parents give informed consent when they know about each stage and are closely involved in the child's care. 'Consent' often describes signing a form before a major procedure. Some consultants believe that consent forms are unnecessary (they are not used in Norway) because the patients' voluntary presence in the hospital implies consent to anything deemed medically necessary.

Yet many patients go into hospital in order to discover the diagnosis, and then to consider the proposed treatment options. Their condition or treatment plans may change. They may want to refuse certain routine procedures. Most of all, they realize the full meaning of their choice as they go through the experience. Awareness changes over time; information is partly static. 'Informed consent' is almost a contradiction in terms because consent is given to future events which cannot be fully predicted or explained in advance; becoming informed is a continuing process.

Written agreements help to protect people's rights. Yet they can be a time trap, binding people to promises which they later regret but believe cannot be questioned, such as details of postoperative care. The hospital (like an elected government) may assume that written consent grants a mandate for many details which patients are not aware of at the time of signing. The contract can reduce families' ability to take an active part in later decisions. Patients need the protection of a formal agreement, but also some freedom of negotiation throughout their time in hospital. This section describes a few of the ways in which families and staff in the two cardiac units negotiated the consent process.

Jane's father, a lawyer, explained the difference to him between primary and secondary information. Like many parents, he was primarily concerned with value judgements, comparative chances and risks, with evaluating and preparing for possible harms. Jane was one of the first babies to have the switch operation for transposition of the great arteries.

What you want to know really is: What's the problem? What's the diagnosis? What's the remedy? What are the chances compared with other surgical procedures? What are the chances of success? What are the risks attendant on it? You want to know how serious the defect is. What the consequence would be if it wasn't remedied. I don't think you want to know about the techniques, or plastic tubing or whatever, because that's just mechanics.

I think they have an obligation to give you sufficient detail to enable you to understand. It helps you to prepare yourself for the possibility of harm. You don't want so much information that you're confused and a decision is impossible, but you want to know as much as you can reasonably be expected to take in.

In contrast, doctors quoted in earlier chapters tended to prefer to talk precisely about the 'mechanics', and to avoid the anxiety and uncertainty of trying to evaluate risk. Certainties are easier to explain, such as the exact nature of a lesion, and the *how* rather than the *whether* of treatment. Yet to parents these are often secondary issues, only useful in so far as they explain the primary ones.

Like adult patients, parents vary greatly in how much they want and are able to understand. Many families were very carefully informed by doctors, nurses, and therapists in the heart units. Parents of older children had years of knowledge and experience. As one mother said, 'I'm fifteen years older now than when my son first came here, so I'm more confident about asking questions and getting the answers.' A bus driver's wife said,

I want to know all the intricate details for myself, as if I could do the operation. I can cope better if I know. A lot of parents don't want to know, but doctors should be able to tell the type of parents they're dealing with.

She contrasted the frank information given in the heart unit with evasions in a hospital where her son had previously been treated for six years. 'Some doctors think that all parents are dim. They just try and stop you worrying—unnecessarily as they think.'

Paul's parents said,

It was fantastic, wonderful. In intensive care they told us, 'Come as often as you like, stay as long as you like.' Everyone, nurses, doctors, and anaesthetists would come up and say how well Paul was doing. They'd answer questions about every little bleep. . . . We were so lucky. . . . It's a wonderful place here. Everybody is so skilful and so kind.

After rapid diagnosis and treatment Paul recovered, according to the staff, 'exceptionally quickly'. Successful surgery may lend a rosy glow to parents' memories of how they were informed, just as problems may cast back critical shadows. Shared pleasure in Paul's recovery encouraged his parents and the staff to talk together.

Many parents expressed mixed satisfaction and criticism about how they were informed. Surgeons in theatre did not always have time to send out detailed information for other staff to give to parents, who found this stressful. 'I think they have no *idea* of the trauma you go through. I think it is diabolical that no one tells you after surgery how it went', said one mother. At one of the hospitals, surgeons took over the postoperative care. Some parents did not understand why 'their' cardiologist no longer seemed to be caring for their child or talking to them.

Parents may take weeks to realize the meaning of risk, and to change from wanting the child to survive at any cost to thinking that the cost is too high. They may have to witness realities which they could not accept as warnings, or to be certain first that everything possible had been attempted. When children did not respond to treatment everyone had great difficulty in knowing what to say. Michael's parents looked ill with anxiety when he was still unconscious three weeks after his operation.

He's had no surgery for eight years because they couldn't do anything. Now they've tried a very unusual operation, they've never done it before. We didn't have a choice really, they said he'll just go downhill otherwise. The surgeon said he'd come and talk to us afterwards, but when we saw him in the corridor he just avoided us. All he said was, 'We didn't expect it to go well and it hasn't.' But we didn't realize that, they didn't tell us that before.

Physicians, surgeons, nurses, and playworkers at the Children's Hospital spent much time informing and preparing families. Michael's parents were probably very clearly warned about the risks and complications. Yet warning of an 'eighty-per-cent mortality risk' is very different from the inner labour of imagining what this actually means, a task which only the parents can do for themselves, and which Michael's parents were struggling with after the operation. They seemed too absorbed in their anxiety even to contact their employers, although they both expected to be dismissed. 'But losing the job would be nothing to losing him.' They expressed the need of many parents to be supported and informed throughout their child's time in hospital.

Some parents seemed to regard honest information as a kind of prop that helped them to endure suspense. Lisa's mother only mentioned her severe anxiety and depression in relation to Lisa's earlier operation when she was 'absolutely terrified' and Lisa was very ill for nine weeks after surgery.[90] An army officer's wife, she gave an impression of building up confidence before the next day's battle.

Now I'm a walking encyclopaedia, so I am very much more relaxed about the whole thing. I mean last time, I was going, 'Aah! aah!' [*gives loud gasping breaths*] but now I'm quite relaxed about it because I understand so much more. I'm very lucky, I've got my child, other people haven't. So I think we're very lucky.... Obviously with this one which is the total correction there's a far higher risk—85 per cent. 85 per cent get through it so—fine. That's better than 50. So you just ... you know at the moment I'm fine about it. Tomorrow I shall just be ... that's all I shall think about, that my child isn't the 15 per cent.

I don't regret ever giving consent or ever saying that it shouldn't be done because I know it has to be.... There are far worse children here so it gives you some security, some perspective. There's not so much to worry about your own child. Why am I making ... why am I feeling so sad about my own child, when there's other people with far worse situations? Far worse—I'm very lucky so—that's it.

The medium of the message

Parents varied not only in what they said they were told, but in what they wanted to know and how they responded to the information. Sharon's mother appreciated a balance of optimism with pessimism.

Like doctors—some have a better way than others. One said to me, 'I think we're fighting a losing battle here.' It was just her temperament, but I thought what a dreadful choice of words. One doom merchant said, 'You do realize how ill your daughter is?' Of course we do. You want to be told the bad and the good things. Most of the staff as people are okay. Martin's the best doctor you could have. He came over to tell me personally. He's human. He feels for you. You can talk to him. You feel attached to them, you've been through so much together. You're so dependent. They take their time to go into detail. Start with the good news and then—'but we'll have to be very careful'. Somehow he's got the right way. He's frank. Not some kind of tin god but he's a dad as well on the same level.

The range of potential information was vast. Some junior doctors talked during a coffee break about babies being packed in ice while the heart is stopped during surgery. The metabolic rate slows down so that the brain does not consume oxygen. Babies therefore need not be put on to heart-lung bypass machinery, which would take up too much room around the tiny heart to allow the surgeon access. One doctor said:

I can't understand how the heart can be stopped and the child be clinically dead for forty minutes. If someone collapsed in a snowdrift and died you wouldn't be able to resuscitate them later. How is it possible? Death is mysterious and indefinable. It's metaphysical. And surgery is barbaric. Parents don't get the counselling and support they need. Maybe in the clinics someone really sits down and tells them the risks. But so often afterwards parents say, 'If only we had known.'

Parents thought that the doctor's pace and manner were important.

I don't feel daft when I ask Dr G a question. He seems to realize you don't understand at first but he doesn't mind repeating at all. He has that nice nature, whereas with Dr H, I said, 'Yes, I understand', so that I wouldn't look a fool, although I only understood a bit. When you're worried it goes in one ear and out the other. Unless it's me. I am thick. Dr H said to ask as much as I like, but sometimes it's his attitude, always seeming busy, rush, rush, rush. He spoke very fast. I think it's not what they say but the way they say it. If they seem nice and relaxed you can take in more. You've got time to think. If they speak slowly to you they seem as if they're more concerned.

There isn't always time to go slowly, yet rushing so that information is not understood is a waste of scarce time. One father said,

Although they make an attempt to explain in lay terms—but then they start using medical terms—like 'constriction', 'ligation', 'granulation of the wound'. If they use one word you're a little unsure about, your mind pauses at that one. You reflect. You try and work out what that one means. They gallop on at a racy pace and you miss the next part. If they slow down to draw, you can keep up with them.

Some doctors used diagrams and coloured sheets, which saved time and clarified confusing concepts, such as:

Doctor: And there's a thickening of the valve.
Mother: Oh, I thought it was a narrowing.
Doctor: Well, that's the same thing.

A drawing would show how thickened valve tissue narrows the passage through which the blood flows. 'The consultant wrote and drew the diagram upside down while he talked, so that it was the right way up for us, as if he was seeing it from our point of view. That was so helpful to me,' said one mother.[91]

One way to save medical time is to involve many other staff in informing families at different levels, as happened in the Children's Hospital, where patients were usually admitted four days before the operation. Sarah's parents explained how the play preparation helps children and parents.

Father: They spent a lot of time with us, starting with trying to tell the child, which was very educational for us because we then had to prepare ourselves to answer the questions she would have. The playleader gave her a book of photographs [following a child through surgery]. She asked us if we wanted to see it first. We were a little anxious that it might be too much for Sarah [aged four] because up to that time she hadn't shown any fear, but we let her see it. I think she was a little upset by some of the pictures. But then the playleader asked her if she wanted the teddy who'd had open-heart surgery. So she dressed up as a nurse and put on a mask and the playleader worked with the teddy and showed her all the tubes.

Mother: She worried like anything when she read about the injections, that she would have two and it would hurt. The book said it honestly. But finally, after the playworker let her actually give a real injection, you know using the same needles as the nurses do, to the teddy, doing that over and over again seemed to quench her fear. We thought we'd better read about it so we had the printed booklet which the sister wrote. It was very, very useful, though I think we learnt as much from the play book.

Father: It's all so simple, and more—I think the way it's done, it brings you much closer to . . .

Mother: Yes, the human side. Somehow it's easier, reading through the book you know your daughter's reading. She's very inquisitive and she wants to know.

Father: I think this play and the nurses do more to get you psychologically prepared, how to cope with it. The doctors' interaction tends to be more technical, medical. You know, not in a sort of cold way, but—we felt prepared watching Sarah play.

Adult patients could be more involved in practical preparation. A cancer surgeon asks his patients to draw their impressions of treatment. If they draw images of poison and mutilation he tries to help them to adopt more positive attitudes, so that they see their treatment in healing images. He thinks that patients' subconscious beliefs powerfully affect their ability to benefit from treatment.[92]

Practical methods help families to understand technical information through growing awareness of its personal meanings. Although informed consent is sometimes dismissed as an impossible ideal, as far as a lay person can judge I thought that many parents were highly informed about their child's condition and treatment, and that some doctors and nurses listened to families in order to be well informed about each child's needs.

Emergency proxy consent

This chapter began by asking whether emergency proxy consent is possible. There is not always time to develop awareness, but there are ways to increase parents' understanding during emergencies.

Antenatal discussions. These are held in some hospitals to help parents to develop their views on medical research and treatment for normal and abnormal new-born babies. When certain congenital defects are detected before birth, possible treatments can be discussed. Parents' conclusions may be recorded in the mother's medical notes or in her birth plan. This creates a background from which to approach emergency neonatal decisions, although the conclusions before birth will be hypothetical and tentative and may change dramatically after the birth.

Defining options. Requests for consent can be confined to the least possible essentials so that families are not asked to sign open-ended forms. Some new-born babies are sent off to a surgical unit with a blank form signed by one parent. A physician in the Children's Hospital told me: 'Usually a form is brought in with the baby. Most often the problem is known and the form is for—well they would know it's for heart surgery, not just for anything. But sometimes it has to be general, permission for any investigation or treatment we think is necessary.' If consent is not reasonably informed, signing a form can be worse than an empty gesture. Ignorant parents may be coerced into agreeing to decisions which later cause remorse. In rare cases when it is impossible to talk with parents, it would be honest to dispense with the form. In British law 'in an emergency, the administration of life-saving procedures on any patient without obtaining consent is a matter for the clinical judgement of the doctor concerned'.[93] When parents are asked to consent only to the fewest possible procedures, later decisions can be discussed as they arise, instead of open-ended consent being assumed. Adequate standards of consent depend on the baby having a resident or regularly visiting parent.

Finding time and space. Some decisions are made in moments, such as whether to put a baby on to a ventilator. Other 'emergencies' may stretch over days. Babies are sometimes rushed off for treatment when delay would not harm them, and would allow time to talk with both parents, preferably together.[94] Even if the mother is unwell, the father can usually be consulted. More care could be taken to avoid separating families. Several brief sessions could occur over a few hours or days, giving families time in between to absorb, question, and reflect. 'When you go away and think about it and *talk* about it, that's when you think of questions to ask,' said one mother. These approaches are adopted if professionals believe that involving parents in emergency decisions is possible and worth while.

Expectations. There is a widely held premiss that parents are unable to give consent in an emergency; as if, unlike other species, we lose the use of our faculties during sudden danger. If this were true, surely the human race would not have survived for long. Parents said they were 'not totally aware', yet like Mark's mother at the same time they gave evidence that they understood certain matters very clearly. Some people may be overwhelmed; others may be conditioned to expect to be confused. On remembering a sudden, shocking crisis, many people recall that they were intensely aware, and saw with a strange clarity what was happening, what it meant, and what outcome they most urgently wanted (or voluntarily consented to).

Mark's mother, remembered instantly grasping the primary issue: 'I thought he was going to die.' Instead of starting with secondary details, trying 'to explain what they thought was wrong', the paediatrician might have started with this primary concern. He could ask Mrs Brown what she was thinking or feeling, and then what she wanted to know. Later he could introduce information in response to her questions. Peter Maguire, a psychiatrist working with cancer patients, has shown how doctors and nurses can use counselling skills when breaking bad news.[95] When patients are helped to talk about their feelings, they can understand the crisis more clearly and quickly, and professionals can learn which kinds of care and information to offer. This skilled approach does not necessarily take more time. It uses time in a more effective way.

Informed proxy consent involves understanding the nature and purpose of proposed treatment, the risks, benefits, and alternatives. Those considering consent should be told whether they are consenting to treatment and/or to research. They should be told that consent includes the option to refuse, and should be asked to signify their decision. They should have the opportunity to discuss issues which the particular family and the professionals concerned consider to be relevant. The range of information on complex surgery is still being developed, and is so great (such as in the numerous biochemical reactions which cannot be understood or predicted fully) that doctors work in partial ignorance.

Informed proxy consent therefore involves only a basic understanding, which varies enormously depending on the ability and attitudes of families and health professionals. Legal definitions of informed consent are a compromise between protecting patients but also setting standards which doctors can reasonably achieve. I suggest a working definition of informed proxy consent as a standard to aim for, which is intended to enable families to understand each procedure, and to help them to adjust to failure and injury should these occur. Informed proxy consent is the absence of serious ignorance or misunderstanding about how the treatment is likely to affect the patient. This definition is unsatisfactorily vague, and has to be balanced with the risks of unduly pessimistic warnings to families. Consent practices vary so much that setting rigid minimal standards can just add to the confusion. Informed consent is really a symptom of something far larger and more complex: the relationship between families and health professionals. Attempts to improve consent practices must attend to this relationship, which is further explored in the next chapter.

Voluntary consent: willingness

Consent is supposed to be informed and also voluntary. After receiving and evaluating the evidence, and thinking out a conclusion, the other stage for patients and parents is to become committed, and to *want* the chosen decision. Like awareness, voluntariness is largely invisible. It is sensed rather than observed, and is most clearly evident in its absence, when patients are obviously being coerced against their will, and their consent is not voluntary. The first part of this chapter considers aspects of the meaning of voluntary consent. The next part summarizes its history. The third part is about consent to medical treatment and research. Then, after looking at tensions between objective science and voluntariness, I will discuss observing and practising voluntary consent in children's surgery units.

Aspects of voluntary consent

Becoming committed

Janet's parents described their experience of giving voluntary consent, while she was recovering a few days after surgery. Janet was ten months old, and had been treated in five hospitals. Her parents thought that they had been very fully informed about her heart condition and the choice of treatments. Eventually they agreed to major corrective surgery, and described the day before the operation.

Mother: Various doctors asked us if there were any more questions. And we really didn't have any more.

Father: No, we were so keyed up about the operation, and that was it, we'd made our minds up. . . . When the surgeon came with the form I felt it was perhaps a little rushed, to be honest. I did clarify with him, could we back out at the last minute. He said, 'All this is to do really is a consent form, oh yes, you can back out the minute before she goes down.'

Mother: But he did ask you why you had asked that question.

Father: I said, 'Well, nothing really.'

Mother: You didn't know why you'd asked it.

Father: I was very apprehensive.

Mother: I think we were both very, very tense.

Father: It took me a while, five or ten minutes to get the courage up to sign it. He was talking to me, going over the operation and things I'd already known about. I let him carry on while I was thinking it over. I plucked up the courage and then I signed it.

Mother: I wouldn't have signed it, I couldn't. I just hadn't got the courage to actually put my name in. If it had gone wrong, I don't know how I would have felt if I'd actually signed it.

PA: Would you have blamed yourself if things had gone wrong?

Father: Well, we had several talks, not only with doctors but also with a minister, and I think he made it very clear to us, well, he counselled us and really we came to the decision, whatever decision we made, it would be the right decision, because we were making it in Janet's interest, not for any other motive. So whatever decision we came to, we felt that was the right decision and we couldn't possibly reproach ourselves for it.

Mother: Even if she had died, I think in time I would have accepted that it might have been the right thing, but I don't think I would have done then.

When there is high risk, and the best course is uncertain, the voluntary aspect of consent becomes more obvious. Families and professionals waver between options. As Stephen said in the first chapter, 'I was half way. I didn't know what to pick.' In these dilemmas, more information does not help families who have had ample time to evaluate the details. Through absorbing information and realizing its personal meaning for them, families know deeply what they are consenting to. Janet's father said, 'That was it, we'd made our minds up.'

The final stage is to become emotionally committed to a decision, to let go of other hopes, and fearful indecision, and be content that this is the best, or the least harmful, choice. Then parents and patients who are old enough to understand can begin to prepare for the uncertain future, although not everyone responds in this way. Yet only when this stage is reached, are parents free to consent voluntarily to decisions which they believe to be in their child's best interests. This may be to high-risk surgery, or to withholding life-saving treatment.

Voluntariness relates to willing and wishing which are different from thinking. Although seeing perfectly good reasons for doing something, we can still lack the wish and the will to carry it out. Janet's parents spoke of the energy required for voluntary commitment, the tension that seemed to be dragging them back, which was difficult to explain. Janet's father could not say why he wanted to be able 'to back out at the last minute'. They spoke of the courage required to accept the risk of harm and loss, courage which Janet's mother felt she did not have.

Janet's parents faced a hard decision.[1] They knew that the operation was not necessarily life-saving, and had been told that without surgery Janet might live 'until her early twenties' but with progressive lung disease. If the operation went well, Janet could expect a much healthier and longer life. If it did not go well, she might die, or might endure worse health. Janet's heart defect occurs most often in children with Down's syndrome, which she had. Her parents knew that her doctors held strong and different opinions about whether or not surgery might benefit Janet; they had read the debate about this operation published in the *Lancet* at that time.[2] During this kind of uncertainty, doctors tended to be less directive and to leave the final decision to the parents.

An emotional choice

Voluntariness is connected with personal values and emotions. Janet's parents thought that corrective surgery fitted with their hopes for their fifth child to have as long and fulfilling a life as possible. Her mother said:

We took the emotional choice to opt for the operation. Late teens and early adults we feel is really the peak of anyone's life. And that was the time when she was going to die. We want her to do as much as she possibly can do. I think if we hadn't chosen to operate, the choice wouldn't have been there for her, because as a sick, invalid teenager there's no way she could hold down a job. It's bad enough if you're an invalid and you've got normal intelligence. But to be a Down's person as well, you've got a label on you straight away. But she hasn't in our house.

Janet's parents believed that as long as they attempted to make the best possible decision for their daughter, then they need not feel totally responsible, since the consequences were beyond their control. Janet's mother thought that it would be difficult at first for her to separate decision and action, responsibility and guilt: 'I don't think I would have done then.' In the same way, she agreed to the idea of surgery at a rational level, but found it very hard to feel willingly committed at an emotional level. She wanted the proposed end, a healthy child, but not the means towards it, dangerous surgery.

A moral choice

Janet's parents implied that the burden was eased for them by their Christian faith. Whatever they decided would somehow be 'right', even if she died and if the rightness was not clear to them. Their religion was central to their consent. It set their guiding principle 'in Janet's interest, not for any other motive'. This helped her father, at least, to feel less threatened by self-reproach, and therefore better able to consent willingly.

Parents considering high-risk surgery were forced to be aware of their child's fragile hold on life, and the limitations of human aid. Many felt conscious of a powerful force, benign or indifferent, which affected how responsible they felt. A Jewish mother, whose son was in Janet's position, did not wish him to have surgery, but wanted 'the Creator' to decide how long her son should live. Another family asked Rabbis to decide whether their son should have his operation. Two parents whose children were frequently very ill spoke of survival of the fittest and their feeling that the children should not have been born and should not survive. Voluntariness is strongly influenced by personal morality and, for religious people, by their beliefs.

A free choice

So far, voluntary consent has been described for what it is (opting, wanting, willing, preferring, becoming committed) or for how it is experienced. The classic description, in the Nuremberg Code, also stresses what voluntary consent is not:

1. The voluntary consent of the human subject is absolutely essential. This means that the person involved should . . . be so situated as to exercise free power of choice, without the intervention of any element of force, fraud, deceit, duress, overreaching, or other ulterior form of constraint or coercion; and should have sufficient knowledge and comprehension of the elements of the subject matter involved as to enable him to make an understanding and enlightened decision.[3]

The few written accounts of voluntary consent also stress the constraints on free consent. The longest work on consent discusses such external pressures at length and concludes:

These many confusing associations surrounding the term 'voluntariness' are too much, we believe, to combat successfully through a conceptual analysis that attempts to tidy up its meaning, and hence we avoid the word entirely.

We substitute a conception of noncontrol that does not have the history and connotation that burdens [*sic*] the terms 'freedom', 'voluntariness' and 'independence'.[4]

This quotation moves away from the active patient to the surrounding circumstances. The patient is so far forgotten, that voluntariness is illogically defined by its exact opposite, 'noncontrol', whereas the essence of voluntary consent is that it *is* control, by the patient through his or her 'free power of choice'.[5] Attempts to 'tidy up' meanings and dismissal of concepts because they are 'confusing' are not helpful if, as the authors say, they prevent the topic of voluntariness from actually being considered.

Another way to begin to understand untidy, confusing realities is to accept their complexity while attempting to realize part of their meaning. Since voluntariness is invisible, seeing it through an analogy may help. Volition and voluntariness both include a sense of movement forward towards a chosen direction, like a sailor following a chosen course though partly driven by such forces as the wind and tides.[6] Similarly, the patient follows a chosen course in two senses: the final goal and the means towards it. The goal may be good health after hazardous treatment, or it may be to endure illness with as little discomfort as possible for the brief life remaining. Although affected by many pressures, patients may be said to have voluntarily consented if the final goal and the main means towards it are what they most want or least fear. A change of direction is voluntary if the patient chooses the change.

Voluntariness can be inhibited by several influences which may alter the chosen direction against the patient's will. First are the unavoidable effects of the illness or treatment, such as unwanted major surgery if the patient is to gain the longed-for goal of good health. There may be complications after the operation leading to extra treatment before recovery. (The Nuremberg definition does not cover these since it refers only to research.) These are not deliberate coercion, but inevitable circumstances like the weather. If they are the only way forward to the chosen goal, then in a sense they are chosen voluntarily although reluctantly, as a sailor would choose a relatively unwanted route if it was the only way to reach the journey's end.

Second is social change, such as in medicine over the last fifty years, so that patients now hope to survive, whereas formerly they would expect to die. Families sometimes feel compelled (by their own or their neighbours' or the media's rising expectations) to risk treatment when they are not convinced that the benefit exceeds the harm.

Third is the way health care is provided. Surgery is surrounded by many routines which patients find uncomfortable and sometimes unnecessary. They consent to the operation (the main direction) but not to all the routines (details of the course steered towards their goal).

Fourth is the influence most commonly examined. The course may be altered by medical information and influence, such as: force, duress, or pressure to consent, deceit by misinformation or omission, overreaching in over-emphasis of hoped-for benefit and under-emphasis of risk, or other ulterior form of constraint or coercion, such as doctors refusing treatment unless a patient agrees to certain conditions. These pressures may be deliberate, or unintended, or they may be unavoidable if, say, medical knowledge is limited.

All four influences can inhibit voluntary consent. I suggest that the meaning of voluntary consent is that, as far as possible within inevitable pressures, the pilot-patient is able to exercise 'free power of choice' of direction, released from avoidable constraints. The patient's 'enlightened choice' of direction depends on informed comprehension of personal needs and of medical information.

Voluntary consent in the child's interest

Adequate proxy consent is based not necessarily on what parents want for themselves, but on what they believe their child needs, and in some cases what the child wants. These two wants of the parents and the child may differ. For example, leg lengthening is a new surgical technique offered to very short people. The treatment lasts a year, and is painful and very disruptive to the whole family. Ten-year-old Lesley had achondroplasia (dwarfism) and was determined to have the treatment. Her parents did not want to cope with all the problems this entailed, and said they would never choose for Lesley to have the treatment, she had to decide for herself, but they wanted to support whatever choice she made.

Voluntary consent links with growing awareness. Chapter 1 described how issues can be examined either by splitting them into parts or by seeing the whole. Critics of patient consent tend to split it into separate stages: diagnosis, planning treatment, informing the patient, the consent form is signed, treatment is given. The value of voluntary consent is shown when the stages are seen as related parts of a whole process that can benefit the child and family, as shown in the next example.

A paediatrician reported that babies with spina bifida too severe to be treated surgically used to be kept in her hospital until they died. In 1976 two parents took their baby home for his short life and slowly this was seen 'as a pattern to be encouraged'. A recent survey of eighty bereaved parents found that those who had been able to care for their baby at home looked back with less sadness, and many had a positive view of their child's life. Parents whose baby had stayed in hospital were sadder and thought that their baby's life had been of poor quality.[7]

The study implies the value of voluntary consent in several ways. When hospital staff listen to families instead of imposing decisions on them, together they can plan more beneficial care for the child. Discussion becomes part of therapy, and is enlarged beyond whether to try to 'cure or to kill' into how 'to give the child as good a life as can be offered, short though it may be'. Parents and physicians may then have time to work through their initial anger or denial of the severity of the defects, to become reconciled to the inevitable outcome, and to decide voluntarily not to attempt hopeless surgery.[8]

Some parents are divided between 'wanting everything possible to be tried' to save their child, and guilt that continuing treatment is not helping the child. The longer the effort had already been, the harder it could be to admit that it was all in vain. One mother, who wanted every reasonable attempt made to preserve her daughter's life, wrote months after the child died: 'Anger, rage, resignation, depression, wanting to kill yourself, self-pity, and nightmares about the pain inflicted on your child trying to save her life, they go through your mind very often. Grief is a very personal thing. It is a living hell.'[9] No one can be certain what is 'reasonable' until after the event, so that willing consent is compromised by conflicting wants.

Sometimes it seems that the technical care is 'a giant step forward for mankind' which leaves behind families' social and emotional welfare and harms them, whether or not the treatment succeeds. ('Family' of course includes the patient.) There are gaps between what might technically be achieved and the price of suffering which families are willing to pay. Voluntary consent concerns closing the gaps by trying to ensure families' willing, informed commitment to harm, or by moderating the treatment into choices which families can accept.

Parents' voluntary consent is important because even young children may sense and benefit from parents' willing commitment, just as they may react adversely if parents resent the treatment. Children cannot be treated in isolation. They depend on years of loving care which cannot be compelled and can only come voluntarily from the parents. In the United States, foetuses have been taken into state care and delivered by Caesarean section against the mother's will. Some of the babies returned to hospital seriously abused or neglected.[10] These cases demonstrate the futility of attempting to benefit children by forcing parents to accept surgery and its consequences against their will. Professionals who disrupt parent–child relationships can do great harm.[11] Satisfactory ways of repairing the damage have not yet been found, and it is very difficult to arrange alternative parenting care. Seeking parents' voluntary consent can therefore be in the child's interests.

The history of voluntary consent

Before anaesthesia was developed, doctors were likely to have been very aware of the voluntary consent of their conscious patients before and during surgery. In 1767 a British court found: 'It is reasonable that a patient should be told what is about to be done to him, that he may take courage and put himself in such a situation as to enable him to undergo the operation.'[12] Yet until this century, there were few records of patient consent, and we cannot be sure exactly what was meant by such phrases as 'the patient agreed'.[13]

Consent in medicine began to be recorded in twentieth-century court cases. Patients who sue surgeons for assault or negligence, are supported by the Anglo-American legal view that, 'Every human being of adult years and sound mind has the right to determine what shall be done with his own body.'[14] The courts have to consider admissible evidence, not invisible states such as voluntariness. So they concentrate on the medical information given to patients, to determine whether they knew what they were undertaking. Courts are therefore concerned with informed, rather than voluntary, consent.

In the national and international medical codes, which are short statements about recommended standards of ethical practice, voluntary consent is noticeable for its absence. For thousands of years, codes in the Hippocratic tradition stressed the doctor's duty 'to prescribe regimen for the good of my patients'.[15] This tradition assumes that 'good' is defined by the doctor, not by the patient, whose request for abortion, for example, should be refused. Doctors are expected to plan and prescribe the best treatment, not to offer patients free choices.

The legal and medical guidelines both concentrate on doctors' active responsibility. This is only practical, in order to promote high medical standards which are to some extent enforceable. Yet this emphasis does imply that patients are passive. Doctors' information is assessed, but not patients' responses. Informed consent is rather passive, voluntary consent is active.

Many national medical codes have been agreed, but only the international codes will be considered here, as representing general attitudes. One code is different from all the others, the Nuremberg Code,[16] as if the world suddenly became aware of principles with a black and white intensity that soon faded. Nuremberg's concerns are remote from today's medical care.[17] The guiding principle of all the adults I observed was to serve the best interests of the child patients, the exact opposite of Nazi exploitation. However, the Nuremberg Code is still relevant in that it seriously recognizes medicine's power to harm as well as to benefit, and the greater the potential for benefit, the greater the potential for harm. The Nuremberg trials demonstrate the dangers of scientific ideals of the objective, rigorous quest for knowledge, if taken to extremes.[18] Nuremberg is the only Code to mention 'voluntary consent', which it does in its first clause: '1. The voluntary consent of the human subject is absolutely essential.' In 1947, Nuremberg set voluntariness before information. This important emphasis is lost in the more often quoted Declaration of Helsinki 1964,[19] which only refers to 'freely given consent' after eight clauses about research design and information. Both these codes are about medical research, not treatment.

Codes about medical treatment, and about research which offers some therapy, appear to value the physician's 'judgement'[20] and 'conscience'[21] more highly than the patient's consent. Helsinki implies that the patient-subject's refusal may be overridden: 'The doctor must be free to use a new diagnostic and therapeutic measure, if in his or her judgement it offers hope of saving life, re-establishing health or alleviating suffering. This view was repeated in the American Belmont Report as recently as 1979.[22] Although the intention is to prevent state interference in medicine, the clause can mean that neither the state nor individuals should question certain medical decisions. It is as if, when trust in medical judgement fell in 1947, trust in the ordinary person's judgement rose. By 1964, trust reverted to medical expertise and away from relatively ignorant patients. Another difference is that the Nuremberg Code was written by a range of professionals, whereas Helsinki was declared by the World Medical Association.

The Nuremberg Code is also unique in stating that the subject 'should have sufficient . . . comprehension of the elements of the subject matter involved as to enable him to make an understanding and enlightened decision'. This assumes that ordinary people can understand medical details. It also suggests that there can be personal elements, in which the patient is most expert, besides purely scientific ones. At least Nuremberg, unlike Helsinki, does not specify the 'elements' as purely 'scientific principles', in which only the doctor is expert. Today, debate on consent[23] is mainly about how medically informed consent can be, and little attention is paid to voluntary choice.

The tragic reasons for which the Nuremberg Code was devised, its attempt to defend humanity against human evil, create a logical trap. Codes and laws are necessary to prevent abuse, because human beings harm one another. It is risky to assume that anyone will not harm others. Therefore, ultimately, no one can be trusted to make decisions on behalf of another person. The only real safeguard is each individual's freedom of choice, protected by rules respecting self-determination and non-interference. The trap is that no defence against harm is offered to patients such as babies who cannot make decisions, and who depend on the agency of others, which is the very potential danger that the Code seeks to prevent.

Voluntary proxy consent is a paradox.

Of all the tyrannies a tyranny sincerely exercised for the good of its victims may be most oppressive. . . . Those who torment us for our own good will torment us without end for they do so with the approval of their own conscience.[24]

Although acting for another's good can cause the greatest harm, it can also lead to the greatest benefits. Doctors and parents are hardly expected to intend harm to children. The sense that they are voluntarily committed to a wise decision may give parents greater confidence to encourage and support their child throughout distressing treatment, so that it may in itself be a therapeutic good. Yet a sense of cosy voluntariness may mask blind assent to misguided and cruel procedures. So although voluntariness is a vital part of valid consent, it is not enough, and must be combined with critical awareness.

Voluntary consent to research and to treatment

Research may be defined as careful, systematic investigation, and therapy as healing care. They are very different activities, yet in many ways they overlap. Much treatment is partly experimental and much research is integrated with treatment, such as in clinical trials. Doctors and patients want to perceive research and experimental treatment as therapeutic. For instance, a high-risk new treatment may be regarded as the patient's only hope. Some of the parents I observed were eager for their child to take part in research: 'We want to do anything we can in return for the help we have had, anything that will help other children.' Doctors have been found to overestimate the hoped-for benefits and to underestimate the risks of their research.[25] A study of medical researchers found that when they gave potential research subjects more information about the harms, risks, and uncertain benefit of the project, fewer people agreed to take part in trials. The researchers themselves felt uncomfortable, and less willing to do research.[26] Possibly they needed to keep up their own optimism, and to perceive their research as directly therapeutic.

Healthy volunteers are regarded as very different subjects from sick patients who may benefit from research. Yet many volunteers also stand to benefit, indirectly or in the future. Some may also be under great pressure to help research into conditions that affect their close relatives, such as thalassaemia or cystic fibrosis.

Doctors consider that all accepted therapies which have not been through controlled trials ought to be tested. The discipline of systematic research is thought to be a major safeguard of patients' interests. Yet the doctor–patient relationship, when the patient's welfare is expected to be the first concern, can conflict with the researcher–subject relationship, which serves the interests of research first, sometimes to the discomfort of patients. Research and treatment complement yet conflict with one another.

Medical guidelines on consent and, in Britain, ethics committees concentrate on consent to research. In practice, consent to treatment is only slowly being accepted by clinicians.[27] There are still debates in Britain about whether patients should be informed that they have cancer. Consent to research will only be accepted fully when consent to treatment is accepted and this has to include the patient understanding the illness being treated. Researchers and some ethics committees still argue 'against seeking informed consent to avoid causing unnecessary distress to the patient in making her aware of the precise prognosis of her condition [breast cancer] and the uncertainty of surgeons about the appropriate treatment'.[28]

Consent to treatment could be regarded as even more important than consent to research. People who are ill, anxious, and dependent on their doctors are more vulnerable than healthy volunteers. The more ill the patients, the higher are the risks and known harms they may agree to, in the hope that new cures may be found.

Yet clear definitions of consent to research do not always easily apply to treatment. With simple cases of research, the choice is two-dimensional: the hoped-for benefits of the research results versus the possible harms of procedures. Consent usually holds no hope of personal gain, and therefore refusal holds no fear of loss. However, consent to research which involves treatment is three-dimensional. Patients balance

1. the hoped-for benefits with
2. the risks and also
3. their illness or defect.

They may have to decide whether to go on being ill rather than risk dangerous new treatment, or whether to try almost any new remedy for an intolerable condition. Through being ill, patients are likely to be more intensely aware of physical risks and benefits than healthy subjects are. Some have far more hope of gain if they consent, and fear of loss if they refuse.

Patients' consent to research involving treatment also involves understanding on three levels:

1. the nature and purpose of the treatment, the benefits, risks, side-effects, and alternatives;
2. medical uncertainty—that no one is certain of the harms and benefits of the treatment, how severe or likely to occur the risks may be, or how well the treatment compares with alternative ones;

3. the research programme—such as a double-blind trial, in which neither patient nor doctor knows which treatment is being given.[29]

When consent to research is reported in medical journals, it is often not clear which levels have been discussed with the subjects, although full discussion at any one level would include the other two. The levels challenge different aspects of patient–doctor relations. They may reduce patients' confidence in their treatment (1, 2, 3), and (unfairly) in their clinician's competence (2, 3), and in their clinician's personal concern for them (3). Patients may sense a tension between being cared for as a unique patient, or being used as a statistic in a trial. Doctors are therefore under different pressures to present information to patients in order to gain their willing, confident agreement.

Modern medicine involves difficult compromises: between deciding when there is sufficient knowledge about new therapies to risk using them, or to hold back cautiously and yet watch patients suffer who might otherwise benefit; between telling patients truthfully about risks of treatment yet raising much anxiety about dangers which may not occur.

Balancing harm and benefit, and the individual and collective interests of patients, is particularly complicated in paediatric cardiology. About thirty years ago, cardiologists working on middle-aged, acquired heart disease had little interest in the totally different congenital heart defects of children. Today, almost all these defects can be alleviated or corrected. Yet steps forward can have a high price. Medical lectures are illustrated by slides of graphs showing the 'learning curve'; mortality rates for a new operation fall sometimes from about 100 per cent, down to 50, then 15 per cent over a few years as the whole cardiac team improve their knowledge and skill, discover new techniques, and learn from mistakes. One intensive care sister told me:

The difficulty of the work hasn't changed much over the years. The cases that we used to think were so difficult are easy now. But we are treating more and more complicated new cases who would have died a few years ago.

New operations carry high risks at first, then are accepted as reasonably safe, until after a few years the long-term risks may begin to show. Children's heart specialists spoke of their work as experimental, 'no one knows what the effects will be in thirty years'. Drug trials are regulated, but new surgery techniques need not first be approved by an ethics committee, or even be explained to patients. The subject is more private and literally in the surgeons' hands. After long discussion at medical meetings about surgical options, based on careful review of the available data, the surgeon may say, 'I will decide when I get in there and see what is going on.' Sometimes only an autopsy will reveal the defect precisely.

There are dilemmas about how freely to admit failures of new treatment. For example, at one medical meeting I observed, doctors discussed a boy who had had a new kind of operation five years earlier, to prevent lung disease. Now he, and the twelve other children in the study, showed more serious signs of lung disease than patients who had conventional shunt surgery. The meeting agreed that no more of the new operations would be performed. This example raises questions about how much families can or should be informed about new surgery, both beforehand, and in retrospect when long-term effects are revealed.

Another meeting discussed how to identify beforehand the children who will 'succumb' to a particular operation. These children were already mortally ill. If conventional surgery could not help, a new technique although of very high risk would offer the only hope. This raises questions about whether, and how, to say to parents, 'We are almost certain your child will die from this surgery, but she will die anyway and we think it is worth trying something. The new operation might give your child a better chance of survival or it might be even less likely to succeed than the usual method.'

There is a growing debate about whether doctors should shield families from this responsibility and anguish, or whether patients and relatives, or the general public, lawyers, or the media ought to share in influencing these decisions. The debate is not only about how much information to give, but how far it is wise, respectful, or kind to ask families to share in making fatal decisions. One cardiologist told me:

I consider that we are paid to make decisions, it's part of the job. If parents agree their child should go to surgery and the child dies, they will blame themselves, and it's a decision they will have to live with for ever afterwards. Sometimes it helps if they can blame somebody else. I think we have to accept this.

Some nurses shared this view. At a nurses' meeting a sister said:

One doctor implied that the parents' view would be taken into consideration. Others thought this was impossible, for parents to decide whether their child should live or die. The consultant said to the parents, 'No, not that horrendous question. It's my decision. You know nothing of heart defects. I'll decide. I'm the expert.'

I think that was too big a decision to leave to parents of a new baby. And parents' motives are very different from the person going through the treatment.

The difficulty here is that parents still know that, even if passively, they allowed doctors to make the decision. Parents could refuse. They still have to sign the consent form, 'the death warrant' as a few parents described it. Doctors make decisions by thinking through all the relevant data and making a final assessment and recommendation. Parents have to decide whether to accept the recommendation. Their decision is based on understanding enough of the medical argument, and fitting it with their personal knowledge of the child, so that they can become voluntarily committed to the conclusion. If families are not involved in making decisions, through the dialogue between medical and personal understandings, they may misunderstand, or bitterly disagree with, or be unprepared for, 'imposed' decisions which they have to live with.

Information and voluntariness can seem to conflict. Patients who know less about the risks of treatment are likely to accept it more willingly. However, although they may embark willingly on a course of treatment, those who have unexpected difficulties during treatment may also endure more pain, anger, anxiety, and slower recovery rates.[30] Preparation is thought to help patients to cope with problems. Voluntariness may also help, in that patients may tolerate difficulties which they have agreed to undertake, for a purpose they believe to be worthwhile, more easily than difficulties which they resent as imposed on them. One example is the criticism of three cancer trials by Evelyn Thomas, a patient who found that she had been involved in the trials. Her objection was not to the research, she supported that, but to being used as a subject in the trials without her knowledge or consent.[31]

Yet as the need of very ill patients for freedom of consent increases, pressure also rises on doctors to reassure distressed families, and themselves and their colleagues, with hope. Many doctors consider it their duty to protect patients from the distress of alarming information (informed consent) and of painful choices (voluntary consent). One clinician justified such protection because 'anxiety in a patient is always undesirable, especially when a serious illness such as cancer has just been diagnosed'.[32]

This is surely unrealistic. Seriously ill patients are helped when their inevitable anxiety is treated sympathetically, not when it is denied. Denial may protect doctors rather than patients. It ignores the reality that patients have other sources of information, such as personal experience. Painful illness and treatment can cause patients even greater anxiety if the clinicians do not seem to anticipate or recognize the patient's experience. Patients also learn from one another. Knowing that other women were having counselling, Evelyn Thomas was deeply worried that she was not seeing a counsellor because she was not expected to live long. Much unnecessary fear could have been avoided if she had been informed that she was in a randomized trial on counselling.[33]

Randomized trials complicate voluntary consent, particularly trials involving patients who receive either no treatment (as in the counselling trial) or placebos. When I asked, 'What does "placebo" mean to you?', some nurses replied, 'It's a trick, a fake.' A doctor discussing a vaccine trial in which babies were given placebo injections replied, 'We have placebos to ensure control, to screen for the placebo effect. Each group must seem to be treated exactly the same.' Placebo meaning 'I will please you' is of questionable relevance to injections for babies. It is frequently interpreted as the patient passively being pleased, or deceived into being pleased, by dummy treatment. An alternative view would see 'placebo' as the patient actively wanting improved health, being committed to, and pleased with, the medical treatment, and releasing self-healing energies which work in harmony with it. This activity is likely to be enhanced when patients feel willingly committed to chosen treatment.[34] Randomized blind trials ask informed patients to dispense with the chance of sharing in the choice of their treatment, and with the pleasing certainty that they are having the most effective treatment or, in some trials, any treatment at all. When it is not known which is the most clinically effective treatment, controlled trials can express care and respect, both for individuals in the trial (who are honestly informed about medical uncertainty) and for all who may later benefit from the findings (about which treatments are beneficial,

ineffective, or harmful). However, valuable knowledge can sometimes only be gained at the cost of assigning patients to treatment
groups which they would not willingly choose. A singer discovered
too late that she was in a group having a breast cancer drug which
adversely affects the voice and which, she felt, destroyed her life;
clinical effectiveness, that may only be measured crudely by survival
rates, can conflict with personal choice. A pilot study of women with
breast cancer suggests that when there is a clinical choice between
mastectomy and lumpectomy, recovery rates improve when women
make their own choice.[35] The subjective reasons for the women's
choices are the kind of bias which correctly controlled trials seek to
exclude, but which is part of the positive placebo element of effective
therapy.

People with AIDS are challenging randomized blind trials, which
treat humans rather like laboratory animals who cannot take part in
decisions.[36] They argue that, as few choices remain open to them,
they should be allowed to share in decisions about their treatment,
and should be free to choose whether to risk taking potentially
dangerous drugs. AIDS research subjects are testing their drugs
privately and discarding placebos. Active medicines are being shared
among patients in the hope that little is better than nothing. Some
people have enrolled in the same multi-centre trial at different
hospitals, so as to increase their chance of having an active substance.
These activities sabotage blind, controlled trials. They indicate that
taking voluntary consent seriously involves rethinking traditional
scientific methods in research on humans, although attempts so far
to reconcile voluntary consent with randomized trials have been
criticized as poor science and poor ethics.[37]

Many diseases, such as high blood pressure, relate to personal
behaviour. Treatment is effective when doctors and patients share
information about healthier ways of living, and when patients adopt
new habits. The patient actively promotes health (or disease). Making and keeping voluntary decisions are the keys to health. Yet not
everyone wants to be informed or to make choices, and increasingly
doctors are being asked to respond to patients' differing needs.

So far, I have looked at practical aspects of how voluntary consent
is being or ought to be achieved according to medical and legal
guidelines. The next section explains further the tensions between
voluntariness and ideals in medicine and research by looking at
underlying beliefs.

Objective science and voluntariness

Voluntary consent is an invisible, elusive process. Yet science tends to concentrate on matters which can be clearly demonstrated. Scientific traditions can work for but also against voluntariness, and this becomes clearer when current ideals of objectivity and autonomy, and tensions between science and care are critically examined. Many of the points made here about objective science also apply to medical ethics.

Two approaches to science have been explained by Evelyn Fox Keller, a mathematical biologist.[38] They are similar to the two approaches outlined in chapter 1. The first, objective, approach values detachment. It separates the observer from the object of study, ignores feeling and value judgements, and measures truth by its distance from subjectivity. The second approach is to become fully absorbed in the object being studied, through thinking, feeling, and intuition being intensely aware of the unique whole. One scientist has described the second approach as touching 'something central to another person, or to a subject, and one feels silent and grateful . . . because one was allowed to penetrate a layer of understanding which remained impenetrable to others. . . . If you really want to understand about a tumour, you've got to *be* a tumour.'[39]

Objective science rigidly controls and dissects objects in order to use them, such as to test a hypothesis. The second approach aims flexibly to appreciate objects in their own terms, 'to listen to the material', to 'let the experiment tell you what to do'. Organisms do everything we can think of 'better, more efficiently, more marvellously. . . . There is no such thing as a central dogma into which everything will fit,' because nature's variety surpasses human imagination. Scientists who impose their own theories and search for data to fit their preconceptions miss reality and its meaning.[40]

Scientists work in countless different ways and many, who in theory believe in pure objectivity, practise a richer response to their subject-matter. Subjectivity is not the same as bias. The subjective scientist who is aware of personal perceptions and takes them into account is in closer touch with reality than the scientist who imagines that ignoring feeling and values is the same as excluding them. All data are perceived through the senses and are inevitably filtered through the grid of former experience. A reminder of how we are controlled by assumptions so ingrained that they have become subconscious was given by a woman who recovered her sight after forty years of blindness. A few days later she asked, 'What are those black and white stripes on the houses opposite?' They were windows. We cannot avoid some degree of subjectivity because we see what we have learned to expect in ways that we have been taught to understand.

A classic image of the scientist is of someone examining cells through a microscope. This image emphasizes distance and difference between the observer and the observed. However, when any possible connections and similarities are denied, moral constraints are loosened, opening up the possibility of violence and exploitation.[41] Treating human beings as if they are mindless research material creates problems. If scientists unconsciously assume a 'correct' model of research data as inanimate and unresponsive, then responding to human subjects' unwillingness or anxiety can seem to threaten scientific integrity. The impersonal ideal of pure science which aims to exclude empathy (as subjective and emotional) risks reducing scientists' awareness both of the warning signs of research subjects' distress and also of the researchers' own compassion.

Empathy interferes with pure research in that it may lead scientists to help distressed subjects to withdraw from the project. Losing research subjects tends to be seen negatively, as biasing and reducing the results, and as likely to increase the length and costs of the study. Yet it could be seen positively as a sensitive response to distressed patients. One of many possible examples of the different values of science and of care is twenty-four-hour urine collection. This could be classed as a non-invasive, problem-free procedure. Yet collection from toddlers involves attaching bags to them. Some toddlers strongly object, and the bags fall off. Collection has to be restarted and the children may spend stressful extra days in hospital. The research conflicts with good paediatric practice which avoids non-essential interventions, and discharges children as early as possible.

The ideals of objectivity have great advantages in medicine. They enable effective means of diagnosing, treating, and preventing disease to be developed, and the best methods to be chosen impartially. Yet scientific ideals also present problems for voluntary consent. Voluntariness eludes scientific analysis. Like other intangible issues it therefore tends to be ignored in the physical and social sciences, and thus can seem to be unimportant. Theories within which voluntariness can be defined and understood remain undeveloped, so that we know very little about it.

Psychological effects of medical research were studied in a group of diabetic children.[42] Even in this group, carefully selected for their emotional stability, some children suffered unpredicted and serious emotional problems arising from the clinical trial. Consent forms were signed by one parent, but sometimes the other parent disagreed. In some cases there was serious family discord about the research. The researchers concluded that 'children and their families engaged in research will require continuing emotional support' and that provision for this should perhaps be built into the design of clinical trials. Significantly, this seems to be almost the only study to consider, monitor, or report psychological factors, so that we know very little about patients' voluntary involvement in research.

The psychology of objectivity

Keller shows further tensions between objectivity and voluntariness. She argues that objectivity is a form of bias, based on a psychological need for detachment and control over oneself and others. It fears intimacy. Scientists are cut off from research subjects (animate and inanimate) and also from their own feelings. (The Nazis denied the distress felt by their research subjects, and their own sense of compassion and shared human vulnerability.) Scientists who invest in 'impersonality, claim to have escaped the influence of desires, wishes and beliefs', impulses associated with childhood.[43]

Each child's psychological development can be traced as the gradual separation from the mother and family through growing independence. The child learns the meaning of objective reality, painfully realizing that the world around is not part of the baby's own self, and cannot be controlled magically by wishes. Throughout childhood the boundary between self and other is ever more firmly defined.[44] Psychoanalysis reveals how the child is torn between longings for powerful yet lonely independence, and loving yet restricting intimacy.[45]

Traditionally, maturity has been regarded as total, independent autonomy based in a pure, objective understanding of the world.[46] A new understanding sees mature autonomy not as separateness, but as confident relations with others. Then the self is fulfilled rather than diminished by intimacy, and objective understanding gains from subjective experience.

Autonomy too sharply defined, reality too rigidly defined, cannot encompass the emotional and creative experiences that give life its fullest and richest depth. Autonomy must be conceived more dynamically and reality more flexibly. . . . Emotional growth does not end with mere acceptance of one's own separateness; perhaps it is fair to say that it begins there.[47]

Interplay 'between the inner psychic space of "me" and the outer social space of "not-me"' has been described by Donald Winnicot, the paediatrician and psychoanalyst, as what 'more than anything else makes the individual feel that life is worth living'.[48] This depends on a strong, enduring sense of self, overcoming a childish egocentric view of the world, and confidently undertaking the risk of being close to others and so possibly being harmed by them. People who insist most emphatically on pure objectivity and autonomy may be those who feel most anxiously defensive about a weak sense of self, seeing intimacy as a regression to childish dependence instead of a heightened adult 'aliveness'.[49]

These ideas have been summarized briefly because voluntariness can only be understood with some reference to its psychological meanings. As a final example of a psychological understanding of objectivity, an extreme avoidance of subjectivity through obsessive control can lead a person to lose all contact with, and trust in, his or her innate, spontaneous will.

In his psychology, self-direction is distorted from its normal meaning of volitional choice and deliberate, purposive action to a self-conscious directing of his every action, to the exercise, as if by an overseer, of a continuous wilful pressure and direction on himself and even [on] his own wants and emotions.[50]

Under this harsh regime . . . the consequence is loss of conviction: truth is inferred rather than experienced, the basis for judgement and decisions is sought in rules rather than feeling.[51]

Personal volition is replaced by external scientific and moral laws. In other words, voluntariness is mistrusted and repressed by narrow ideals of objectivity.

Keller defines objectivity as an authentic, reliable view of reality.[52] This can include empathy in order to gain a richer understanding of oneself and others in their own right. If rigid objectivity excludes empathy, it presents psychological and practical difficulties in respecting voluntary responses, one's own and other people's.

Science and care

There are differences between the ideals of objective science and of subjective care. Research on humans is justified by its intentions for future, general benefits. Yet researchers and subjects can differ in their understanding of 'benefit', 'acceptable harm', and 'justified' research. Nazi experiments are sometimes dismissed as poor science, badly designed work providing no useful knowledge. This is not true,[53] and falsely implies that inhumane research is also inevitably unscientific. Yet much valuable medical knowledge has been gained through methods now judged to be inhumane. Semmelweiss's work has rescued countless women from puerperal fever. When he became convinced that infection was spread by obstetric staff, he demonstrated this in a controlled trial, examining twelve patients after washing his hands and twelve without washing, as was customary then. As he expected, all the second group died, thus supporting the hypothesis.[54]

To identify scientific standards with humane standards is to miss the difference between the two ideals. Scientific ideals of clear, precise analysis, avoiding undue enthusiasm for untested ideas, are one aspect of medical excellence. In contrast, the ideals of care seek emotional involvement and shared values and experiences. The patient is used as a research subject in one setting, and treated as a vulnerable dependant in the other. Medicine as a science and as a caring profession at times has to balance conflicting ideals.

The Nuremberg emphasis on voluntary choice may have been soon forgotten (it has not been repeated in later codes) because such awareness of the potential dangers in science devoid of humane care was too painful, and too inconvenient, for Western society to tolerate for long. Informed consent is mainly about basing decisions on objective medical data. Voluntary consent involves both scientific and personal values, and can be a means of working out tensions between them in order to serve each patient's best interests.

Assessing voluntariness

The question remains: Did Janet's parents give voluntary consent? The answer could be considered from three viewpoints, which will be discussed in turn, the views of: the people giving consent; the doctors who inform them; or any observer, such as a nurse, lawyer, or relative. Each view depends on personal beliefs about how far families can and should be involved. Some people who say that they consented voluntarily seem to have low expectations about how much they could or should be involved.

The parents' view

Janet's parents explained to me that they thought their decision was informed and freely made. They did not feel under pressure from the consultant to agree to anything against their will. In a long interview, they described their changing opinions. At first her mother was shocked that Janet had Down's syndrome and 'didn't want to be close to her'. Later, her parents' hopes for their daughter changed as she became 'just one of our children, she has an equal place in our lives'. All Janet's grandparents thought that she should not have surgery, 'because the problem is solved when she's older' by her early death. In response to this, Janet's parents 'were hurt and horrified, because it's not just a question of the longevity, it's also a question of the quality of life. We couldn't just sit back and see her go slowly downhill.' As their relationship with Janet changed, her parents' choice of medical treatment changed.

At first, they had difficulty in trusting the many doctors they met, partly because the diagnosis changed, as Janet's condition is difficult to diagnose, and also because opinions as to the best treatment differed. This led to them to consult other sources. 'We would thrash about and get as many books as we could.' Eventually, 'Dr B gave us three choices: complete repair, banding and then complete repair, or do nothing at all, and he gave us the outcome as he felt it would be in all three cases.'[55] Eventually Janet's parents 'took the emotional choice' to have surgery, but left 'the medical decision' about the type of operation to the doctors.' They chose the goal, but wanted clinicians to decide the route, 'because we didn't feel we knew enough to make that decision'.

They also wanted to avoid a precise commitment, because they disagreed with one another. Janet's mother preferred the lower risk banding operation, 'I just wanted her a bit longer without having to face the risks.' Janet's father preferred corrective surgery because the banding surgery 'wasn't really solving' the basic problem. Janet was admitted for the banding operation. However, one book[56] advised against this.

Mother: It was fantastic, because the book actually said they didn't recommend the banding . . .

Father: for an A V canal . . .
Mother: and that in fact was what she was coming in for, as we were reading the book . . .
Father: on the way to the hospital . . .
Mother: because we were only given it that morning. . . . Over the weekend we saw various doctors who said they didn't want to do the banding . . .
Father: quite independently of what we said, we didn't influence them at all. [*He repeated the book's explanation of the problems that could result from the banding.*]

The new information challenged their decision to leave the precise decision to the consultant, in case surgery was offered which they now questioned.

PA: What would you have done if the doctors wanted to band?
Mother: I think we would have still trusted the doctors at the time.
Father: We would have trusted the doctors at the time. . . . It's all very well reading up about things in medical books, but when one really comes down to it, one puts one's hands in the doctors and in the hospital here.
Mother: I think we'd discussed that if they were still going to go ahead, we'd go along with it.

Guidelines on consent to research imply that informed consent and voluntary consent tally, that people need only agree to decisions which they thoroughly understand and support. While this may be so with medical research, Janet's example suggests that with complicated treatment, patients' logical choice is not always the same as their voluntary choice. Sometimes they suspend judgement because they do not feel qualified to judge. Decisions involve not only data, but decision-making rules. Although many parents, especially fathers, felt obliged to learn the technical details, they still relied on doctors to interpret the details, to set them in an order of priority, and relate them to the particular patient within a wider framework of medical experience. Medical opinions about Janet's care had changed several times over the months. When there is clearly disagreement between doctors, at some stage families have to take the risk of trusting in a particular doctor's judgement.

Janet's consultant recommended corrective surgery, and estimated the risk at 'eight or nine to one of her surviving, instead of the earlier estimate of four or five to one'. With twice the chance of safe recovery, Janet's mother was happier to agree to corrective surgery. Both parents seemed satisfied that their consent to Janet's operation was as voluntary as possible within the limits of the choices open to them.

The consultant's view

Janet's consultant told me that 'the climate of opinion' had changed since the Arthur case.[57] More parents wanted to have their Down's baby 'treated as normal'. In cases like Janet's,

You make the decision for them that you feel they want to make. I can sense them out. I think it falls roughly into one third want something done, one third are open, and one third do not want surgery, and you can see it. If you start talking about surgery, and the techniques and the risks, and they start fidgeting and getting—and twitching, you can sense that they don't want surgery, and then you'll say, 'Well you *can* operate but I consider it is the best decision to leave it. They can be very well, these children, without surgery.'

I think you have to be flexible, but if we operated on all Down's children with serious congenital heart defects, that would be one in six of our patients. With limited resources, I think it's reasonable that where you have to make a choice, you operate on normal children before Down's children.

I would be equally happy if they did not operate [on a Down's child with Janet's defect]. I tried to present the choices without bias, but that's impossible. I am open about it.

In Janet's case, her consultant seemed to consider that her parents were able to give informed and voluntary consent. Also, it was becoming easier for parents to do this, since the hospital policy had changed into being more responsive to parents' differing wishes.

An observer's view

Each observer's view may differ. Some would consider that Janet's parents should have been free to insist on corrective surgery if this was not offered. Others may think that her parents had no more right, and far less knowledge, than her doctors had when deciding Janet's future.

There were the practical limitations of medical knowledge. No one could exactly predict the benefit and harm to Janet of each option. I gained the impression that despite difficulties great efforts were made by everyone concerned with Janet to achieve as informed and voluntary a proxy consent as possible.

The observer's view is limited because so much is invisible: expectations, satisfaction, and the 'free power of choice'[58] of voluntary consent. Just one invisible aspect will be considered here, power.

Power is the positive, nurturing force of healing and overcoming disease. Patients have this power in self-healing, and in taking decisions. Yet power can also be coercive and can restrict voluntary consent. Stephen Lukes explains three kinds of coercive power, which I will summarize with medical examples.[59] He acknowledges that trying to see the invisible can be criticized as unscientific and dangerous. Yet he thinks that there are worse problems in ignoring unseen dimensions, and we need to find some means of exploring them.

The first kind of power is obvious coercion, such as when a doctor provides or withholds treatment knowing that this is not what the patient or parents want. In the past, with Down's children with Janet's condition, although some parents were very unhappy about their child's ill health and asked for corrective surgery, some doctors would only offer corrective surgery for non-Down's children. The second coercion is when doctors provide treatment which patients are unlikely to want, although the doctor may not have asked. So, for instance, the doctor may block or avoid cues from parents that they want to discuss alternative forms of treatment. The third kind of power is when patients are unable to choose a treatment which they would have chosen if they had known about it, but they do not even realize that they have not been given the choice. Some parents were not aware that corrective surgery was a possible choice. Lukes considers that power is unique 'in its self-concealing tendency' because the more hidden power is, the stronger and more effective it can be. Patterns of power can be traced through seeing how invisible relationships are expressed in minor details, such as in the way parents are involved or excluded in wards and clinics, in practical care and decision-making.

Voluntariness is 'sensed' as Janet's consultant said, rather than proved. Its absence is more easily noticed (in stated or implied resistance) than its presence. To ask patients directly whether their consent is voluntary could increase pressures on them to seem to be willingly compliant, if they are reluctant to seem to be critical. Although voluntariness is hard to assess, it may be indicated in some of the following ways.

Knowing the risks and hoped-for benefits, patients are content that the final goal (the expected results) and the means towards it (the treatment) seem to them the best or least harmful option. They have no strong objections to the chosen treatment, and do not state or imply unwillingness in principle. They may express agreement, and explain how the decision fits with their moral values and religious beliefs, their hopes and plans. Patients are able to discuss their reservations with their doctors. If necessary and possible, the treatment is modified to suit patients' wishes. They have time to accept the proposed treatment plan and to let go of other hopes, clearly knowing the other options.

Not all these criteria occur in every case, and not all are clearly demonstrated. Patients may very much want the hoped-for goal yet fear the means towards it. Yet, like Janet's mother, they may fear withholding treatment still more. Voluntariness is elusive, subtle, and complex. Much is lost if it is dismissed as an impossible ideal. Patients benefit through attempts to achieve consent which is as voluntary as possible, when their reservations are used in working towards the solution which they are most willing to accept.

8

Trust between doctors and families

Trust is often assumed to be something that just happens between patients and doctors. Yet in practice trust is very complicated, elusive, sometimes hard to establish and sustain, and subject to many influences. This chapter is about the place of trust in consent to dangerous treatment.

'Trust', wrote one doctor, 'means less risk of misconceptions' and is also a 'marvellous time saver' because it can be a substitute for long explanations. Doctors should therefore be good leaders, and 'improve morale' with a show of confidence, 'not just blindly dish out "complete honesty" and tell everybody everything they "have a right to know"'. The trusting patient is contrasted with the questioning patient. Why should patients want to be informed, unless in 'bad faith' they mistrust medical competence?[1]

Some writers see trust as a duty.

Doctors need freedom to act upon their judgement of what is best for their patients. . . . Morally speaking the relationship ought to involve trust on the part of the patient and fidelity on the part of the doctor.[2]

This advice implies that 'what is best' is always unanimously agreed. Yet if there is only one best course and if doctors always follow it, informed consent is a polite token of respect but not a precaution against avoidable harm. It is ornamental but hardly useful. Patients' mistrust is then made to appear irrational and unjust.

Trust is not a duty which we 'ought' to feel. No one would argue, surely, that doctors and patients 'ought' to trust drug companies. Trust is partly an instinct, and partly a complex kind of testing guide, like litmus paper. Trust is a mixture of thinking and feeling, personal and impersonal responses, often a struggle between doubt and hope.[3] The parents talking in the heart units indicated some of the invisible patterns of trust in the consent process.

Trust as conviction

Joanne aged eight enjoyed cycling, swimming, and roller-skating. Her mother described bringing a seemingly healthy child into hospital for investigations.

Well I suppose we forget she's ill, but really basically she has got this heart disease, so they are taking care to see that she doesn't become ill. Dr A said, 'Come in,' and you can't turn round and say, 'No,' can you really? So we've just come in as a matter of course. And we'll have to—well we don't *have* to—but we will abide by their decisions. They've always done right by her in the past. So, um, hopefully we don't have to worry. [*Laughs nervously*]

They'll tell us tomorrow morning. My husband will be here, because, um, I get a bit upset, if there's something I don't want to hear [*laughs*] and then you can't really take it in, can you? We know the long-term prognosis might not be that good. Dr A doesn't know if there's anything else they can do for her. So whether that means her standard of life will go down, or it will stay the same, we won't know till tomorrow. But he's prepared us. He's very good and he's very truthful—well to us he is, but then we've always asked him to be.

Our faith is in him as a person. I'm not saying that these others are not equally as—clever, but *our* faith is in him. We just feel more confident. He's known Joanne from the word go, and when she was so terribly ill it was him who helped her through, so therefore our faith is in him. It gives me security. When we've seen him in a clinic, not someone else, I go away feeling more reassured. I suppose it's psychological, but that's how I feel.

Mrs McKay's view of trust was shared by many of the parents I interviewed. Heart disease is invisible and often deceptive when the child seems perfectly healthy. Families therefore have to trust far more in medical assessments, especially when these contradict visible evidence and when the news is something they 'don't want to hear'. Trust is more than intellectual conviction; it also consists, as Mrs McKay said, in 'psychological' states of confidence, security, and reassurance.

Trust in information, the informer, and the context

Trust takes time to develop at several levels. A managing director said that agreeing to emergency medical decisions for his son presented 'two very great differences' from making business decisions.

I'm supposed to know something about my business; I know nothing about medicine. The second thing is that I know something about the person who is giving me the information in my business and I know nothing about the person who is giving me the information in the hospital. Well, I had met the consultant twice. No problem, I had every confidence in him, but it's a difference.

Charles's father distinguished the information from the informer. Knowing the informer helps towards 'being on the same wavelength', and having a clearer understanding of personal meanings and perhaps habitual omissions or exaggeration. Misunderstandings can easily arise during early meetings. For example, Charles's father said he was horrified on being shown round the intensive care unit to see mess and rubbish around an empty cot. As this was one of the few aspects of the unit he felt qualified to assess, it shook his confidence in the unit. Later he learned that cots were often not prepared until just before the next baby was admitted; accepting the unit routines restored his confidence. Such misunderstandings are less likely to occur, or can be explained more easily, when families and staff have had time to get to know one another.

Knowing the informer also helps on the second level of knowing how much to trust their information. Not yet having this experience, Charles's father relied on the experience of others. 'I had to find out within twelve hours who was the best surgeon for transposition of the great arteries. I phoned a cardiologist I knew in Denver, he phoned England and found out it was the surgeon here.'

As Charles spent months in the unit, despite many difficulties, his parents' trust developed. They appreciated the honest admission of problems. 'It's good and brave and the right thing to say they don't know when they don't know.' 'I've never found that I was missing information, there was an overflow of information.' 'The best people tend to attract the best people to work around them in a centre of excellence like this.' 'The nurses were all cheerful, they were all busy, and we're very grateful because it was such a good system. It's a very good team and that reduced our stress.' Trust concerns believing in the information, the informer, and the surrounding circumstances, such as the image and ethos of the unit.

Personal trust

Parents' trust in the doctor's character and attitude towards their child is extremely important to them. They tend to justify (and perhaps to strengthen) their trust by remembering how it has been validated 'in the past', as with Joanne. They value continuing personal care 'from the word go', by one familiar clinician. One example is the mother who wrote to me:

We thought Dr A was marvellous and we have never had reason to change that initial opinion. He said, 'To us, Linda is a rare and fascinating case but we will never forget that she is *your* precious daughter.' In that light we were happy that the decision [about surgery] was his, and we have both always felt that this was completely right.

He said, like all the others, what a high-risk operation it was. I said, 'What I want to know is, will she make it?' His reply, putting his hand on my arm and Linda's—'She'll make it.' It was so unofficial but kind. Somehow I felt he was saying, 'No guarantees, but . . .'. I wasn't led to false hope by that, but things weren't so black, I think.

Personal trust looks for a particular doctor with a personal concern for the child to guide the family through the impersonal and threatening world of intensive medicine.

One mother told me how her child had almost died when in the care of her local doctors and was dramatically rescued by expert cardiologists. Yet she still trusted her local paediatrician in preference to the cardiologist who was

too cut and dried. There was no warmth or compassion in what he was saying. He didn't relate emotionally to the child. I always feel happier seeing our paediatrician. He's very positive and can handle the negative side very gently. The heart is very technical but I think cardiologists could handle it in the same way, positively and gently.

At first, this attitude seemed to me illogical. Yet other parents seemed to value warmth and personal concern, qualities they could assess, at least as highly as technical efficiency in the doctors they entrusted with their child's life.

The mothers tended to stress trust as a personal relationship, with an involved doctor who knows their child well. Even mothers who seemed to cope by remaining reserved valued personal trust if it could develop. Emma spent almost all her two and a half years in hospital. Her mother implied rather than stated her own distress. 'One day when she was particularly ill we went home and played scrabble. I shall never play scrabble again probably.' 'I wish the ward staff would treat the parents as *knowing* something about the child. Er, sometimes they are very distrustful of what you say. Some will take quite a lot of notice, but it would be nice if more did. On the

whole most parents know their children better than anybody else.'
Emma's parents found their local paediatrician 'very sensitive to the
question of whether, the possibility . . . might reach a stage where
you wouldn't fight any more—because the misery wouldn't be
worth the . . . We had some doubts.' However, Emma's mother
relied on a particularly close relationship with one doctor. 'Penny
happens to be about my own age and a similar background. One of
our pet dreads is that she'll leave. She's certainly the one I could talk
to of all the doctors we've had, mainly because I know her best and
she knows Emma *better* than any other doctor ever has done.'

Two parents were worried when their mentally handicapped
daughter's operation was postponed several times. Her mother
wanted to show trust and said to me:

Every time they cancelled we'd put on this smile and say, 'Oh, that's okay.'
But there was that lack of respect, no thought for your feelings. I think that's
made us a bit bitter. We do this underneath thinking, what we really think
about letting loose and getting aggressive, and on top we tend to be polite.
We're not the sort of people who want to create a fuss.

Eventually Diane had her operation. Her discharge was delayed
because she refused to eat.

Father: She is very unhappy. I'm convinced if she did go home she'd start
feeding. We've known her for six years and we really do understand how
to look after her. But the ward round all stand and talk, then tell you what
they've decided.
   I think the doctors ought to go on a course for bedside manner.
Someone comes running around, has a quick listen to her heart, a quick
look over. Like it's, 'Those are lovely conditions for us to work with.' He's
not bothered, because she doesn't communicate. It's a case of she's a lump
of meat lying there so you roll her about a bit, you drag her off down a
room and forcibly take some blood off her. You're not able to relate to it
so you just sort of ignore it and carry on. If parents dare to create a stink
then they get the same treatment.
Mother: We, um, it was very wrong of us but we started getting a bit
paranoid.

This example suggests that families' trust is nurtured by medical
concern, and willingness to listen, and is undermined if these
responses are missing. Ruth Jacobs[4] shows how denial of child
patients' emotions contributes to their distress. The staff in an
orthopaedic ward worked to technically high standards, but they

avoided close relations with the family, and treated the child as a 'work object'. The units I observed were far more open and welcoming than Jacobs's hospital. Yet mistrust was still a problem, when parents felt they were not equal partners with the staff, and that they could not honestly express their views.

Personal rapport has practical implications. It is easier for families to start conversations, and to ask questions, if the doctor seems responsive. When asked which doctor she preferred to ask for information, a mother replied, 'Sandra, because she's approachable. She'll smile at you in the corridor, but the others just look through you.' Their relationship with the individual doctor strongly affects the families' sense of trust.

Impersonal trust

In contrast to the families' view of personal trust, professional views of trust tend to be impersonal in several ways. When families and staff bring different values and expectations about trust into the consent process, misunderstanding and disappointment may result.

Doctors expect families to trust in the tertiary medical framework, as an institution that is 'as safe as the Bank of England'. They work in teams so that patients benefit from a range of expertise, with continuing support through the local primary health team, local paediatric team, and the specialist referral team. Families are encouraged to trust all the colleagues, and to contact the appropriate level of care, not to rely on one doctor. I asked one of the six consultant cardiologists in the Children's Hospital if families were confused by the shared care. He replied, 'Oh no, because we all know each other so well.' His confidence in the team approach overlooked families' different expectations.

Mistrust of personal involvement pervades academic Western thought, in medicine and ethics and all the natural and human sciences. Sociologists, for instance, criticize doctors' intrusion into patients' private lives as medicalization of daily life, as medical dominance, surveillance, oppression, and interference. Graphic examples illustrate the dangers of such intrusion.[5] Yet the opposite extreme, impersonal medicine, presents at least four problems. Crucial social and psychological factors in disease are ignored and illness is defined simply as physiological problems treated with drugs or surgery. The doctor is then the active expert and the patient the passive dependant. The expressed need of many patients to include personal issues is denied. This denial leaves unresolved problems and anxieties. When 'treacherous, destructive' emotions are opposed to trustworthy reason, trust in human nature (which combines thinking and feeling) and therefore trust in oneself as well as other people, is undermined.

One surgeon questions the common mistrust of emotional involvement. He thinks that cool detachment is a defence against failure and pain, but

it just buries the hurt on a deeper level. I used to think a certain amount of this distancing was essential, but for most doctors I think it goes too far. Too often the pressure squeezes out our native compassion. The so-called detached concern we're taught is an absurdity. Instead we need to be taught a rational concern, which allows the expression of feelings without impairing the ability to make decisions.[6]

Peter Maguire, a psychiatrist, has shown how hospital staff unconsciously but 'consistently use distancing tactics with their [dying] patients to try to ensure their own emotional survival'.[7] He concludes that if staff are 'to risk getting close' to patients, they could be harmed by the experience unless they are supported in developing new means, personal and team-work, of coping with the strain. Themes of risk and trust run through his paper in the problems of overcoming fear of oneself, of patients, and of colleagues, in order to be able to talk openly about distress. As a nurse in one of the units said, 'I am personally very frightened of dying and find it hard to cope with the older child dying because of my fears.'

Professionals have doubts in two areas: in their personal and professional ability to respond to the patients' distress; and in contemporary medicine, questioning how much harm it causes, and how much good it achieves? In these two areas, misgivings perhaps most commonly and urgently arise in specialties such as intensive care of children, where mortality and morbidity rates are high, treatment can be distressing, and long-term benefits are uncertain.

Doctors persuade as well as inform, conveying optimism to patients and colleagues, and overcoming doubt. Writing about medical innovations, Arthur Kohrman, a neonatologist explains the dilemma.

We have been on a technophile course in medicine; both the promise and the limitations of technology for the solutions of the eternal human problems are just now coming into focus [raising new problems. Intensive care medicine] is the most visible testimonial to the limits of and the problems created by technology [and doctors] are necessarily the most committed believers in its possibilities. They . . . can serve as lightning rods for the frustration and anger of a society in the process of adjustment to disillusionment.[8]

There were undercurrents of doubt in the units. Nurses and social workers spoke of the stress in cases of prolonged uncertainty about whether a child would die or be permanently brain-damaged. The staff disagreed on how long attempts to keep children alive on ventilators should continue. In out-patient clinics, after families had left, some consultants would tell me the risks and adverse side-effects of treatment, and of their frustration at not being able to alleviate problems. After a series of such patients, one consultant said to me, 'Sorry, a disastrous morning.'

Impersonal trust in the value of medicine is an essential part of medical work. Medical students have to take on trust the vast body of taught and textbook medicine, most of which they cannot test personally. The neat certainties of scientific theory and data offer a form of refuge from doubt, and are often dressed in euphemisms. Just one instance is the term 'risk/benefit' which stresses certain benefit against uncertain harm. Inverted, a similarly loaded phrase would be harm/hope.

Tension between personal and impersonal trust

Doctors sustain impersonal trust in the enterprise of cure partly by avoiding too close an involvement in personal care. 'Care' originally meant anxiety and sorrow (as in careworn); part of the meaning of 'to care for someone' is to identify closely with him or her. To trust in their patients' responses, to identify with them and share their sorrow, makes doctors in high-risk medicine deeply conscious of its limitations and harms. Junior doctors in the units who had doubts about intensive medicine planned to work in general practice or community medicine which they saw as more concerned with personal care. Those who remain confident about high-risk medicine are caught in a contradiction between personal and institutional trust. A way of escaping the contradiction is to refute parents' criticisms, and to mistrust their 'over-anxiety' as the inevitable but transient price of future health.

Parents also felt a conflict between impersonal and personal trust. Charles's father spoke of consultants who, he felt, walked 'like bishops in the cathedral atmosphere' of the hospital. He said he needed to sense this dignity and authority, which inspired his trust and respect. His need links with doctors' impersonal faith in the institutions and enterprise of medicine. Yet although Charles's father found comfort in medical authority during the anxious months when his son was very ill, he was also disturbed by some of its effects.

Privacy is very important to me. It's these sort of very serious discussions about the baby which in my view should never be in a room where someone else, not directly involved, can overhear because—your, if your eyes are on stalks, and you're thinking about who is listening . . . If we were in the public ward, it clammed me up. It made me absolutely schtum and angry. . . . That something so serious . . . er [that the doctor] had not gone to the trouble of thinking what my feelings would be and that it might therefore be desirable to have the conversation in privacy. Because if he was not prepared to do that, er, what did this imply about the rest of his decision-making capability? . . . If he was going to treat the parents like this maybe he would treat the baby—a bit . . . The whole thing is so dreadfully stressful.

This example raises the questions: Why could not a successful, upper-class man ask for the privacy he wanted, and feel able to talk on equal terms with doctors?

Families seem to need two forms of trust which are partly incompatible. Patients with a very serious condition depend on having faith in superior medical knowledge; this sets clinicians apart on a different plane. Many families spoke of their great faith in impersonal surgeons as if their very remoteness inspired confidence. Yet remoteness jeopardizes personal aspects of trust, such as being able to talk honestly or critically. The first, unequal kind of trust works when clinicians are aware of families' wishes, but it inhibits families in explaining their wishes. If these are ignored, trust is shaken and tested. The distancing, which many families partly want, then restricts their attempts to resolve problems. The second, equal kind of trust encourages families to talk more fully with doctors; it offers the security of shared understanding rather than of awe. Yet this security could also discourage honesty when parents fear to disrupt a close relationship by being critical.

Some fathers I interviewed tended to stress impersonal forms of trust, speaking in a businesslike way. 'In my daughter's case there's no problem. She would have died if she hadn't had surgery, so whatever the risk it was worth having a crack.' They discuss their child's case as they would talk of a problem at work, as if doctors are senior members of the hierarchy, and as if the object is to agree on a trustworthy contract. Medical seniority increases the expertise available for the contract and its reliability, and sets the limits on how much responsibility the client need take. Detachment indicates professional integrity. The hierarchy offers reassurance but can also prevent disagreements from being sorted out if they arise. While they need to trust in superior medical knowledge, many mothers also want to step outside hierarchies and to talk intimately about their child's daily problems, rather as they would discuss a family matter with relatives. Part of the difficulty for Charles's father may be that he was unused to being a junior, non-expert, and critical member of a hierarchy, struck by the tensions between personal and impersonal forms of trust.

Trusting patients and parents

Patients are expected to trust doctors, yet trust may only be possible when it is reciprocal. Some doctors' trust in parents is limited. One consultant said:

I don't expect much of parents. Some are good witnesses and some are vague and not terribly helpful. When you don't know the family and you're making all sorts of observations and decisions about surgery . . . In episodic events I may rely on them, but I tell them what is likely to happen, that the child may become blue, so if it does happen they are reassured that I knew it was likely. There has to be trust between the parents and physician, to reassure parents that you know what to predict. It's a way of handling it and involving parents. I don't rely on their opinion. I prefer to go on objective clinical data. I assess the likely progress and plan accordingly. Parents want to know how we can manage it.

Trust is here conceived as one-way, not as mutual. Parents trust doctors' objective expertise, yet doctors mistrust, do not rely on, parents' opinions. It is difficult for parents to notice very gradual changes, such as in their child's colour, and for doctors to assess the very varied reports from parents. However, some children at home depend on their parents realizing, in time, when they need emergency life-saving hospital treatment. Parents therefore need to be clearly informed about signs to watch for, and when they know these, they can give clearer reports, and so help to increase doctors' knowledge of the child's state of health.

Some consultants felt it would be wrong to trust patients with certain information. After one fifteen-year-old left the clinic, the doctor said,

I can't see any future in people knowing they may suddenly die. That's a little bit of medical paternalism. I don't know how explicit to be about the risk of sudden death but I think talking of a dilating aortic aneurysm gives them a flavour.

Trust involves respecting the other person's viewpoint and, during the stress of treatment, if this respect is missing, trust between child and parents can be undermined. Terry aged three was crying at his post-operation clinic check.

Mother: He's frightened just a little bit but he's doing fairly well.
Father: He's a mummy's boy and we can't get him away from her. . . . He cries a lot. Do we walk away and leave him crying a lot at playgroup?
Consultant: Oh, what you'd do with any other child. My own son got up to the same tricks.
Mother: It's trusting people that's the problem. Oh, have you got our new address?

This example included four reasons for Terry's crying, and why his parents might have responded to it as a serious sign of distress, not as 'tricks'. Terry was unsettled by his recent operation, by moving house, starting at a new playgroup, and his mother had just had another baby. When patients cannot express their own need verbally, the responsible adults have to trust in the patient's warning signs and in their own responding empathy.

Trust is built on compromises between intrusion and detachment, as shown in the following relaxed discussion. The mother and doctor gave me an impression that they shared amusement about the policing role of medical surveillance. Simon, whose condition had been thought too severe to treat, eventually survived two operations, and attended an out-patient clinic, grotesquely thin but cheerfully smiling.

Mother: With weight gain—er—or not weight gain. Any idea how much I should expect him to put on, or when I should worry, or not worry?
Doctor: I think we're more concerned with whether he looks well. If he's smiling and responsive and not pale and sweaty.
M: Right.

D: The weight gain *per se*, I wouldn't use that as the only indicator of well-being. Er, is that . . . ?

M: Yes, that's a lot better. [*Laughs*] Er . . .

D: Well, obviously we'd like him to—well people use weight as an index of health . . .

M: Mmm.

D: And as an index that the parents are looking after the child properly and all that.

M: Yes.

D: We have no doubt about all that. [*Both laugh*]

M: I keep waiting for someone to phone up and say, 'That mother's starving her child.'

D: [*Laughing*] That's right. . . . He might put on weight in the second year.

M: Oh well, at least we might get there. That's the hopeful thing.

The explicit talk implicitly acknowledges the mother's anxiety that she may seem negligent and that her son may soon die. As well as being technical, the doctor's words are confirming and moderately optimistic. The transcript cannot convey the sense of shared understanding through the whole encounter. Sentences did not need to be finished in order to be understood, and many were begun by one speaker and finished by the other. Part of the need which many parents seemed to bring to the cardiac units was for reassurance about their felt inadequacies, both in having a child with a heart defect and in the care they gave their child. They found acknowledgement, rather than avoidance, of these issues helpful.

The opposite view to fear of interference is expressed by Martin Buber.

In human society at all its levels, persons confirm one another in a practical way in their personal qualities and capacities and a society may be called human in the measure to which its members confirm one another.

The two-fold basis of our life is: the wish to be confirmed as what we are, even as what we can become, by others, and, our innate capacity to confirm one another in this way.

That this capacity lies so immeasurably fallow constitutes the real weakness and questionableness of the human race; actual humanity exists only where this capacity unfolds.[9]

The capacity depends on taking the risk of mutual trust. A nurse teacher told me how when a child dies,

I feel sort of shaking and not really knowing what to do or where to turn and wanting to run away. Sometimes the parents have supported me almost.

[After one child died, his mother] just came and put her arms round me and said, 'Oh, Bridget, I'm glad it was you that was here.' . . . In a sense . . . my shell had gone . . . Whereas if they thought we didn't care it would be easier but it would be wrong. I'd rather us show our feelings . . . I try not to wear a shell but I always want it to be around . . . Well, it's—what do soldiers wear? A sort of shield. It's very seldom I need to resort to it.

Other nurses wrote of helping newly bereaved parents through 'allowing them quietness and to open their hearts if they so wish'. 'We learn each day to show more sympathy. Some nurses are naturally gifted, some need to learn and are unsure how to help. This can be uncomfortable, and support and counselling is needed for the nurses.'[10] 'Rational concern'[11] is developed by nurses who trust themselves and their patients to respond to distress positively, instead of purely in criticism or despair.

Reciprocal trust develops when the relationship between efficient professionals and helpless patients changes into shared responsibility. Nurses in Nottingham wards arrange for some young patients over eleven years to administer their own drugs.[12] These trusting practices help to develop mutual respect and confidence.

Trusting in valid judgements

Recent medical advances have reduced medical reliance on patients' trust in some ways, but stretched it in others. Arthur Kohrman, a neonatologist, believes that in earlier times 'both medicine and its clients have collaborated in the mystification process'.[13] The physician's dignified bedside manner encouraged patients to trust without enquiring too closely into the (often ineffective) treatment. Today, as scientific practitioners become more informed and informative the public is becoming aware of 'how uncertain, capricious and idiosyncratic medical practice can be'. Informed consent may be seen as an effort to dispel mystification, and to open up medicine to lay understanding. Yet at the same time, new medical ambitions and complex knowledge create new obscurities.

Advances have occurred because physicians are willing 'to imagine effective lives for children previously thought doomed'.[14] Kohrman thinks that physicians are conditioned into optimism by 'believed prognosis' based on data or on guesses. To 'avoid prematurely foreclosing on hope', doctors may encourage 'unwarranted optimism' which 'seems an even worse, crueller error'. These rapid changes mean 'that there are many gaps in our understanding of societal impact, deficiencies in our ethical constructs, and excesses and imperfections in our practices'. The imperfections challenge people's trust in the medical enterprise and in their own ability to make valid judgements. The strain increases for parents who are allowed to become more informed but not more involved in decisions about their child's care, as Jane Williams's case shows.

Jane had spent all her four months in hospital. Surgery successfully corrected her heart defect, but partly paralysed her diaphragm. She had difficulty in breathing and gaining weight and had a series of infections. At first Mrs Williams told me that she was 'not really sure' whether Jane had caught infection from other patients. 'When I ask the doctors they all say that all the patients with it have different strains.' Later she said, 'They've got to say that to protect themselves. I don't believe it.' She tried to ask that Jane was not nursed by nurses caring for the infected babies.

It wasn't easy because I feel I've got a fairly good relationship with most of the staff. I felt very awkward. And blow me, she catches it again. Barrier nursing—they don't do it properly here. They just play at it. They play with one baby then another. Very often they don't wash in between. Well, I can't say anything. They're being nice. It's like a slap in the face to say anything, like telling them how to do their job. . . . I couldn't report the nurses because I get on so well with them. It's a bit like sneaking.

As she talked, Mrs Williams became more certain about her own judgements. From saying at first that she was a 'bit cross' later she talked about 'doing battle' but gave a sense of the 'battle' being mainly inside herself, in her conflict between wanting to trust and have friendly relations with the staff and needing to trust her own perceptions and to protect her child.

Mrs Williams explained that babies with infections 'usually have an intravenous line' rather than having three to six injections each day. 'They have to put a new line in about every day.' Jane had had so many lines that it was difficult to insert new ones. Her parents received conflicting information. Doctors disagreed about where the lines should be inserted.

They took it out and put it somewhere else because they thought it shouldn't be there. I asked the nurse if they'd tried to put a drip in Jane's head and she said, 'Oh no, they wouldn't put a drip in there.' But later a doctor told me they had tried.

Then they decided to put one into her neck so they took her away to the treatment room. I'd probably have gone if I'd been asked because she calms down much quicker if I pick her up. They got an anaesthetist to do it because apparently it's quite difficult. At last he came out and told Dr B [SHO] that Jane was too distressed, he couldn't get a line in. We heard that because we were sitting by Jane's cot. Dr B stayed at least half an hour in the treatment room with Jane and a nurse. Then they brought her back in here and put her straight into oxygen, a head box. Jane looked ghastly, grey, breathing very fast. I couldn't pick her up for a while. I felt they'd spent half an hour trying to calm her.

We were furious. David told the nurse he wanted to make a formal complaint. Dr B came in and was quite rude and off-hand, and a few words were exchanged on both sides. I was trying to calm Jane down. Anyway David and Dr B ended up amicably, both sides apologising to each other.

We made our point. They knew when Jane has an infection she can't take much stress, she gets upset very quickly. We felt she should have been sedated for something as dramatic as that. It's quite unpleasant. They turn them upside down so blood rushes to the neck. She would find that particularly uncomfortable because of her breathing difficulties.

Late that evening I found they'd tried to put in a line again. On Sunday she was really ill. The nurses told me they hadn't sedated her. I felt the nurses were on our side, even the sister. . . . Because Jane was so upset, they wanted to put her back on the ventilator, and I was very, very angry, because I felt *they*'d made her like that. She was perfectly happy until they tried to put lines in. So they put her life at risk simply to give her antibiotics, on more than one occasion. She has them by injection now and doesn't even wake up, because they couldn't get a line in. I think the consultant told them to try that.

Staff rotas caring for many patients in disconnected stages restrict professional awareness of each child's particular needs. Parents, through continuing care, connect the stages and the cumulative effects on their child. Mrs Williams said that later a doctor spoke 'glibly' about putting Jane on and off the ventilator.

I don't think it's a joking matter. I think the ventilator is the most upsetting, depressing thing. It still upsets me to think about it. When they used to try and take her off the ventilator and they had to put her back on and give her the paralysing drug, that would upset me more than anything.

As Arthur Kohrman commented,[15] recent medical advances (both life-saving intensive medicine and far more open information for families) show up practical and ethical deficiencies. Doctors and families are expected to cope with new technology without the time, resources, and support they need. Great demands are made on mutual trust.

Gratitude for life-saving surgery gradually changed to criticism through a series of seemingly puzzling jolts which awoke a 'battle' of mixed feelings. These could only be resolved if Mrs Williams questioned her trust in the staff and began to believe her own observations and the criticisms the staff made of one another. Through several interviews, Jane's mother described how anxiety and then anger warned her of problems, and gave her the confidence or impetus to think them through. An example was the discrepancy she saw between the ideal and the actual practice of barrier nursing. Although she resolved her inner conflict by coming to believe her own opinions, she had difficulty in resolving her differences with the staff. When the doctors were angry at being criticized, Jane's parents tried to repair the relationship. Mr Williams, a lawyer and far older than the doctor, apologized to her and hid his anger, fearing that 'relations can easily break down completely', and not believing that more equal relations could be established.

Mrs Williams seems to be caught in a double bind, which can be said to have three aspects: a strong complementary relationship between dominant and subordinate people; an injunction that must be disobeyed to be obeyed; inability of the subordinate person to step outside the frame and thus dissolve the paradox by commenting on it because that would be insubordinate.[16] The injunction is that responsible parents should respect and trust the staff, and therefore not question care which they see as inadequate. Mrs Williams saw the only solution as:

to push to get her out. I'm going to keep asking and not let up and if she's well enough I might tell them. We definitely lost confidence [but we] made a conscious decision to hold back a bit, as the way things are going, relations can easily break down completely. Because she's always going to be a patient at this hospital. We felt it was in her interests for us to maintain friendly relationships.

Discussions between professionals and parents contain covert communication about relations between them, and how they share authority over the child. The staff may assume that they have authority and competence which parents doubt but feel unable to question.

'Every language has a structure concerning which, in the language, nothing can be said', except in a separate 'metalanguage'.[17] For example, maths has a language of symbols which can only be discussed in the metalanguage of words. Yet with personal communication we do not have a metalanguage; we cannot step outside the words, thoughts, and feelings we use when communicating. Patients and professionals cannot explicitly talk together about problems of trust without threatening the trusting relations between them.

Mrs Williams spoke of her tension while Jane was on a ventilator.

I used to talk to her when she was awake, and play with her. But most of the time I used to count the heartbeats and how fast she was breathing, and watch the machines. . . . I was always on edge, but I was happier sitting there than being away. I worried more and got more upset if I wasn't there. I think I'm just over-anxious. I worry about every little thing—if Jane vomits, if she goes pale for five seconds. I think the nurses . . . they've got six babies in here and they're used to it. They're never nasty to me but I think they feel I'm overreacting sometimes. It surprised me how quickly her temperature dropped on the gauge when her cover was taken off. I wouldn't have thought twice about that if I'd taken her straight home.

Although she learned partly through watching and listening, it was difficult for Jane's mother to question the professionals' judgement when her criticism was mainly based on knowledge they gave her. Their extensive knowledge was balanced by her particular knowledge of her child. Detached hospital care for many babies partly contradicts the values of involved maternal care for a particular baby. Parents were anxious not to seem to claim more than their child's 'fair' share by some kind of utilitarian measure of the fair. Yet this measure had an impersonal basis: the amount of care one nurse could give to six babies (in the non-intensive care ward). The nurses thought that the nurse: baby ratio was inadequate. It bore no comparison to the almost full-time care a mother gives to one well baby at home. Yet in its light, maternal concern for a sick baby can be classified as 'over-anxiety'.

Patient care was fragmented because of constantly changing medical and nursing staff rotas; senior doctors usually made decisions and junior doctors carried them out. One consultant who took a particular interest in family-centred care also spent time supporting junior doctors. Through listening to them sympathetically, such as when they had many difficulties in setting up a drip, the consultant was more aware of what was happening to patients.

Without this close contact, consultants' decisions were sometimes based on partial information. Close working relations of trust between different grades of doctors enabled closer continuity of patient care. It could be easier for junior doctors to 'admit defeat' and ask a more senior doctor to help. Praising one senior house officer, a sister said that one of her excellent qualities was that 'she knows when to give up trying to put in a line. She knows when the child has had enough', in contrast to some others.

Mrs Williams explained that Jane was using up so many calories with rapid breathing that this prevented her from growing, yet growth would help to improve her breathing. Some doctors thought that putting Jane back on the ventilator or putting extra calories in her feeds would help her to grow. A few nurses said that other heart units did not have these policies. While parents were grateful for detailed information which in many ways increased their trust in the paediatric team, conflicting information could also complicate trusting relationships. Parents had difficulty in sorting out what to believe.

Now I've sort of thought and calmed down. I think they're being unreasonable. Because although she is under-weight, a lot of older heart babies weigh the same or less than Jane. . . . But they make me anxious because of the ventilator if she doesn't grow. . . . I don't think this hospital listens to parents enough. They ask what I think, because Jane's been here a long time, but I feel they're not interested in hearing the answer. . . .

They don't like it at all if you do question a decision or disagree with something they want to do. I felt, if they wanted to put her on the ventilator, as part of a plan to make Jane better, I wouldn't mind so much, but they seem to be grasping at straws. I think the junior doctors' judgement is very poor. . . . They feel they must *do* something. They haven't got the confidence to look at a baby and say, 'She looks all right we won't do anything,' which senior doctors often do.

If a baby's only in for two weeks, parents don't realize a lot of what is going on. But you get to know why they do certain things when you've been here longer. For example, when Jane was breathing at about ninety they used to sedate her a lot to make her resps[18] come down. When they were trying to put the line in, we asked why she hadn't been sedated. Dr B said she couldn't be sedated because of her breathing problems. You get conflicting advice. That kind of thing happens a lot.

If Jane ever needed another operation I'd ask a lot more questions and be a lot more wary. I've found they often only tell you if you ask questions, and you don't know what questions to ask—not being a medical person. I think the senior registrar is very, very good. He actually sits down and draws pictures, and tries to make you understand, and he's very patient and explains things thoroughly, more than once if you want, and he listens to me.

Families and clinicians want the same end, the patient's healthy recovery. Yet families tend to see each means as partly an end in itself. Barrier nursing, drips, injections, all have important effects on the patient. Means partly determine ends. Intent upon the end, doctors may underestimate the pain of the means, if medical and nursing care is fragmented. They may forget that they are using the body as a means of obtaining certain results, instead of always treating the patient with as much care and respect as possible.

Parents' growing reservations about the harm of treatment lead them to realize that consent includes seriously considering disadvantages of, and alternatives to, treatment. Although she will be 'more wary', Mrs Williams still sees the only course as 'to ask more questions' rather than to state her views. Inequality, not only of knowledge but also of status, jeopardizes respect and veracity in doctor–patient relationships. Junior doctors may feel threatened and defensive, consultants have to defend their juniors.

Mrs Williams believes that attempts to improve care for patients risks damaging the goodwill on which that care partly depends. How can she achieve more considerate care for her child by inconsiderately criticizing the nurses? Obligations to the child are bound up with obligations between the caring adults, and are influenced by how much the adults are able to trust in their own and one another's judgements.

Trust as active belief

Trust involves putting a precious possession into someone else's power, and so risking harm, loss, or betrayal. Two things of greatest value to parents are their child's welfare and their self-identity as their child's primary care-takers. Yet children's surgery is inevitably dangerous and has to exclude parents from certain stages of care. One mother began a letter to me about consenting to her child's operation with:

It is extra difficult to write about an emotional upheaval of such immense proportions. It is also somewhat disturbing to mention them as they tend to be pushed to the back of one's mind. To many parents this must be one of the most traumatic occasions of their lives.

A patient going for surgery is like someone who has decided to jump off a burning building, having checked as far as possible that the building is burning (diagnosis), that there is no other way out (alternatives), and that there is a safety net (treatment and prognosis). Eventually the only way to test the truth is to take the risk, entrusting oneself helplessly to the skill of those holding the net. Trust impels patients to choose surgery as the lesser danger. It works as a kind of hinge moving them from questioning independence into voluntary dependence and suspension of disbelief.

Questioning can seem to be mistrustful, yet reasonable discussion between doctors and parents develops only when each trusts the other to be talking and listening with honesty and respect. Relationships are then tested and developed, paradoxically through seemingly mistrusting, critical challenges, such as asking for a second opinion which can lead to fuller acceptance of the first opinion if it is confirmed.

Proxy consent is complicated by questions about who is the best judge of the child's interests, especially if these may conflict with the family's interests. Doctors' belief that they ought to act as the child's advocate can restrict them from confiding in parents. For example, the parents of a baby of ten months did not want her to have palliative surgery. This would keep her alive only for a few years, and might lead to 'the nightmare' of a series of operations which could not cure her. Shamira's father wanted to protect her and the family from this distress. The consultant wanted to keep open the option of surgery, reminding the parents that Shamira's interests must come first, and warning them of future distress. They might later want to choose life-prolonging surgery but find that progressive lung disease made this impossible. So the consultant put forward arguments for surgery, but said to me when the parents had gone: 'It is very difficult for all of us. The parents are set against surgery because they know there is no cure. I think they've been brave enough to do what I would hope to do but I'm not allowed to say.' This implied that in order to keep faith with the child, the doctor felt an obligation to counter the parents' arguments and to keep open the option of surgery by not entrusting the parents with a personal viewpoint.

In discussions about surgery, two forms of doctor–patient relationships intersect. Patients who question the doctor as teacher asking, for example, about the cause and nature of the disease, express trust in his or her expertise. When patients question the

doctor as provider of treatment, and ask about the effects of interventions, it can be difficult for them to avoid implying suspicion
about medical skill. They risk alienating doctors when they are
dependent on their goodwill. They increase their insecurity, not only
because they fear *appearing* to the doctor to be mistrustful, but also
because they fear *being* mistrustful when they need to nurture their
trust on which they will have to depend. As risks increase, fear may
inhibit questioning because the higher the risk of death from surgery,
the more likely are patients to die without treatment. Opinions differ
on the appropriate balance of information and trust, and the time to
switch from questioning autonomy to vulnerable faith. Some parents
said they questioned more carefully on behalf of their child than they
would on their own behalf. A proxy fits uneasily between patient and
staff, intensely sharing both the patient's fear and risk, and also the
staff's responsibility.

Whereas some staff seemed to interpret consent as completely
entrusting the child into their care, many parents wanted to share
responsibility and to renegotiate traditional boundaries, such as in
asking for more access to the pre- and post-operation areas. One
mother told of her relief that she was able to keep her promise to her
four-year-old daughter, who later died, 'that I would stay with her
until she had had the anaesthetic. . . . If my child had died during the
operation as far as she knew I would have been with her.'

When parents spend weeks or months moving between doubt and
hope they are concerned with fidelity: how to fulfil their obligations,
towards their child and also to the staff. Adverse, conflicting feelings
have to be worked through in order to arrive at a state of trust, while
sense is made of contradictory advice and fragmented care, as shown
in Jane's case.

Signing the consent form is not necessarily a sign of complete
transition from doubt to assurance. Mixed feelings may continue for
long afterwards. Although parents may believe in the doctors' good
faith that they have given the best possible advice, this is not the same
as being certain that the treatment will benefit the child. One mother
thought that the doctors 'who were extremely kind' wanted to
prevent her from worrying. 'But I never believed them. I would have
preferred to have known what really happened, but then I don't
know if they knew themselves.' Anxiety, an inevitable part of
awareness of the child's problems, can increase if doctors avoid
discussion or offer reassurance which parents do not believe. A

tension is set up between needing to trust doctors and disbelieving what they say, between feeling anxious and appearing to be reassured.

Anxiety rises before and during operations. Some parents sat up with their child through the night before surgery, expecting that this might be the child's last night. When the child is in theatre, 'Your mind is just not anywhere, and you're clock-watching the whole time, thinking, "What are they doing now?"'

When Janet survived her operation, her mother said, 'It was the most wonderful, marvellous news. It was absolutely incredible. It's like a dream still. I keep saying I can't believe it's reality. I just never thought she'd come out of it.' Learning to believe in cure was a process of gradual adjustment, the rearrangement of beliefs, similar to the previous process of coming to accept the need for surgery.

Trust is a series of transient states which eventually resolve into certainty about harm or benefit. Perhaps the fullest analysis of trust or faith has been made by religious writers who believed that, after resurrection, relative faith would resolve into absolute certainty; modern surgery offers a close analogy. As Karl Popper believed,[19] evidence can never offer complete proof; ultimately there has to be the leap of faith to bridge the gap between evidence and belief—until the time when the theory may be disproved. Trust is a mixed, ambiguous tension between doubt and the hope of certainty. Several parents said, 'I won't relax till we're all safely home.'

Modern concepts of truth as scientific evidence can obscure how subtle and complex truth is, and how we depend, in obtaining any information, on trusting our own confusing perceptions and other people's. Truth and trust share a root meaning of belief, and this older meaning helpfully challenges narrow ideals of truth as independent, objective fact. Truth as belief reconnects the observer and observed, thinking and feeling, proof and faith, by acknowledging that we know through struggling to understand our perceptions. Jane's case illustrates how parents work to evolve and sustain beliefs about what is actually happening, when much of the evidence is invisible or contradictory.

Words on trust and truth, written before truth came to be identified only with objective fact, convey the struggle towards trust including, as Janet's parents found, belief in miracles.

> On a huge hill,
> Cragged, and steep, Truth stands, and he that will
> Reach her, about must, and about must go;
>   .   .   .   .
> Hard deeds, the body's pains; hard knowledge too
> The mind's endeavours reach, and mysteries
> Are like the Sun, dazzling, yet plain to all eyes.
> Keep the truth which thou hast found.[20]

Since trust is invisible, it may partly be understood by using Freud's method of showing feeling through allegory. In a biblical story[21] Balaam, a prophet on important business, is riding his donkey along a narrow way. The donkey stops and refuses to go on although Balaam beats and threatens to kill her. At last Balaam realizes that she has seen an angel standing in their path, pointing a sword which would kill him if they moved forward.

Richard MacKenna[22] suggests that Balaam represents authority, all the rules and theories we are expected to follow. We are the donkey, burdened down with all that we 'ought' to do and believe, but occasionally aware of truths which contradict Balaam's instructions. Linking trust and ought implies that we ought to trust Balaam in the form of medical authority. Yet this can mean denying new awareness in which we cannot help trusting and which inevitably causes us to doubt authority.

Trust can be more than a passive response to medical activity. Trust in her awareness of the angel impels the donkey to act by making her own rules. If defined as an obligation, trust can turn into a form of coercion, a reason for not informing patients, and a source for doubting families of guilt and inner conflict, as Jane's mother felt. Trust then moves from being a source of awareness (of the angel) to being used as a means of suppressing awareness (as Balaam tries to do when insisting that the donkey obey his authority). To see trust as a duty denies its dynamic and involuntary nature. Trust is a powerful, warning instinct, so deeply part of human nature that it cannot be static and institutionalized.

The notion of medical fidelity can be used as a further restriction on patients' critical judgement. Fidelity means keeping promises, but the trusting patient is expected not to exact promises and instead to leave the doctor freedom of choice. This can shift the meaning of medical fidelity into keeping faith with impersonal medical ideals which may differ from, or even be hostile to, patients' personal preferences.

Trust in the consent process

Arguments for and against patient consent are based on many assumptions about trust. To understand consent it is necessary to question assumptions and to see the paradoxes in trust. Doctors tend to trust in theoretical and technical knowledge, in utilitarian values, and in professional detachment. To many families and nurses, trust is a personal experience, partly immediate, partly developing through struggle and difficulty. The tension between these two approaches can complicate consent.

Trust is not a duty to be assessed as strong or weak, or to be measured inversely by high or low anxiety. Patients' high anxiety about their condition may increase their trusting dependence on their physician. Trust and anxiety can work together; both can aid growing understanding, and adjustment to illness and recovery. The appropriate measure of trust is whether it is true or false, valid or invalid. Valid trust relates to what each person believes is worth trusting in. If a patient refuses proposed surgery, the surgeon might interpret this as mistrust in his or her technical excellence or goodwill. The patient may greatly respect the surgeon's skill and goodwill, but still decide that the proposed operation does not fit her own case. Subjectively and often subconsciously, trust assesses evidence, experience, motives, and values. If the evidence is intangible or disputed, people have to work to develop and hold on to their personal beliefs, as Jane's and Janet's parents did. Firm beliefs are held by people who trust in their own judgement, tested through personal experience.

Kantian ethics has advanced conscious theories of respect for patients. Yet paradoxically its emphasis on reason, logic, and demonstrable evidence undermines subconscious, practical respect for ordinary thinking, feeling individuals, and their partly intuitive emotions such as trust. Recognizing the part of trust in informed consent shows how reason and emotion work together through the consent process in ways that cannot all be reduced into words. Lessening the gap between the ideal and the practice of patient consent depends on accepting rational feelings as valid sources of knowledge, and valid parts of our human identity. This includes valuing 'negative' feelings such as anxiety. When doctors, nurses, and families acknowledge this integrity of human nature, in themselves and in others, more equal and reciprocal trust between them becomes possible.

Rather than attempting to measure intangibles such as trust and anxiety, it is perhaps more useful to consider two things: the reasons for each patient's beliefs seen within their own framework of values; and the conditions which affect trust between patients and professionals. Trust is encouraged when patients and staff:

  can talk without deceit or concealment;
  respect each other's viewpoint;
  risk giving confidential information;
  feel free to ask 'silly' or critical or intimate questions;
  can admit ignorance;
  do not need to be defensive or hostile;
  are willing to re-examine beliefs;
  can agree to differ;

while trusting that they will not lose the respect of the other.

9

Ethical medicine and bioethics

To the beginner, trying to understand bioethics can be like wandering in a jungle. After a while, well-known and quite basic ideas can be traced in the tangled undergrowth of deontology and other exotic species, but at first it can be very confusing. This chapter is written for beginners, as well as for anyone experienced in bioethics, in the belief that moral questions in medicine should be discussed in a common language which everyone can use. (Bioethics is the ethics of science, medicine, and health care, and is a singular noun like mathematics.)

The first section is an example of an ethical dilemma. Then bioethics will be defined, and the main frameworks and principles will be considered critically. The aim is to show how theories in bioethics can be used to help patients, but can also be unhelpful, particularly towards child patients. After sections on conventional bioethics, an alternative approach to ethics is considered. Ethics is discussed here, towards the end of this book, because the theories will be reviewed from the perspective of practical experiences, including examples from earlier chapters. (The index lists page references to the children mentioned.)

Existence or health

Tom Ayres, aged three years, was brain damaged after having heart surgery. His mother considered that future surgery was against Tom's interests.[1]

Their whole thing at the hospital is to help save life. I think he's got no life whatsoever, and he should be dead. But my husband is saying, 'Do everything that you can.' But it's not going to help Tom.

The Ayres' first dilemma illustrates the centuries old debate: whether to sustain life at any price, or to decide that a life can be so empty or unbearable that death may be preferable.

We both passionately believe in what we're doing. My husband loves his children so completely. He thinks we must let Tom go on and on and on—as a cabbage. I think he's had enough as well as us. He's skin and bone. Sometimes his eyes look as if they're saying, 'Oh, for God's sake, Mum!' Who wants him to live with a brand-new corrected heart?

Mrs Ayres thought that Tom's paediatrician was very supportive, but that he too was trapped in the dilemma.

I would like to talk to someone neutral, but there is no one. Our paediatrician said, 'I'll back you in all you decide, Jenny, but you've got to decide with your husband, there's nothing I can do till then.' It's affecting our whole family life, even the grannies are split over it. I don't feel we'll ever come together, there is no sensible compromise.

Today's technology has complicated practical choices by keeping mortally ill and disabled patients alive. Through the enormous effort and cost directed towards postponing death, modern medicine has also complicated moral choices. It raises conflicting expectations that we should not only live longer but also be healthier. Morality and health are closely connected; 'look after yourself', it is our 'duty' to ensure our own and our children's health. Yet we do not know how to reconcile the values of health and of life when they conflict.

New technology affects some parents' second reservation: that some doctors are biased towards intervening because, even if treatment will not benefit the child, the knowledge gained may benefit other patients. Mrs Ayres feels 'held to ransom' by such medical pressures, as if she is restricted until the price can be paid and the key found to release her from the dilemma.

I feel we're being held to ransom at the hospital. It's not to benefit Tom, but for research. That's no good, no benefits, except to others. I don't want him to be a guinea-pig.

A third concern is that hospital staff aim to save life in routine, defensive medicine. It is easier to define the general policy 'save life', and to get everyone to agree and act on this policy; it is harder to agree on what is a 'minimally tolerable life', and what should be done if an individual patient seems to be existing below this level. 'Minimal health' is an uncertain, contentious, subjective idea. It could dangerously disrupt hospital routines, such as emergency resuscitation procedures, which are designed for efficient general care, and to prevent litigation. 'I think it is a problem for the hospital. He had a red sticker on his file, "Don't resuscitate", but they did.'

Fourthly, Mrs Ayres felt helplessly unable to control decisions, because the consent form is vaguely worded and assumes that parents agree with one another.

Can they operate without one parent's consent, and who counts most? I'd hate to think my husband can sign the consent and in the background I'll be screaming, 'Don't do it.' There's such a vagueness on the consent form about 'any other necessary doings'.

Fifthly is the strain of caring for a child who barely survives. Mothers see how all the family is affected, not only by the drain on their own energy but also by the strain of daily life with the sick child, with the continual practical impact of realizing and grieving over the child's restrictions.

Tom was on twenty-two drugs. It took me hours to get them down. He'd bring some up and I'd wonder what he'd kept down. So I have decided to stop stuffing all that garbage down him. It makes me mad when people say I'm lucky not to have to explain to Tom. He is at home *all* the time. I never get a break. Emotionally and mentally *I* find it far worse.

Through living so closely with Tom and sharing what she sees as his futile suffering, Mrs Ayres considers that his death may be the best course for Tom and the family. Doctors work to a rapid time-scale, seeing the child fairly briefly and making quick decisions. Yet for the family, time can move very slowly, shedding a quite different light on small, yet deeply significant details.

How can theories and methods in bioethics be applied helpfully in cases such as Tom's?

Defining bioethics

Ethical medicine is an ancient tradition of people trying to resolve medical dilemmas guided by their moral values. In contrast, bioethics is a new professional discipline guided by academic philosophy and law. It covers a wide range of theories and disciplines, from moral philosophy to campaigning for patients' rights. I use the term 'bioethics' here in a narrow sense of the extreme, formal end of medical ethics, dominated by law and moral philosophy, by theories of duties, utilities, or abstract rights, and by the 'Belmont principles'.[2] Bioethicists stress the principles of justice, of respect for personal autonomy, of beneficence in doing good and avoiding harm to those affected by medical treatment and research.

Four perspectives on, or contributions to, medical ethics may be defined as:

health professionals' knowledge and experience;
patients' and their carers' needs and expectations;
bioethicists' and lawyers' theories and analytical skills;
social scientists' data and observations.

I am writing from the fourth perspective about the third perspective, partly to show how patients benefit if all four approaches work more closely together.

First, the three main frameworks in bioethics will be reviewed. As each approach has been fully advocated and criticized in many volumes,[3] they will be considered only briefly here.

Frameworks in bioethics

Duties or principles are the main concern of deontology, especially the duties of respect and justice, of beneficence (doing good) and non-maleficence (not doing harm). Unlike other frameworks, deontology claims to uphold certain minimal standards of good and right behaviour.

Deontology is influenced by Immanuel Kant's view that duties should be universal. 'Act only on that maxim through which you can at the same time will that it should become a univeral law.'[4] Yet 'universal' rules tend to ignore women and children (as shown later), and the rule that you should only do to one child, such as Tom, what you would do to any child ignores his individual circumstances.

Kant also believed that it is 'precisely the fitness of [the rational person's] maxims to make universal law that marks him out as an end in himself'.[5] This means that a person can make any law, which is justified as long as it is universal. Deontologists claim to insist on basic moral standards, but they cannot do this. First, because they can make their own laws. Second, because no unqualified moral law has yet been universally agreed (even one as basic as 'do not kill'). Third, because when duties conflict, there is no rule about which one (such as respect or justice) should come first. Fourth, as will be shown, each duty has conflicting meanings.

So although deontology stresses important principles, it can confuse rather than clarify debates about patients' care.

Utilities of benefit and harm are the concern of utilitarianism, which aims to increase benefit or happiness and to reduce harm. Utilitarians try to search flexibly for the correct or best answer to each dilemma, weighing harm and benefit in each case. This avoids enforcing the rigid, sometimes harsh duties of deontology. Yet it can excuse wrong doing, if it masks or even condones harm to a few in order to benefit many, or if it permits present harm for possible future benefit. Utilitarians might conclude that Tom's family would be happier if he died, or that he should have experimental surgery that might benefit future patients. These arguments would seem immoral to some deontologists.

Disagreements in Tom's family indicate that happiness cannot be clearly agreed, defined, or predicted. Firm decisions cannot be based on the hope of elusive happiness.[6] When doctors and parents disagree, it is uncertain whose definition of benefit should predominate, especially when child patients' own choices are not known.

Rights theory acknowledges that individuals' needs may conflict, and so it fosters tolerance, equality, and liberty. Rights are usually declared by, or for, oppressed groups, unlike deontology's duties which are usually stated by dominant groups. So although rights are the obverse of duties, rights tend to be more specific, and can helpfully challenge old assumptions.

Yet inconsistent rights can equally well be justified, such as Tom's right to treatment or to freedom from over-intensive treatment, his right to life or to an end to a life that is 'demonstrably so awful'[7] (if this is the case). Contradictory rights complicate and weaken each assertion, because rights tend to be stated as simple beliefs. However clearly asserted, a right means little unless supported by those with the power to satisfy it. When rights are asserted as slogans, rather than as subtle arguments, implacable confrontation can develop between those who support and those who dismiss the right. This can harden opposition instead of helping to clarify and resolve disputes.

Claims about rights to resources can be divisive, yet if rights are to be fulfilled, they depend on a belief in common humanity. Babies' rights to life-saving intensive care, for example, tend to be discussed in competitive terms about who qualifies, with much disagreement over borderline cases. So asserting and debating rights can pose problems for achieving them.

These frameworks in bioethics offer many useful insights yet they each have limitations. The next section considers further problems in details of the frameworks, in the principles of justice, respect, and beneficence.

Bioethics principles

Justice

Justice can be defined in contradictory ways, each of which seems unjust to its critics. Justice as equality concentrates on the central features common to many cases. 'Blind' justice ignores individual circumstances, treating everyone equally, refusing to make exceptions. Exceptions would betray both the integrity of impartial justice, and the standards which justice exists to defend. For example, if euthanasia were legally permitted in one case, this would remove defences against abuse in many potential cases.

However, justice as equity sees that in many ways we are unequal, having different needs and resources. One rule for all can harshly reinforce unjust inequalities. Justice as equity therefore considers particular issues in each case, although justice as equality would see this as unfairly biased.

Even if the meaning of justice as fair distribution could be agreed, long debates in Tom's case could follow: on the nature of benefits such as medical technology, social support, time, respect; on how they may be shared between Tom and his mother, Tom and his siblings, or between Tom and other children in need; and on who has the right to make a consent to decisions about sharing resources.

The philosopher Janet Grimshaw criticizes ethicists' regard for justice as abstract equality. She thinks that we cannot ignore in moral thinking,

the context of social relationships and of human nature, and . . . of certain beliefs about desirable social goals. There is no 'real' or 'fundamental' meaning of justice . . . which some process of 'conceptual analysis', all by itself can discover.[8]

It seems unlikely that a solution to Tom's case could convince and satisfy his whole family. The dilemma reaches beyond clear reasoning to deeply held personal values and feelings. Abstract justice cannot produce universally agreed decisions, and justice which ignores conflicting personal values may enforce but cannot convince.

The Ayres family appear to have debated Tom's case exhaustively, and yet to conclude that 'there is no sensible compromise'. Some ethicists would argue that the family is too involved, and their dilemma should be referred to an impartial, detached ethics review committee.[9] This argument assumes that moral problems can be understood more clearly when the abstract bones of a dilemma are separated from the flesh of the personal context. In order to 'think clearly' moral philosophers do 'mental house cleaning', clearing away the 'rubbish' of social circumstances and subjective definitions to define terms precisely. Philosophers' 'speciality is clear thinking, not factual investigation'.[10]

However, Grimshaw asks 'What clear thinking is it that philosophers are supposed to be specially good at?' 'Discussion of "meanings" cannot be divorced from consideration of the "facts" to which they apply.'[11] This is partly because meanings are slippery and subjective. We cannot avoid using language loaded with personal meanings and values, and therefore we cannot talk in purely objective terms. There are not even neutral terms for 'child', 'patient', or 'mother'. Ethicists who think clearly would first examine the moral assumptions within words instead of imagining that these words can be neutral.

Grimshaw thinks that 'no amount of mental house cleaning' is going to provide a neutral resolution to questions of power, dependence, and painful choices between competing values. She quotes an elderly male philosopher writing about abortion in 'neutral' terms of 'we': 'If we are glad we are alive, we are enjoined not to terminate any pregnancy which will result in the birth of a person having a life like ours.'[12] The 'we' assumes 'that we are a community of equals who have simply to make moral decisions'.[13] This ignores the real position of the woman forced to consider abortion, or to spend her life caring for a severely handicapped child. It also ignores all the pressures on her due to the unequal relations between men and women. David Hughes's mother and Tom's mother see these daily realities as part of the moral decision about their sons' treatment. The 'trivial' details of daily life,[14] which philosophers want to dismiss as rubbish cluttering up the real issues, do not just complicate moral dilemmas. These details partly constitute moral dilemmas. The daily drudgery which Tom's mother believes to be pointless, and her sorrow for Tom in the endless small ways in which he fails to thrive, continually pose for her the moral questions of whether she can or should share in perpetuating his existence.

There is a danger that bioethics will be seen as a set of rules which people obey purely through reasoned conviction, and which offer clear solutions. This would restrict voluntary choice, rather than helping people to make more aware decisions. Moral rules are based partly on personal beliefs and are only convincing to those who share the basic premiss. If rational argument could convince, then philosophers would convince one another. Patently they do not. No moral rule seems comprehensively to allow for every case, yet also to be consistent and unanimously agreed. For example, *The physician's duty to the sick* states:[15]

1. A physician shall bear in mind the obligation of preserving human life.
2. A physician shall owe his patient complete loyalty and all the resources of his science.

The duties conflict when patients ask for abortion, or euthanasia, unless 'bear in mind' simply means 'think about' and not 'observe'. A reminder to 'think about' preserving life seems so bland as to be hardly necessary. The Code is also ambiguous. 'Loyalty' can mean loyalty towards the patient's interests as perceived by the patient, or else as perceived by the doctor. The two perceptions can be very different as, for example, between obstetricians who want to invest all the resources of science into childbirth, and women who do not want this. When patients compete for scarce resources, doctors cannot owe each patient 'complete loyalty'. Rules attempting to promote justice have practical limitations.

Respect for the rational person

Bioethics' emphasis on rationality works against child patients. It implies that reason alone can provide the source, defence, and purpose of a just morality, and that children's dilemmas can be apprehended and resolved solely through reason. There is also a tendency to assume that children are not yet rational and therefore have no direct part in the consent process. Each chapter so far has shown how splitting reason from emotion creates problems for patients and families. They need a medical ethics which challenges this split. Yet much bioethics tends to reinforce the divisions.

Philosophers see reasoned analysis as a defence against false beliefs. Although such analysis is helpful, throughout history deluded and evil beliefs have been elaborately justified and wise beliefs have been apparently refuted. Kant was one of many philosophers who dismiss emotions as transient and unreliable. Yet both thoughts and emotions can be passing or permanent, mistaken or well-founded.

Chapter 7 considered the extremely objective person who directs his every action 'as if by an overseer, of continuous wilful pressure on himself and even on his own wants and emotions',[16] who seeks the 'basis for judgement and decisions in rules rather than feeling'.[17] All this applies to Kant. Cut off from the inner self, Kant looked to external duty which is in 'no way based on feelings, impulses and inclinations'. He warned against 'far-reaching ingenuity', and believed that 'we should not act from our own interests or from another's' but only from the 'supreme principle of duty'. Duty is constant, like blind justice: 'In morals the proper worth of an absolutely good will . . . lies precisely in this—that the principle of action is free from all influence by contingent grounds.' Kant could not 'warn too strongly' 'against the slack, or indeed ignoble, attitude which seeks for the moral principle among empirical motives'.[18]

Some of Kant's views are now discredited as the prejudices of an eighteenth-century burgher, indicating that abstract duty is not an infallible source of a universal morality.[19] Young and sick children rely on adults also to look inwards, with far-reaching ingenuity, sensing their needs through empathy, as the mothers of Mark and Jane, and as Sam's nurse tried to do. Children also depend on adults to act in their interests, and from more potent motives than impersonal duty. Kant's idea of an impersonal moral response would be pathological in parents and nurses. Many patients need precisely the personal responses which Kant dismissed.

There are further limitations in bioethics' definitions of the rational person. Instead of considering human nature in all its rich complexity, philosophers tend to confine themselves to aspects of humanity which they believe are not shared by other species. They then compound this unfortunately restrictive approach, by assuming that our few unique qualities are our only really human ones. These qualities, summed up as reason, are the only ones which are supposed to define us as persons. The favoured definition of a person is John Locke's definition.

We must consider what *person* stands for;—which, I think, is a thinking intelligent being that has reason and reflection, and can consider itself as itself, the same thinking thing, in different times and places; which it does only by that consciousness which is inseparable from thinking, and, as it seems to me, essential to it: it being impossible for any one to perceive without perceiving that he does perceive. When we see, hear, smell, taste, feel, meditate, or will anything, we know that we do so.[20]

Philosophers often omit Locke's last sentence, which complicates the definition, showing that even in animals, feeling and thinking, mind and body are inseparable. Some species share almost all our abilities, such as to communicate, make choices, relate, hope, remember, and relish life. A squirrel, gauging the distance and strength of branches in relation to its body weight, neatly illustrates Locke's definition. Philosophers tend to overlook this, or to label animals' abilities as 'mere instinct' instead of appreciating how complex instinct can be.[21]

The belief that only human persons are rational is linked with Kant's principle that only rational persons are ends in themselves and therefore worthy of respect.[22] Bioethicists then claim that only humans who can be, or can become, rational persons should receive life-saving treatment if in need. This can lead on to the claim that beings such as animals, human foetuses, anencephalic babies, and, to a few philosophers, normal babies[23] are non-persons. Ending their lives is justified as moral, besides being convenient.

Bioethicists discuss personhood almost as if it is a clear, clinical condition. Yet personhood is so vague that it is impossible to define precisely, or to identify, or assess in many cases. Babies develop as persons when treated as if they already are persons. Babies who seem too neurologically damaged ever to become rational persons make unpredictable recoveries. Maureen Oswin[24] has shown how handicapped children dismissed as 'vegetables' can experience rational emotions such as happiness, profound sadness, and close attachments. A 'person' is also partly a social concept. Labelling someone as a person is a subjective matter. When we attribute or deny personhood to other people, we judge our own humanity, as the Nazis showed.

John Harris attempted to narrow Locke's criteria for personhood into beings able to use language and to state preferences.[25] He believes that only fully rational persons, who are able to state that they value their own existence, actually can value it. He then assumes that there is a moral difference between these persons and non-verbal 'creatures that cannot value their own existence'. The latter 'cannot be wronged [if they are killed] for their death deprives them of nothing they can value'.

One reply to these arguments would be to discuss the ignorance in which they are based, and how sophisticated, and aware non-verbal beings such as new-born babies are.[26] Another reply would point out Harris's tenuous logic. (How can he know that non-verbal beings do not value their own life?) A third reply would question the assumption that only disembodied reasoning has moral worth. (If rationality were moral, it would surely show altruistic concern for 'non-rational' but sensitive beings, rather than immoral disregard for them.) A fourth would ask how 'persons' can possibly be defined without mention also of their physical and emotional capacities, personal relationships, and unique identity. A fifth would discuss the dangers of losing the meaning of 'harm and benefit' to patients when personhood is confined to the intellect.

However, the sixth reply (which is why it is important not to be diverted into the others) is that these unproductive arguments in bioethics wander far from the central issues. They confirm Bertrand Russell's remark that 'the purpose of morals is to enable people to inflict suffering without compunction'.[27] The debate in bioethics about the person assumes that the central question is: Does this human being have any right to treatment? With the possible answer: No, because this being is not a person.

Yet such discussion would make no sense, for example, to Richard's parents and the professionals caring for him. Their central question is: What is the appropriate treatment for Richard? Leading on to the tentative questions: What will help him to have a tolerable life now and in future? If death is almost certainly inevitable, how long should attempts at cure continue? Might he survive, but be so damaged that his life will be too empty or painful to wish on any potentially active being (human or not)? If so, would it be preferable, for him, not to prolong his life? If attempts at cure cease, what other treatment will be given while he lives? How can those caring for Richard be helped in their work? What might help to make Richard's parents' lives tolerable if he dies, or survives with gross handicaps?

The 'rational person' debate overlooks children's needs and capacities. It lends a spurious certainty to the most complex, tentative questions, but contributes little to the real discussion. It is therefore not a useful basis for discussing medical dilemmas involving children.

Respect for the autonomous person

Informed consent is justified as a form of respect for autonomous persons. Yet bioethics' interpretations of autonomy discriminate against the consent of children and their proxies.

Kantian respect stems from the imperative: respect persons by treating them 'never simply as a means but always at the same time as an end'.[28] This imperative, not to use people, is a defence against abuse of patients and research subjects, yet it leaves loopholes. When respect is set as the highest principle which should not be compromised by 'paternalistic' beneficence,[29] it is defined as offering patients the choice to accept or refuse treatment.[30] The purpose of patient consent is then to respect this right to autonomous choice. However, many patients are deemed not to be autonomous, so consent would seem to be irrelevant to their case. When respect means not presuming to make decisions on another person's behalf, proxy consent which does exactly this can be seen as a contradiction in terms of the *raison d'être* of informed consent, and to have no justification.

In contrast, clinicians tend to interpret respect as providing the best treatment.[31] Yet respect is too vague a concept on which to base complicated discussion about what is the best treatment for, say, a severely ill baby. Clinicians can argue that however dangerous or unwanted a medical intervention, if it is intended to preserve life and the hope of future autonomy, then it is a form of respect.

In bioethics, respect is usually interpreted as non-interference. Caring support can then seem like disrespectful interference. Bioethics tends to avoid discussing positive interactions, such as care, and instead stresses negative ones such as respect for privacy. That this is a fairly recent value, is shown by the original meaning of privacy as privation and the usually fatal punishment of being excluded from society. Of course respect for patients' privacy and dignity is important, as well as care to avoid unnecessary interference. Yet patients dependent on society for life-giving care have other important needs, such as for injections or bedpans, and they can only be respected if these needs are met. The strict bioethics meaning of respect as non-interference is therefore of limited use to dependent patients.

The contradictions within 'respect' illustrate the basic problem in academic bioethics. Although concerned with patients in dependent relationships, it is based on ideals of independent individualism, in which the highest value is autonomy, or a kind of isolation. As MacIntyre writes:

Modern societies oscillate between a freedom which is nothing but a lack of regulation of individual behaviour, and forms of collectivist control designed only to limit the anarchy of self-interest.[32]

Individualist philosophy does not fit with dependent patients living within networks of relationships, or with the ties between sick children and the caring adults.

The work of Locke and Kant on rights and respect considered only one type of person: the independent, property-owning man. Their theories are 'universal' only in so far as they apply to all men in this category. Kant excluded children, 'women in general', and all subordinate men. They have no 'civil personality' because they obey and depend on others, and therefore cannot be autonomous.[33] Locke had to deny rights for women because he based rights on a property-owning patriarchy which would cease if women were independent.[34] Autonomous persons were a privileged élite set in unrealistic isolation. (Kant ignored his dependence on his own servants, for example.)

Bioethicists' attempts to apply this kind of 'respect for persons' to almost everyone therefore has complications. Instead of extending the meaning of 'person' to fit real people, they try to fit people into the original concept of the rational, autonomous person. Patient consent then tends to be discussed either as if patients are not partly emotional and dependent, or as if, when they are very dependent, they have no autonomy, so that respect and consent cannot apply to them.

In the Kantian vision of autonomy, we rise above feelings and contingencies into the realm of pure reason, where the correct choice, which it is our duty to make, is clearly seen. This is why Kant says: 'I need no far-reaching ingenuity to find out what I have to do in order to possess a good will.'[35] In seeing no conflict between will and duty, Kant ignores the complications in voluntary consent felt, for example, by Stephen, and by Janet's and Jane's parents. Vic Seidler explains Kant's vision of autonomy by showing 'Kant's conception of the person as fragmented' between the worlds of reason and of feeling. Only in the rational world are 'our freedom and autonomy guaranteed to us', because in the feeling world we are driven and constrained by our needs, desires, and human inadequacy.[36] Kant's stress on iron duty assumes that we can only choose freely when we rise above our feeling nature. Duty then reveals the only rational, and therefore autonomous, choice.

Alice Miller also indirectly explains Kantian psychology which mirrors the extremely objective scientist in chapter 7.[37] Kant's maxims echo the child-rearing books of his time. Miller reviewed three centuries of these protestant, mainly German, manuals. Their common theme is violently to crush children's will and feelings, and to enforce their unquestioning obedience, respect, and duty towards their masters. Miller then shows how this morality nurtured the Nazi state. Nazi leaders obeyed Kant's precepts, such as respecting persons, by defining those they tormented as non-persons who threatened the interests of persons.[38] Denying vulnerable feeling in oneself lays the groundwork for an evil morality.

Ultimately, Kantian respect and autonomy are lonely, antisocial ideals. Human relationships seem to be feared because they involve dependence and intimacy. 'Using' others (as means) and being used by them are assumed to be forms of abuse, instead of being seen as potentially rewarding and autonomy enhancing, indeed as the only means of actually relating. Kant prized the detached, equal 'relation of rational beings' (as if between disembodied minds) and he rejected human nature. For instance, he insisted that sexual relations are worse than suicide because 'complete abandonment of oneself to animal inclination makes man not only an object of enjoyment [*a means*], but still further an unnatural thing, i.e. a loathsome object, and so deprives him of all reverence for himself'.[39] Ethical medicine reveres the body as part of the self and honours the diseased patient. Yet Kantian bioethics is founded on the theories of a misanthrope.

Bioethicists would probably reject Kant's extreme conclusions, yet few challenge the premises which lead towards them. They tend to share Kant's emphasis on autonomy devoid of feeling, on respect as non-interference, and on the primacy of the lonely individual. Their explicit and subconscious theories about human relationships deny realities such as the child's dependence on the parents' loving care, or the intricacies of trust, and so they cannot acknowledge the value or complexity of proxy consent.

Autonomy literally means 'self-law', which can be interpreted in two ways. In bioethics the usual meaning is 'self-rule' in which reason controls other aspects of the self, as Kant required, to prevent the person being ruled by feeling or impulse. Another meaning of 'self-law' would include honouring the natural laws which enable the self to thrive. For example, if left to decide for themselves, healthy babies know how often they need to feed and rest, or to practise an activity until they perfect it. In many ways babies are autonomous beings. Feeling and impulse can work in harmony with good sense and rational judgement. Denigrating natural laws as a threat to rational autonomy, as Kant perversely did, can set the mind against the body and result in misery and ill health which undermine self-fulfilling autonomy. The ethical care of children includes respecting their natural autonomy, when making decisions for them and increasingly with them.

A common legal view advocates 'the basic right of the child to be entitled or empowered to come to an enjoyment of autonomy'.[40] All possible means should therefore be pursued to enable them to reach adult autonomy. Yet hope of future autonomy can become a coercion which tolerates very high costs of painful and dangerous treatment, and denies children any present freedom to withdraw. A few children in the units, after repeated surgery and with a very poor prognosis, wanted to stop living. One mother said of her eleven-year-old son, 'He wants just a sleep. No more pain or sadness.' Gwenda's mother said to her, 'You know what will happen if you don't have this operation.' Her eleven-year-old daughter replied, 'I'll be flying up in the sky with the birds. No more needles or operations. I want to go home.' Both children needed their present autonomy to be respected in balance with realistic hopes for their future.

Kant's narrow view of autonomy as rigid obedience to duty conflicts with the more usual, modern view of autonomy as the freedom to make any choice.[41] The broad view tends towards relativism, in which 'anything goes' and one opinion is no more valid than any other. Respecting autonomy then means respecting anybody's opinion simply because it is their opinion. This can go to non-rational extremes. Bioethics which stresses individual autonomous choice avoids imposing general definitions of harm and benefit. Yet without agreed meanings, bioethics itself becomes relativist, more concerned with norms and etiquette, than with real ethics. Then, however elaborately argued, a personal decision is arbitrary and like a plant without roots, because there is no constant, agreed, common ground regarding good and evil.

It is hard to see why autonomy should be so highly valued in bioethics. If all that matters is the person's right to choose, but not the validity of the choice in terms of human benefit or good, then autonomy seems an empty freedom. If all that matters is continued survival (to prevent autonomy from being ended by death) regardless of the kind of life being preserved, then survival seems a dubious benefit. Relativist autonomy is hostile to proxy consent. If everyone is entitled to a personal opinion, consent is just an exercise in respect for the patient's own opinion. The child's 'non-autonomous' opinion does not count, and the parents' opinions are reduced to 'just any other view' no more valid than any other.

The value of proxy consent falls when consent is justified as respect for the patient's abstract autonomy, but rises when consent is seen as a means of furthering benefit, preventing avoidable harm, and trying to work towards the best possible decision. Autonomous choice is then not arbitrary, but rational, based in lasting, personal beliefs, on careful analysis of feelings that are in touch with human need. Harm and benefit are understood as felt experiences, not vague abstractions. 'Respect for autonomy' is so important that child patients depend on richer interpretations of this term, which serve them instead of excluding them.

Beneficence

Beneficence is doing good and preventing harm. In Kantian ethics, beneficence is not perceived as a response to the particular other person, in the context of his or her life, enriched by benign feeling or impulse. Instead it is reconstructed as a set of rules or obligations towards the generalized other person (act impersonally as you would to anyone).[42]

Kantian mistrust of feeling as a threat to autonomy, and mistrust of the varied personal response as a threat to justice, pervades bioethics. Its reasoned arguments are supposed to prevent abuse and rampant self-interest.[43] So bioethicists reconstruct living relationships in terms of rational rules and duties or rights, like butterflies pinned to a card. For instance, beneficence

will be treated as a *duty*, and thus as distinct from mere mercy, kindness and charity. [It] asserts the duty to help others to further their important and legitimate interests. ... The line between a duty and a moral idea is not always easy to establish, and beneficence has proved to be the most troublesome moral duty to place firmly in one of these two categories.[44]

Beneficence is troublesome in a liberal morality (that is, one concerned with liberating autonomous individuals) because it weaves interdependent, social ties. Beneficence is the main principle in utilitarianism, in which it is reconstructed even more impersonally not as a kind of relating, but as a set of utilities—benefits and harms to be weighed and calculated. The phrase 'legitimate interests' begs the question as to what is legitimate and who is qualified to assess it in disputed cases. Tom Ayres's case raises questions of defining harms and benefits to Tom and his family and how these may be evaluated and compared.

Many issues in beneficence have already been referred to under justice and respect, so this section will just consider one issue: problems of understanding harm and benefit to child patients who cannot state their views. It is vital to connect physical, mental, and emotional experience, firstly, because to the patient harm and benefit are felt experiences (of pain, loss, humiliation, grief, or joy, relief, happiness, achievement, healing, fulfilment); secondly, because the only means of understanding non-verbal patients is through a thinking-feeling empathy.

One of the main dichotomies mentioned through this book, is the mind–body split underlying the pursuit of pure reason. Before we can connect thinking and feeling, deeply held assumptions dividing them have to be overcome. John Searle, lecturing on reconnecting mind and body,[45] appeared to bridge the gap, but then fell back into it by assigning everything either to physiology or to consciousness. So he referred to his body as 'hunk, junk, brute force' (as stupid) and to the human brain as the only form of intelligence (just as in the 'person' debate discussed previously). In this scenario, all matter is mindless, and all reason is powerless—sets of thoughts like particles somehow get shunted through the brain by physiological impulses.

Reality is nothing like this. Everything can perhaps be reduced to power/energy and knowledge/intelligence, and both forces pervade everything. Mind and body are united in complex fusions of energy and intelligence. For example, abstract thoughts are full of mental energy, growing, multiplying, branching off in all directions uncontrollably. The physical body has amazing intelligence, as in the mononuclear phagocyte in human blood[46] which produces over a hundred chemical substances, and migrates around the body, responding appropriately such as by destroying harmful bacteria or cancerous cells, or by healing wounds and tissue, apparently without any reference to the brain. The process may be mindless but it is not stupid. Order, meaning, purpose, ingenious and beautiful design throughout matter express their own autonomy and intelligence. Once this is appreciated, connections between the child's physical and emotional well-being, and mysterious ties of empathy between human beings can begin to be appreciated.

Proxy consent, which tries carefully to debate the vulnerable patient's interests, is at least as important as the consent of independent people who can look after themselves. Much of the proxy's knowledge stems from weakness, from sharing aspects of the patient's illness, pain, dependence, and anxiety, as adults quoted have shown. There are certain kinds of knowledge which can only be gained through such weakness.[47] Kantian autonomy, and impersonal, rational utilitarianism abhor the sensitive vulnerability and the physical and mental feelings which are the source of the knowledge that informs proxy consent.

Like the child who pointed out that the Emperor had no clothes on, children's dilemmas show up inadequacies in present emphases in bioethics. The next sections discuss problems raised by the profession of bioethics, the value and limitations of clear reasoning, and the tendency to separate decision from action.

Methods in bioethics

Clear reasoning

Bioethics is a rapidly growing profession; its members write, lecture, run courses, and sit on ethics committees. Some American ethicists charge fees for advising doctors on cases. Eliot Freidson[48] has shown how a profession is created when its members claim to have unique and necessary skills. In doing so, they create an ignorant and dependent laity which, by definition, lacks these unique professional skills. Bioethicists claim to be skilled in clear thinking.[49] They clarify debates through skilful analysis, define terms, and guide others past illogical traps towards valid conclusions. Such guidance can be very useful. Yet it does presuppose that those involved have not already thought through each issue clearly, and that each issue can be reduced to clear arguments and decisions.

Bioethics committees serve the interests of medical research subjects and (in North American hospital and institutional review committees, but not generally in Britain) of patients, by setting minimal standards and so preventing abuse of vulnerable individuals. However, patients are seldom members of these committees.

In claiming to think 'uniquely' rigorously, and sometimes to represent and speak for patients, professional ethicists imply that other people cannot do this. Clear reasoning in bioethics can in some ways work against the interests of patients.

There is the risk, especially when discussing individual patients' dilemmas, that ordinary people's abilities will be underestimated, and that decisions powerfully affecting their lives will be moved outside their control. Discussion may be translated into esoteric terms (such as whether the patient is a person) which confuse and handicap both patients and doctors. Patients' own meanings may be lost, and issues of vital importance to them excluded. Patients risk being recreated doubly as lay people, both medically and also now morally. Informed consent is at the centre of moves towards more equal relations between doctors and patients. Yet patients and their proxies risk being demoted and usurped, particularly by American ethicists.

Decision and action

When detached objectivity is valued, there is a tendency to separate decision from action, the end from the means of achieving it. The abstract justice of a conclusion, such as *whether* to turn off life support machinery, or to inform patients that they are dying, is sifted out from the myriad activities of *how* to implement the decision. Decisions made by courts, ethics committees, or sometimes by senior staff are carried out by junior staff or by families who have to live with the reality of decision. Bioethics tends to stress the theoretical question: 'What ought to be decided?' or 'Should the baby live?' rather than the practical question: 'How can we work together towards the best solution?' Yet means and ends alter one another, so that separating decision from action is not always helpful. People change. The unwanted handicapped baby becomes a valued member of a close family, or the whole family experiences intolerable strain and sadness.

The dramatic decisions debated in bioethics cover relatively few dilemmas. The majority of profoundly handicapped babies survive without ever needing a ventilator that might be switched off.[50] Decisive action is probably impossible in Tom Ayres's case; he will go on living for some time, affected by small decisions about how much medical support he should be offered each day. To concentrate on the few big decisions diverts attention away from everyday reality. Morality is like a jigsaw puzzle. Bioethics concentrates on the title of the jigsaw (to permit or prevent certain procedures). The people involved attend to the pieces, and continually face moral questions about how each piece should be fitted in, and how it affects the whole present and future picture. While Tom's mother gave his drugs, she questioned the purpose, alternatives, and possible consequences, until at last she decided to stop. Jane's mother wanted each part of treatment 'to be part of an overall plan, not grasping at straws'. Richard's nurses and doctors were unsure how to prepare his parents for his death. The plan is not just an abstract theory, it is a practical movement in many small stages.

Bioethicists tend to suggest that dilemmas can be resolved as long as people think clearly enough. However, a dilemma means choosing between two precious alternatives.

There are indeed crucial conflicts in which different virtues appear as making rival and incompatible claims upon us. But our situation is tragic in that we have to recognize the authority of both claims. There is an objective moral order, but our perceptions of it are such that we cannot bring rival moral truths into complete harmony with each other and yet . . . to choose does not exempt me from the authority of the claim which I choose to go against.[51]

Inevitable choices shown in earlier chapters include: balancing the individual and collective interests of children; fighting to defeat death while having to accept inevitable mortality; choosing between hope and realism; allocating medical time to technical or to social concerns. Each competing value holds essential advantages and also disadvantages. They are antagonistic yet complementary.

When there are no clear, predictable answers, those involved do not need imposed, facile decisions. They need support in coping with uncertainty while they gradually work towards their own answers and connect the overall decision with the interim parts.

A comprehensive framework

The three frameworks outlined in this chapter, of duties, utilities, and rights, are ultimately inconclusive and open to extensive criticism. Some philosophers believe that disputes between the separate frameworks 'can be resolved only if the principles of bioethics are integrated into some larger theoretical framework. We need moral theories and not just bioethical principles.'[52]

However, attempts to create a comprehensive 'prototype for all knowledge' (so far unsuccessful) have been criticized as deeply authoritarian. To assume that there can be one neutral answer for all similar cases is to deny individual people's interests and values. Such a prototype 'creates a masked form of legitimation of structures of domination', and covers over problems of unequal power and resources.[53] It is likely to be the greatest threat to the autonomy of patients and doctors.

Bioethicists are seldom introspective, rarely questioning why they want to reduce the awesome variety of human morality into neat, impersonal categories, or want to construct universal principles, or why they value objectivity and duty, and denigrate attachment and emotion. The sociologist Alvin Gouldner writes of this kind of reductionism as stultifying and 'life-wasting'. He believes that people 'surmount tragedy when . . . they use what they have and are, . . . even if this requires them to ignore cultural prescriptions, or to behave in innovative ways undefined by their roles'[54]—or rules.

Bernard Williams criticizes futile contemporary moral philosophy which gives an impression that 'all the important issues are off the page somewhere'.[55] Its abstracted purity creates unreal dichotomies.

Almost all worthwhile human life lies between the extremes that morality puts before us. It starkly emphasises a series of contrasts: . . . between force and reason, persuasion and rational conviction. [It implies] that without its ultimately pure justice there is no justice. Its philosophical errors are only the most powerful expression of a deeply rooted and still powerful misconception of life.[56]

Attempting to burrow down to the common roots of inconsistent branches of bioethics (if there are such roots) would, I suggest, produce a medical ethics that:

is even more abstract, remote, and impersonal, so reinforcing instead of challenging the very qualities in medicine which distress people;

disregards the practical moral concerns of patients and those caring for them;

is confined to reason and ignores other kinds of human knowledge;

redefines medical dilemmas into esoteric concepts and language that confuse patients and health professionals;

provides facile solutions which, even if elaborately justified, cannot convince everyone they affect.

The ethics of justice and of care

The rest of this chapter is about an alternative approach to medical ethics. Deontology tends to look backwards towards traditional duties and authorities. Utilitarianism tends to look forward to the consequences of a decision, calculating future benefit. Children need a medical ethics that also looks at the present, that:

  is practical, involved, and personal;
  centres on the moral concerns of patients and those caring for them;
  learns from the thinking-feeling knowledge of everyone concerned;
  clarifies problems in everyday terms that ordinary people can use;
  helps people to work together towards solutions.

Bioethics resists the kind of medical ethics just described, partly because of assumptions about authority and morality. Before an alternative form of ethics can be widely accepted, there have to be new understandings of authority and morality. These will now be described, partly in order to explain the alternative approach.

Beliefs about authority

Medical ethics is in danger of becoming a closed shop for experts. Ironically for a philosophy centred on respect for autonomy, bioethics appeals to the common belief that ordinary people need experts to solve their complicated problems. Antonio Gramsci thought that 'it is essential to destroy the widespread prejudice that philosophy is a strange and difficult thing just because' specialist philosophers do it.[57] He believed that at a basic level

'everyone' is a philosopher and that it is not a question of introducing from scratch a scientific form of thought into everyone's individual life, but of renovating and making 'critical' an already existing activity.

Then we can move on to 'the second level, which is that of awareness and criticism'. We do this by working out our own understanding of the world through questioning, acting, and learning to know ourselves.

Gramsci knew that 'critical understanding of the self takes place through a struggle'. Jane's mother showed the difficulty of working out what she believed was really happening through her own reactions. Difficulty is not always a signal to give up and call in experts. It is part of learning 'in order to arrive at the working out at a higher level of one's own conception of reality'[58] and then to put beliefs into practice. This task is best achieved when the families and professionals learn together how to respond to problems and to provide even better care.

Critical, active ethics is practised when bioethicists stop being expert authorities, and join the struggle of learning to know themselves. Yet this can only happen when beliefs about impersonal morality, which prevent self-knowledge, change.

Beliefs about morality

Psychologists such as Piaget and Kohlberg traced human moral development through stages: from the child's personal response in helping and pleasing others; into subordinating relationships to rules and reason; and finally towards the adult stage of observing universal principles. 'Adult' morality is concerned with impersonal, universal justice. It respects detached objectivity and autonomy, and frames moral rules to protect them.[59]

However, many people are found to stop at the early stage of the personal response. The moral psychologist Carol Gilligan suggests that instead of being regarded as inferior, their morality can be seen as different but valid.[60] This morality is about personal care, valuing relationships, and learning through feelings such as trust and concern. It takes the risk of becoming involved.

The psychological appeal of bioethics is that it is 'proper, adult' morality, offering the hope of objective certainty, and clear, fair decisions from detached vantage-points. These can be valuable. Yet the psychological need of patients is also for caring involvement to help them to cope with uncertainty, risk, and tragic decisions.

Gilligan's theories about moral stages are based partly on research which found that women tend to see safety in personal contact, and danger in distance from other people. Men are more likely to associate closeness with violence and risk, and to see safety in separation.[61] The research suggests that attitudes towards objectivity and autonomy are deeply influenced by the psyche. The two approaches are not typical of all men and women, but can be understood as broadly expressing the masculine and the feminine principles which may both be inherent in everyone.[62] When women become more involved in medical ethics, and when men become more aware of their feminine side, the one-sidedness of bioethics based on justice and respect is seen more clearly. Impersonal justice can seem callous, and 'frightening in its potential justification of indifference and unconcern'.[63]

In many dilemmas, people are not wanting to act wrongly, but are uncertain how to act rightly. It therefore does not help simply to impose rules supposed to prevent wrongdoing, or to perceive a dilemma as a self-contained problem that can be solved by logic. The problems may be too complex.

The moral problem arises from conflicting responsibility rather than competing rights and requires for its resolution a mode of thinking that is contextual and narrative rather than formal and abstract. This conception of morality as concerned with the activity of care centres moral development around the understanding of responsibility and relationships, just as the concept of morality as fairness ties moral development to the understanding of rights and rules.[64]

Care combines with respect, because respect literally means relooking and reknowing, recognizing essential human wisdom which goes beyond bioethics' cognitive reasoning. 'Care, respect, trust, time together, and a progression of disentanglement and of decisions are the path to appropriate actions,' said Simon's paediatrician. In cases like Tom Ayres's, he would bring everyone concerned to talk together. The paediatrician could act as the 'neutral' person Mrs Ayres needed, helping everyone to understand each other with new insight. Traditions in science and philosophy which mistrust emotion and intuition have to be overcome, so that people learn to trust themselves and the others involved in each dilemma. Then they think and sense their way together towards moral solutions which are negotiated, not imposed. Feelings such as empathy and anxiety inform and motivate the moral response of care, as Mark's and Jane's parents, and Samuel's nurse explained. Morality is 'the ability of people to engage with one another in such a way that the needs and feelings of others come to be experienced and taken on as *part of* the self. [These] experiences structure moral feelings.'[65] Adults do not care for sick children simply from duty. Beyond rules and pure reasoning, morality is complicated and enriched by our needs and desires, perceptions and values, emotions, experience, and disposition. Moral dilemmas are understood through a thinking-feeling understanding of 'the person' (oneself and others, child or adult).

Understanding 'the dynamic of human relationships then becomes central to moral understanding'.[66] This is because 'apart from our relationships there would be no moral necessity so that a perspective on relationships underlies any conceptions of morality'.[67]

Similarly Pellegrino and Thomasma recognize that besides the minimal defence of rules, and the essential consideration of benefits, the character of the physician and his or her relationship with the patient is of primary concern.[68] They add self-effacement to the usual list of medical virtues, and describe virtuous physicians as those who try to act rightly by habit, regardless of whether the act is noticed by anyone. Their portrait fits the views of the parents in the cardiac units who want to be able to trust doctors for their personal as well as their professional qualities.

Their 'Medical Oath for the Post-Hippocratic Era' includes clauses on: acting 'primarily in behalf of my patients' best interests and not primarily to advance social, political, or fiscal policy, or my own interests'; helping patients to share as fully as possible in decisions which affect them; helping them 'to make choices that coincide with their own values or beliefs'.[69] When doctors make space for families to share in medical decision-making, a vacuum is created unless families are willing to play their part. Many of the clauses on the physicians' obligations apply equally to parents making decisions for and with their children.

The hierarchy and the web

Gilligan describes two moral approaches as a hierarchy or a web.[70] Autonomy is about being apart, being protected from the threatening other by rules, finding safety in being at the top of the hierarchy and therefore in control of the rule-making. From this vantage-point, such as on an ethics committee, one can look down on problems with detached objectivity, and avoid getting emotionally involved by remaining rational and 'on top' of them.

The opposite image is of a web that coheres through human connections. Morality is perceived as being involved, caring for others, finding safety within reciprocal, close relationships. Moral dilemmas are considered in context, seeing the patient's individual history and psychology, seeing possible social injustices and individual suffering. This approach attempts to resolve dilemmas through negotiation, with compassion and tolerance. People are guided by moral thinking, feeling, and intuition, by the essential wisdom in themselves and others, not by imposing the armour of external rules.

The web is 'the vision that everyone will be responded to and included, that no one will be left alone or hurt'.[71] It is the ethics of moral reasoning and caring awareness, unlike the first ethic of cognitive reasoning and blind justice. Traditionally health professionals have been advised to avoid being too personally involved with patients, and of course respect and non-interference are vital protections for both patients and professionals. Yet as recent work in psychiatry has shown, doctors and nurses who lose sight of the person in each patient also lose touch with the value and fulfilment in their work. 'Burn out' is prevented through appropriately personal working relations, not through avoidance of the personal.[72]

Gilligan's ethic of care has been criticized as denying problems of power. One response to medical dominance is to construct a counter-dominance of legally enforced rights, and consumer powers, but this does little for vulnerable patients who cannot assert their rights. Another response is to analyse how medical power is structured and sustained, such as through the myriad ways in which wards and clinics are designed and managed, committees are selected and controlled, resources are allocated, staff are chosen, trained, and supported. It is then possible at many levels to question medical power, to help to reduce dominating, destructive elements, and to enhance its creative, nurturing elements. Health services can be reformed, partly with the help of the people using them.

It is useless, in abstraction, to exhort doctors to respect patients' autonomy if they are pressured to distance and hurry patients because of very heavy case-loads. Ethical issues pervade the health services from small details, such as how furniture is arranged either to encourage patients to talk or to inhibit them, to new developments, such as nurses becoming patients' advocates. Psychology, counselling skills, and emotional support for the staff can contribute more to the moral quality of health care than bioethics debates do. Nursing ethics is rapidly expanding. It would be unfortunate if it were based on bioethics' mistrust of feeling because, in nursing, empathy and care can be seen as 'the essence of morality'.[73] Child patients, particularly, benefit when the hierarchy is complemented by the web.

Ethical medicine

Bioethics is a one-sided kind of ethics based on traditional beliefs in expert authority and morality. It has helped society to become more aware of moral issues in medicine and to debate them more clearly. Yet it needs to evolve into a deeper understanding of humanity, beyond rational detachment.

Ethical medicine combines justice with care, principled decisions with the response to individual need, like two pathways meeting. This can create a richer although more complicated medical ethics. Moral dilemmas are considered by reviewing the child's medical and social needs, in the light of relevant moral principles, through the thinking-feeling awareness of the caring adults. 'Thinking what ought to be done' is combined, as some of the doctors in the units said, with 'sensing what the child needs'. Parents' consent is then not a token gesture, but an opportunity for parents to learn, and also to share their unique and essential knowledge of their child with the paediatric team.

Paediatrics leads the way in this kind of patient and family-centred approach to medicine. It would be unfortunate if bioethics jeopardized this approach. When the responsible adults, whenever possible with the child, contribute different kinds of knowledge, medical, nursing, and personal, the differences between them can be used to search for a resolution which is as rational and compassionate as possible.

When philosophy really is critical analysis, instead of a prop justifying unhelpful traditions, new approaches are practised in medicine and ethics. The final chapter discusses how these practices affect proxy consent.

Proxy consent

The central concerns of this book are the nature, practice, and value of proxy consent to children's treatment, seen mainly through the parents' eyes. Important issues surrounding proxy consent, including the child's view-point and growing competence, medical research with children, and confidentiality, have been considered only briefly. This is partly to avoid repeating detailed discussion elsewhere,[1] and also because so far little is known about children's understanding of consent.[2]

This concluding chapter considers who is qualified to make proxy decisions for child patients, and what the relevant decisions are. It ends by summarizing the main features of proxy consent.

Proxy consent and the experts

A sixteen-month-old boy had been on a ventilator in a Chicago hospital for nine months. His parents and doctors had long wanted to end apparently hopeless attempts to preserve his life. The hospital lawyer advised that this would be illegal. Eventually the father kept back the staff at gun-point, while he disconnected the ventilator and held his dying son.[3]

Among many comments on this case, it was alleged that the event would never have occurred had the hospital had an ethics committee to advise that the lawyer was mistaken. However, this would seem to compound the problem: that impersonal experts can powerfully influence such personal decisions which have been agreed by all the adults caring for the child. The case raises questions about who has the expertise to make medical decisions for children.

Medical dilemmas can, in a sense, be approached from a high or a low perspective, as illustrated at a conference session on euthanasia.[4] Some speakers looked down from a vantage-point of high moral principle. An English lawyer asserted that euthanasia is wrong and unnecessary because clinicians can now relieve all pain and suffering.

In order to prevent the kinds of abuse perpetrated by the Nazis, declared a German professor, the state must enforce absolute standards that forbid euthanasia. (Nationalizing morality would seem likely to repeat the problems which he hoped to prevent.) Other speakers began from the lowly basis of the patient's need, seeking for the best or least harmful response. A Dutch physician described the physical and mental distress which no drugs can relieve, and the attempts in Holland to respond to the estimated 3,000 to 6,000 requests each year for euthanasia, yet also to prevent abuse. An Australian paediatrician spoke of the lack of effective yet safe pain relief in neonatal units, and of cases in which treatment which might have saved life was discontinued because the cost in suffering for the baby was judged to be too high.

If decisions are made by individuals, rather than solely on principle, should doctors or parents carry the responsibility? The thesis of *Doctors' Decisions* is that doctors are the responsible moral agents.[5] Informed consent is not just a matter of presenting medical facts and options so that patients can select their choice as if from a self-service buffet. Doctors' judgement and experience can also be of great value to patients, and inevitably information is coloured by the medical account and the patients' perceptions. Clinicians are also legally, financially, and professionally accountable for the decision, although they may leave certain final choices to their patients or the parents, sharing moral agency closely with them. This acknowledges the very heavy, if less public, burden of responsibility which parents giving proxy consent also carry. Both doctors and parents are morally responsible for their own decisions.

In describing current medical practices of sharing or retaining control over decisions, *Doctors' Decisions* also illustrates the rapid changes in medical morality over just a few decades. When compared with, for instance, medical textbooks on gynaecology or psychiatry of thirty years ago, the older texts now appear puritanical, even punitive, and in comparison current medical views are liberal and compassionate. Yet this very change demonstrates how transient and uncertain are the concepts of harm, benefit, risk, a worthwhile life, and how these abstractions can only be defined in real terms by including the perceptions of people experiencing them.

In their comments on the doctors' chapters, the philosopher contributors consider that medical judgements are tempered by social morality. One philosopher wants to formalize this regulation, saying that clinical decision-making 'cannot operate in a vacuum [it] cries out for confirmation by social morality' we should 'call in law, philosophy and the like'.[6] Such a shift in emphasis from the 'lower', practical, individual case viewpoint, to the 'higher' detached and collective form of expertise could protect patients from exploitation and doctors from litigation. However, there is the risk that laws or guidelines arising, for example, from a national ethics committee are likely to be defensive and conservative, thus hampering progress in the sensitive response to need.

Those who advocate a national ethics committee tend to belong to the academic élite and to have little direct knowledge of the mass of disadvantaged people they would affect. For instance, the view of one such advocate, that 'the source of all knowledge is the universities',[7] denigrates the essential knowledge gained from everyday experience by all classes of people. The striking change in medical morality in recent decades has little to do, I suggest, with the universities. Doctors are now more liberal because consumer and rights movements, disadvantaged groups, black and disabled people, the chronically sick and their carers are far more vociferous, insisting that a single, dominant 'social morality' of an élitist establishment discriminates against many social groups. Disadvantaged people are introducing practical new concepts of compassion and respect which fit with the burdens and indignities they actually experience. If there is to be a national ethics committee it should not be confined to 'law, philosophy and the like' but should include and be accountable to people from many other backgrounds.

Micro-ethics is now being distinguished from macro-ethics. Micro-ethics considers a moral dilemma as an enclosed logical problem, such as whether a very handicapped baby should be helped to live or to die. Macro-ethics considers also the context of the dilemma. If the baby lives, will there be adequate practical and financial support to enable the child and family to lead reasonably fulfilling lives? What right has the state, or any other authority, to impose decisions on families unless it is prepared to share the resulting burdens? Social and economic policies are recognized as moral issues, affecting children's welfare more potently than micro-ethical debates do.

Moral dilemmas are too important to be left to academic experts; they have also to be understood through direct experience. The following analogy of two very different forms of navigation[8] is a

reminder of earlier discussion on parents' knowledge and the expertise which informs proxy consent. 'Primitive' Polynesian sailors cross
hundreds of miles of open ocean, steering by the stars, winds, and
currents, and on a cloudy night by the sound of the waves lapping the
hull, 'and the feel of the boat as it travels through the water'. The
sailors rely on myriad perceptions and memories, which they cannot
put into words. In contrast, modern European navigators rely on
highly sophisticated instruments, but without these they are lost. We
have no instruments for listening to babies and semi-conscious
patients, or for measuring pain and distress, but we do have 'primitive' means of intuition and perception. Humane care depends partly
on these primordial skills.

   Subconscious beliefs underlying academic theories restrict our
practical and moral understanding of proxy consent. One such belief
is the idea of the body as a machine. In many cultures, until less than
four centuries ago, nature was regarded as an organic unity. Every
part was thought to be alive and sensitive, dependent on and affected
by every other part, from the stars above to the rocks below, in a
great harmonious web of being.[9] Everything and everyone was seen
as all bound together. 'The whole world is knit and bound in itself:
for the world is a living creature [the parts connected] by reason of
their mutual love. . . . When one part suffers all the rest suffer with
it.'[10] These beliefs changed in Europe during the Enlightenment
when philosophers began to separate mind from matter, reason from
feeling, and objective fact from subjective value. Instead of seeing
organic unity, they saw machines. The human body came to be
regarded as a set of inert, static, 'stupid' parts,[11] like clocks.[12]
Harvey compared the heart with a pump.[13] Newton's physics
assumed a model of dead matter being moved by external forces such
as gravity, not by its own inner spirit.[14] Scientists began to be
technicians who controlled and repaired machines, analysing them
by the laws of mathematical logic. A subconscious model of the
doctor as active but impersonal technician and the patient as passive
machine developed. This changed patients' relations with doctors
and their consent to treatment. As trust in medical theories and skill
increased, trust lessened in patients' ability to understand, to share in
decisions, and to heal themselves.

   The mechanical view is useful in many ways, and has made
possible a whole new approach to healing. Yet it is incomplete. The
sharp divisions of the Enlightenment are now being challenged,

for instance by quantum physicists and ecologists. Each part is no longer seen as separate and inert, although the old dichotomies still powerfully influence medicine, psychology, sociology, and ethics. However, as examples through this book have shown, in practice, families and many doctors overcome the Enlightenment dichotomies when considering surgery for children. They take account of both reason and feeling, objective and subjective criteria, scientific precision and awareness of the 'whole child' within the family. They are not just detached observers, but are aware of their own involvement. In order to understand proxy consent, and invisible qualities such as trust, willingness, and awareness, we need to rethink the artificial dichotomies and to see how the separated pairs work together.

Parents' thinking-feeling experience leads to heightened awareness which can only partly be explained. Searching for words, one father who had been afraid that his daughters would die quoted these lines to explain what the crisis of consenting to surgery meant to him. The verse recalls pre-Enlightenment beliefs about relating in love and suffering.

> For it so falls out
> That what we have we prize not to the worth
> Whiles we enjoy it, but being lack'd and lost,
> Why then we rack the value, then we find,
> The virtue that possession would not show us
> Whiles it was ours.
> When he shall hear she died upon his words,
> The idea of her life shall sweetly creep
> Into his study of imagination
> And every lovely organ of her life
> Shall come apparell'd in more precious habit,
> More moving delicate and full of life
> Into the eye and prospect of his soul
> Than when she lived indeed.[15]

When patients cannot communicate, their needs can only be sensed by those most intimately involved in caring for them. Ian Kennedy writes that 'our genuine, conscience-searching agonising' begins in moral intuition.[16] John Harris dismisses moral intuition as dangerously irrational, citing how outrage can reinforce blind prejudices.[17] Yet Harris confuses unreflective egoism with the insights of reflective altruism described in this book by parents, doctors, and nurses. Proxy consent is understood when altruistic intuition is respected as rational and valuable. Conscious adult patients are presumed to be aware of their own inner needs. Yet the needs of very young or very ill patients somehow have to be sensed through means other than pure reason and language, as shown in the two following examples.

Simon's mother described his early months when 'basically nothing could be done and they were just waiting for him to die'. Eventually, she asked if surgery might be attempted.

I think it was one of the hardest things to accept. When he was very ill, then I could understand [not attempting surgery]. But when he started to get better and he had some good days, then you'd feel really helpless, because he'd sort of fight through so many—bad patches, but we had nothing to offer him. He was obviously a fighter and you knew he was not going to give up.

The doctors finally agreed to try very high-risk surgery because 'the original prediction was obviously proving incorrect', but Simon's mother thought that this was partly affected by Simon's determination. For a baby with so many difficulties he seemed to have an amazing zest for life.

In contrast, a senior nurse talked about some babies who seemed to 'want to give up', or who suddenly died for no clear reason. Martin was also only a few months old.

It came to the stage when all the nurses wanted Martin to die, and so did his mother—for his sake. It was a relief to us all when he arrested. But the senior surgical registrar just rushed in and resuscitated him, and he survived a few days longer.

Sensing the child's best interests involves close observation, rational analysis, and also empathy. The two conclusions just mentioned could be criticized as misguided or dangerously subjective. Yet so also could the debates of an ethics or institutional review committee, which may be devoid of direct, compassionate knowledge of the individual child (and possibly be influenced by fear of litigation and lost profits, and by members competing for power and status). Such debates are potentially far more harmful to patients. Individual medical dilemmas may be so tangled and complex, that referring them to a committee can be like trying to saw through a knot. The alternative is for the family and staff around the cot to try the hazardous task of unravelling the tangle, learning from one another about the child's best interests, developing their expertise through direct involvement.

The relevant decisions

Informed consent is usually confined to the extreme end of health care—surgery—in which families are least knowledgeable. Arguments are then dominated by such questions as how much lay people can or want to understand about technical details. The opposite approach would be to ask: In which aspects of hospital care are families knowledgeable, and to which do they also want freedom to consent or dissent, such as in daily routines, feeding, and pain relief? When meals are served by the playworker, only parents may be aware of the effects of nauseous drugs on appetite. So necessary knowledge is lost when making medical decisions unless parents are encouraged to be part of the caring team.

Informed consent is in danger of being treated like a game of chess. When champions challenge novices, the likely result is to show the novices' limitations. This encourages the conclusion that novice patients and parents are generally ignorant in all aspects of medical and nursing care as well as in the most complicated techniques. Parents reach a similar conclusion from the other direction; if their opinions pass unheeded in small matters, they do not expect to be able to influence major issues. If they do not feel free to ask for a chair, how can they question a surgeon's decision?

When I asked parents about consent to surgery, some looked blank as if they unquestioningly left such specialized matters to doctors, but they had plenty to say about the quality of their child's care. Proxy consent should not be confined to formal consent to major procedures, leaving 'low-risk, routine decisions' to physicians, as advised by some experts.[18] Families are also concerned about many 'minor' issues in which they are expert.

Although proxy consent is usually given to fairly simple, low-risk surgery, almost all the examples in this book have been about difficult exceptions because these illustrate the limitations of proxy consent, in how far parents are willing or able to share in medical decisions. They also illustrate what parents can contribute during decision-making. The following summary of main features of proxy consent shows how, if necessary, it can help towards unravelling complex dilemmas.

Informed proxy consent depends on parents receiving and understanding adequate medical information. In the children's heart units, great care was often taken to inform parents, in the belief that they could reasonably understand complex decisions.

Informed decisions also include knowledge of the patients' interests. As the adults usually closest to their children, parents have unique and essential information about them. They help their growing children to speak for themselves. Children's law is based on two values which are assumed to conflict: children's need for nurturance yet also for self-determination. However, these values may be reconciled when parents help children to develop self-determination by nurturing their developing skills. Proxy consent is then based not on 'parents' dwindling rights'[19] but on furthering children's growing responsibilities.

During the consent process, families and professionals inform one another. Simon's mother is informed, partly because she knows her child so well, and also because Simon's paediatrician and other doctors 'helped tremendously by answering all our questions, and *listening*, and spending so much time being very, very supportive'.

Voluntary proxy consent depends on parents being able to make reasonably free decisions, within the unavoidable constraints of the child's illness and treatment. When parents expressed doubts about medical proposals, many doctors discussed these in detail, wanting to help parents to be convinced, and committed to the medical decision, and not to feel coerced into agreeing.

There was less medical interest in adapting decisions to the parents' requests. This was partly because of the imbalance of knowledge; doctors were usually more fully aware of the likely clinical effects of decisions. Some doctors were more confident than others about making value judgements as to which risks were worth taking. Ian Kennedy repeatedly states that doctors are no more expert than anyone else in making moral decisions.[20] Yet constant practice in resolving medical dilemmas must result in some expertise. Kennedy's view implies that technical and moral issues can be completely separated, but this separation is neither possible nor helpful. It can result in deadlock, preventing negotiation between doctors who deal with technical aspects, and patients who deal with value judgements, as doctors have pointed out.[21] Consent is more usefully seen as a process through which families and doctors arrive at medical and moral agreement that satisfies both parties, if necessary with the help of the other professionals directly concerned. If this is impossible, referral to another consultant may be considered.

Since the 1960s, families have been increasingly informed about medical decisions, but efforts to involve them in decision-making are developing more slowly. Voluntary proxy consent will be more widely achieved as professionals and families expect to share decision-making more fully, and become more skilled through practice.

Adequate or good-enough consent describes a realistic approach towards helping parents to make as informed and free a choice as possible. There is no magic line dividing the competent from the incompetent. Rather, there is a range of degrees of competence, with the obligation to achieve as fully informed consent as possible. One example is Sean's mother whom the nurses thought of as 'very simple, she doesn't really understand'. She did seem to have difficulty in understanding medical information, but she was clear about some basic issues. She told me:

I'd feel more guilty and upset than the doctors would, because I'd signed the form. They're only doing their best, their job. But how would you feel if something went wrong with your child on the table? The doctors don't see it like that, that he's my child. They think I'm moaning. I'm not complaining but I have a right to know, to be told what is happening, the good and the bad, and what his condition would be if he didn't have these operations. A heart operation is serious. I feel really guilty when I look at his scars. I've got to have second thoughts about whether to say 'no'. Mothers really should have more say than doctors because you have to carry it all. When he's back home, I do everything. He's mine. I have to take responsibility for him everywhere I go.

Sean's mother saw her rights not in terms of property rights over her child, but as a means of fulfilling her responsibility to him as far as she could.

Proxy consent assesses harm and benefit not as abstractions, but as physical and mental experiences, which matter both during treatment and in their future effects. Close contact with the child deepens awareness and prompts reservations and questions which encourage the adults to scrutinize and sometimes to reconsider their decisions, and their evaluations of harm and benefit. One example is Nimmi. During the weeks when she was on the ventilator, some of the nurses were among the first to say that 'it is cruel to keep going on', and gradually this became a unanimous decision. Another example is Gwenda's parents working to persuade the staff to accept Gwenda's wish to end the treatment and to go home to die. Such decisions involve accepting, besides the almost certainly hopeless prognosis, the 'level of truth' of the patient's suffering. A psychiatrist described the difficulty of listening to the distress of families in the heart units, in this example of one mother's grief.

At one point in tears she spoke to me about her deep shame at giving birth to an imperfect child. I felt this was her level of truth, where she's at, and whatever else she is or does rests on that. [A question is] whether you can take the pain of knowing about their intense suffering. Tears come to my eyes when these people talk. I get the feeling we're peeling away the layers of an onion on both sides. It's a question of whether my truth and their truth does get through. . . . The degree of empathy required is as tough as any kind.

Accounts of parents' and children's distress can be so disturbing that they are sometimes discounted as emotive exaggeration, as constructs unrelated to any reality, or 'atrocity stories'.[22] Obviously like any other group, including professionals, parents sometimes misunderstand, over-react, and unfairly misreport events. However, dismissing parents' and nurses' criticisms and descriptions of children suffering as unfair or untrue would involve dismissing the chance of learning from their insights.

James Robertson believed that were the emotional harm to children of hospital treatment to show as physical bruises, hospitals would quickly change. Because emotional harms are invisible, they tend to be ignored. Robertson made films of children's distress in hospital to demonstrate his case.[23] A widespread reaction of outrage among paediatricians was shared by Dermod MacCarthy. He discussed the film *Laura* with his ward sister, saying how much he hated and disbelieved it, and that distress like Laura's could never occur in his ward. The sister replied that she was equally disturbed by the film, but was convinced by it. MacCarthy went into his ward the next day, and saw it with new eyes. He joined in Robertson's lifelong work to humanize hospital care for children, which involves respecting children's and parents' evaluations of harm and benefit.

One mother wrote of her severely ill daughter:

We should look at what the child's behaviour is telling us. Remembering the difficulty I, as an adult, had in being heard, I am confident that many children suffer from being unheard. Especially because so much of what they have to tell us is said non-verbally. People should ask themselves if they are really 'listening' in every sense of that word.[24]

'Really listening' to someone else's distress can be very painful as MacCarthy found. It is painful for the adults caring for sick children and gaining the knowledge necessary for informed proxy consent and also, perhaps, for anyone reading descriptions of the families in this book. Such listening involves forms of knowledge gained through emotion which are overlooked in Western science and philosophy, but valued in Eastern and Western religions. 'Your pain is the breaking of the shell that encloses your understanding.'[25] New understanding reveals that the 'universal golden rule', that we should do to others what we would wish them to do to us,[26] is not enough. It offers an excuse to ignore the individual. Voluntary proxy consent is committed to decisions intended to fit with the wish and need of the particular child, which may be very different from what we would wish for ourselves.

Proxy consent may involve 'drawing the line',[27] deciding when a proposal is too risky or harmful. Some people are optimistic and determined, valuing life very highly and accepting prolonged treatment. Some children and parents come to see death as a merciful release, and learn to value life and 'to think of time in terms of depth rather than length'.[28] Proxy consent, as Stephen's family said in the first chapter, can be a way of discovering families' attitudes towards aggressive treatment. In making and keeping to either choice (to accept or refuse treatment) families need much listening support.

   Although not all parents put their sick child's interests first, most do so, and no satisfactory alternative to parents' care has been found, except the closest possible substitute. Young children are so dependent that they suffer if their interests are too far separated from, or in conflict with, those of the family, rather as a branch cannot be treated separately from the tree. Sharing medical decisions with parents encourages consistent and continuing care during and after the child's stay in hospital. Modern society increasingly puts pressure on parents to 'give the child a chance' through treatment, whatever the cost. Monica Dickens, for instance, praises prolonged attempts to overcome childhood leukaemia as heroism. She criticizes cowardly fathers who leave their family during the child's drastic treatment.[29] Family separation is one of many consequences of leukaemia and may be associated with the disease rather than the treatment. Yet medical harm at times exceeds the benefit, and family breakdown may then be a sign, not of weakness, but of a reasonable response to inappropriate use of technology if parents leave an intolerable situation. Their sense of guilt about congenital defects is widely recognized.[30] This is increased if they have no power to prevent their child's suffering, and more so if they feel partly responsible for it because they sign the consent form.

Some families are more cautious about treatment than their doctors are, others are more anxious to prolong life with intensive treatment. Both doctors and families are influenced by personal opinions in deciding when the physical, emotional, and financial costs of prolonged treatment outweigh the potential benefit. Disagreements among the medical team demonstrate when this cannot be a purely clinical decision. When differences are discussed, parents and doctors have to explain, justify, and therefore scrutinize their decisions more carefully. As a director of paediatric nursing, Elizabeth Fradd is involved in a few cases when, against the consultant's advice, parents decide that the treatment should end. She aims to help parents and other staff to decide when it is best for the child to 'draw the line' and to withhold treatment. She believes that nurses should listen to and support parents and, if necessary, act as advocates for the family.[31] Disagreement between parents and doctors can be used constructively when, with mutual respect, they discuss together critically how the child may best be cared for.

Proxy consent is both a formal agreement and a process. Clear agreements and consent forms protect both patients and hospital staff. Yet these need to be complemented with negotiations through each stage of the patient's changing condition and treatment, so that proxy consent can be a means of perceiving and then achieving the most appropriate care.

Legal and moral rules provide minimal standards, but sick children need far more than negative safeguards. As Carol Gilligan wrote, we need to move away from the 'paralysing injunction not to harm' into learning through sympathy and shared humanity. 'Seeing the world comprised of relationships rather than of people standing alone, a world that coheres through human connection rather than through a system of rules.'[32]

Proxy consent includes understanding, choosing, knowing that it is possible to refuse, and signifying the decision. Formal requests for consent and signified agreement seem to be seldom practised in the hospitals, except with written consent forms for major procedures. Children benefit when the staff are aware of the need to request permission for many kinds of minor procedures, and when parents are aware of their right to refuse interventions, or to ask for higher standards of care, such as in X-ray and ECG departments.

Proxy consent has to be seen in the context of how each hospital encourages or restricts family-centred care. It is helpful when professionals develop effective ways of communicating with families and with one another, when they share knowledge and try to overcome the inequalities which prevent open discussion. Also important are the design of, and routines in, the wards and clinics, and the attitudes which they express as to whether it is possible and worth while to involve parents in decisions. There will always be a gap between the actual and the ideal standards of care. This book does not aim to demand unrealistically high standards, but to show how even small changes can so much aid the consent process, to the benefit of everyone concerned.

Children need medical and nursing practices, training, and ethics which are responsive to parents' awareness of their child's needs. As this increasingly happens, the practice of informed and voluntary proxy consent moves closer to the theory.

The families quoted in this book were interviewed at a low point in their lives. Yet their time in hospital enabled most of the children to live full and healthy lives. So to put the hospital episode into some perspective, I will end with just one from many examples of parents' gratitude.

I do think it's marvellous, a very good hospital, although there's always room for improvement. You come through it, and have the joy of life and health, and the staff have to go on living through the misery again and again, easing life for other people. There are so many families—if ever the staff knocked on their door, they wouldn't be able to invite them in fast enough. They'd treat them as honoured guests. We'll always be sending photos back there, as so many other parents have to do. There is a bond that can never be forgotten. We've been through so much together.

Notes

Chapter 1. Introduction

1. Warner, J., 'Commentary' on 'Early Experiences of Heart-lung Transplantation in Cystic Fibrosis', *Archives of Disease in Childhood*, 64 (1989), 9.
2. Pot-Mees, C., *The Psychosocial Effects of Bone Marrow Transplantation in Children* (Delft, Eburo, 1989), 3, details commonly experienced distress, and Judd, D., *Give Sorrow Words: Working with a Dying Child* (London, Free Association Books, 1989), illustrates how intense the suffering can be.
3. See the references in n. 2.
4. Hall, D., Stacey, M., *Beyond Separation* (London, Routledge, 1980), 186–7.
5. Gilligan, C. identifies attachment and detachment theories in moral psychology in *In a Different Voice* (Cambridge, Mass., Harvard University Press, 1982).
6. Merchant, C. analyses the five beliefs of detachment, which she terms the mechanic view in *The Death of Nature* (London, Wildwood House, 1982).
7. Oakley, A., McPherson, A., Roberts, H., *Miscarriage* (London, Fontana, 1984).
8. Tolstoy, L., *Anna Karenina* (1873), p. 1.
9. Examples of two leading American texts are: Beauchamp, T., Childress, J., *Principles of Biomedical Ethics* (New York, Oxford University Press, 1983) and Engelhardt, H., *The Foundation of Bioethics* (New York, Oxford University Press, 1986).
10. See the references in n. 9.
11. Wallace, L., 'Informed Consent to Elective Surgery: the "Therapeutic" Value?', *Social Science & Medicine*, 22/1 (1986), 29–33.
12. Illich, I., *Limits to Medicine* (Harmondsworth, Penguin, 1976) and Ehrenrich, B., English, D., *For Her Own Good: 150 Years of Experts' Advice to Women* (London, Pluto, 1979) are two of many examples.

Chapter 2. Consent in the wards

1. Alderson, P., *What the Parents Think*, a survey of families in two paediatric cardiology units (1986). 415 questionnaires were distributed and 278 families replied.
2. Platt Report, *The Welfare of Children in Hospital* (Ministry of Health, London: HMSO, 1959).
3. Openheim, C., *Poverty: the Facts* (London, Child Poverty Action Group, 1988). A report based on government surveys and reports.
4. Local authorities pay social workers, yet if the hospital authorities valued this support they would surely have found funds to supplement it by supporting a social work research project for instance.
5. Tubbs, H., 'Children in Isolation', *National Association for the Welfare of Children in Hospital Update*, 7 (1982), 6–7, and see Taylor, M., O'Connor, P.,

'Resident Parents and Shorter Hospital Stay', *Archives of Disease in Childhood*, 64 (1989), 2.

6. Forfar, J., MaCabe, A., 'Masking and Gowning in Nurseries for the Newborn Infant', *British Medical Journal*, 1 (1958), 76.

7. Menzies Lyth, I., *Containing Anxiety in Institutions* (London, Free Association Books, 1988), 43–88.

8. Alderson, P. (See above, n. 1.) Thirty-one parents wanted to stay 'somewhere near the hospital', 146 in a parents' room in the hospital, 59 in the ward within calling distance, and 64 'in a put-up bed next to my child'. Probably even more wanted to stay in the hospital than indicated in the survey, because in my interviews parents often said they did not want to stay at the hospital. They then explained that they would want to stay, and did so, in their local hospitals, but at the cardiac units they found the accommodation too depressing ('it's near the morgue'), or too lonely ('I need to be with my husband during this crisis', 'I just can't cope on my own'), or too far from their child ('so what is the point of staying?'). Lack of space to stay near the children was the most commonly mentioned feature of the hospitals which caused parents greatest distress.

9. Alderson, P., Comer, B., *Report of Nursing Satisfaction Study at the Brompton Hospital* (1986): a survey of the views of 74 paediatric nurses (58 replies). Forty nurses thought that aspects of child-centred care were inadequate, and several mentioned the shortage and expense of parents' accommodation. Nurses' views are also drawn from my interviews, and I attended psychosocial ward rounds, nurse support meetings, and meetings on stress run by a psychiatrist for the staff.

10. Robertson, J., *Young Children in Hospital* (London, Tavistock, 1970), and Jolly, J., *The Other Side of Paediatrics* (London, Macmillan, 1981).

11. See above, n. 9.

12. At the time of the survey (n. 1 above) most parents could not go with their child beyond the ward. Of 278 returned questionnaires, 12 wanted to stay 'until the pre-med was given', 94 'until my child was taken out of the ward', 61 'until after the journey to theatre', 78 'until after the anaesthetic had been given', 33 did not answer that question.

13. Brain, D., MacLay, I., 'Controlled study of mothers and children in hospital', *British Medical Journal* (Feb. 1968).

14. Byrne, D., Napier, A., Cushieri, A., 'How Informed is Signed Consent?', *British Medical Journal*, 296 (1988), 839–41.

15. Briony had an atrioventricular septal defect but not Down's syndrome.

16. Daly, J., 'Innocent Murmurs', *Sociology of Health & Illness*, 11/2 (1989).

17. See, for example, extensive literature on pain in childbirth, initiated by Read, G., *Natural Childbirth* (London, Heinemann, 1933).

Chapter 3. Consent in the clinics

1. The average for clinics observed with this consultant. I observed 64 clinics held by 11 paediatric cardiologists, and 10 joint clinics.

2. The average for this second consultant (n. 1 above).

3. The drugs are spironolactone, digoxin, and frusemide.

4. Henley, N., *Body Politics* (London, Spectrum, 1977). Personal time and space correlate, the more time people have for one another, the closer they tend to sit and the more they look at one another.

5. Petrillo, M., Sanger, D., *Emotional Care of Hospitalised Children* (New York, Lippincott, 1978). One of many psychology texts which shows how children benefit when they are able to protest.

6. Halmos, P., *The Faith of the Counsellors* (London, Constable, 1965).

7. Joseph had an atrioventricular septal defect and Tetralogy of Fallot.

8. Shanta had an atrioventricular septal defect, Tetralogy of Fallot, and other cardiac anomalies.

9. Kelly had a ventricular septal defect, pulmonary atresia, collaterals supplying the pulmonary arteries, and truncus type one. This was in 1985. Heart transplants have changed the scene, but the issue of when to resort to risky surgery remains.

10. Siegel, B., *Love, Medicine and Miracles* (London, Rider, 1986) is just one of many reports about the effects of patients' responses on the progress of their disease.

11. John had tricuspid atresia, ventricular septal defect, and pulmonary stenosis.

12. Gill, C., Blake, N., *Paediatric Diagnostic Imaging* (London, Heinemann, 1986), criticize their colleagues for causing unnecessary distress.

Chapter 4. Medical decisions

1. These examples may date quickly as new operations become commonplace. Yet they illustrate the general problem of considering surgery at the stage when it is fairly new and high-risk.

2. I observed 9 medical meetings in the Children's Hospital, and 18 in the Brompton Hospital.

3. Halmos, P., *The Faith of the Counsellors* (London, Constable, 1965).

4. Titmuss, R., *Essay on the Welfare State* (London, 1958), 200–2.

5. *Nuremberg Code* (1947) reprinted in Duncan, A., Dunstan, G., Welbourn, R. (eds.), *Dictionary of Medical Ethics* (London, Darton, Longman, & Todd, 1981).

6. Gilligan, C., Wiggins, G., 'The Origins of Morality in Early Childhood Relationships' (unpublished paper, Harvard University, 1985).

7. This observation is based on the clinics, many ward rounds, and the medical meetings and other staff meetings I attended, as well as interviews with five consultants and three senior registrars, and many brief conversations. Some consultants also read and commented on draft copies of this work.

Chapter 5. Professional team-work

1. Each hospital is different, and almost all the examples in this chapter are from the Brompton Hospital.

2. At the Brompton Hospital I observed: 16 paediatric unit meetings; 4 psychosocial ward rounds; 3 nurse support meetings; 5 sessions on stress chaired by a research psychiatrist. I also held 7 long interviews with nurses as well as many conversations with individuals, and groups of course nurses. With the clinical nurse teacher I carried out a survey of the 74 paediatric nurses.

3. Leroy had a very severe form of total anomalous pulmonary venous drainage. The veins taking blood back from the lungs are attached to the right instead of the left side of the heart. Two years later he still needed extra oxygen to help his breathing and was retarded.

4. Alderson, P., Rees, S., 'Caring for Children in Hospital—the social worker's role', *Social Work Today* (Dec. 1987), 14–15.

5. Alderson, P., *What the Parents Think*, a survey of 415 parents in 2 cardiac units (1986).

6. Cornwell, J., Gordon, P., *An Experiment in Advocacy: the Hackney Multi-Ethnic Women's Project* (London, King's Fund Centre, 1984).

7. Manthy, M., *Primary Nursing* (London, Blackwell, 1980), and see also Green, L., 'A Special Friend', *Nursing Times* (3 Sept. 1986), 32–3; and Fradd, E., 'Achieving New Roles', *Nursing Times* (14 Dec. 1988), 39–41.

Chapter 6. Informed consent

1. Law and research on consent are summarized in Kaufman, C., 'Informed Consent and Patient Decision-making: two Decades of Research', *Social Science & Medicine*, 17/21 (1983), 1657–64; and King, J., *Informed Consent: a Review of the Empirical Evidence* (London, Institute of Medical Ethics Bulletin Supplement no. 3, 1986). For detailed discussion on consent to research see Nicholson, R. (ed.), *Medical Research with Children: Ethics, Law and Practice* (Oxford, OUP, 1986).

2. President's Commission for the Study of Ethical and Legal Problems in Medicine, *Making Health Care Decisions* (1982), ch. 4; and *Report of the Royal Commission on the NHS* (Cmnd. 7615, HMSO, 1979), ch. 5.

3. On children's fantasies, fears, and psychological understanding see Petrillo, M., Sanger, D., *Emotional care of Hospitalised Children* (New York, Lippincot, 1978).

4. Wallace, L., 'Informed Consent to Elective Surgery: the "Therapeutic" Value?' *Social Science & Medicine*, 22/1 (1986), 29–33.

5. Clough, F., 'The Validation of Meaning in Illness-Treatment Situations', in Hall, D., Stacey, M. (eds.), *Beyond Separation* (London, Routledge, 1979), 77.

6. Kelley, M., 'Adjusting to Ileostomy', *Nursing Times*, 8/33 (1987), 29–31; and 'Loss and grief reactions as responses to surgery', *Journal of Advanced Nursing*, 10 (1985), 517–25. Stoma surgery creates an artificial anus through the abdominal wall.

7. Siegel, B., *Love, Medicine and Miracles* (London, Rider, 1986).

8. Buørge, G., personal communication (1989) on her work in Oslo.

9. Harrison, H., 'Neonatal Intensive Care: Parents' Role in Ethical Decision-making', *Birth*, 13/3 (1985), 165–75.

10. Faden, R., Beauchamp, T., *A History and Theory of Informed Consent* (Oxford, OUP, 1986).

11. Meadow, R., 'Munchausen syndrome by proxy', *British Medical Journal* (July 1989), 248–50.

12. Kramer, S., 'Splitting and stupidity in child sexual abuse', *Psychoanalytic Psychotherapy*, 3 (1988), 247–57.

13. Winnicot, D., *The Maturational Process and the Facilitating Environment* (London, Hogarth, 1965), discusses good-enough mothering.

14. Newell, P., *Children are People Too* (London, Bedford Square Press, 1989).

15. Woodward, J., *Has Your Child Been in Hospital?* (London, National Association for the Welfare of Children in Hospital, 1978).

16. Neill, A., *Summerhill* (London, Gollancz, 1962), notes that the most home-sick children in his school came from unhappy homes.

17. Kennel, J., Klaus, M., *Maternal Infant Bonding* (St Louis, C. Mosby, 1976), associated separation of parents and children with later child abuse.

18. Capron, A., 'The Authority of Others to Decide about Biomedical Interventions with Incompetents', p. 119, in Gaylin, W., Macklin, R., *Who Speaks for the Child?* (New York, Plenum, 1982).

19. Cruel fashions in child rearing are described in Miller, A., *For Your Own Good* (London, Virago, 1987).

20. Nuremberg Code 1947 in *Dictionary of Medical Ethics*, ed. Duncan, A., Dunstan, G., Welbourn, R. (London, Darton, Longman & Todd, 1981).

21. Nicholson, R. (ed.) *Medical Research with Children: Ethics, Law and Practice* (Oxford, OUP, 1986), 237.

22. Declaration of Helsinki 1964 in *The World Medical Association: Handbook of Declarations* (Ferney-Voltaire, 1986). I have quoted the 1983 version.

23. Gillon, R., 'Medical treatment, medical research and informed consent', *Journal of Medical Ethics*, 15/1 (1989), 3–5.

24. *Canterbury* v. *Spence* [1972] 464 F. 2d 772.

25. Laskin, C., in *Hopp* v. *Lepp* (1980) 112 DLR (3d) 67.

26. *Sidaway* v. *Governors of the Royal Bethlem Hospital and Others* [1984] 1 All ER 1018. A surgeon was not found negligent for not informing Mrs Sidaway of the risk of paralysis from her neurosurgery since this was estimated to occur in less than 2% of cases.

27. *Bolam* v. *Friern Hospital Management Committee* [1957] 1 WLR 582. So far the legal standard of adequate consent is still based on the standard in this case, of what the reasonable doctor would decide to tell.

28. See case referred to in n. 26 above.

29. Scarman, J., 'Consent, communication and responsibility', *Journal of the Royal Society of Medicine*, 79 (1986), 697–700.

30. Kennedy, I., *Treat Me Right* (Oxford, OUP, 1988), 216.

31. See above, n. 26.

32. O'Brien, B., *What are my Chances Doctor?* (Brunel University: Health Economics Research Group, 1986), gives a detailed analysis of calculating risk.

33. Mercer, D., Mercer, G., *Children First and Always: a Portrait of Great Ormond Street* (London, Macdonald, 1986), 197.

34. Faden, R., Beauchamp, T. (above, n. 10).

35. Kennedy, I. (above, n. 30), 313–14.

36. The Guardianship and Administration Board Act (1986) Victoria, Australia, is one of several acts which allow the appointment of guardians who have legal authority to consent to medical treatment on behalf of adults who are unable to make personal decisions.

37. Above, n. 22.

38. Nicholson (above, n. 21), 216.

39. Nicholson (above, n. 21), 233; and US President's Commission for the Study of Ethical Problems in Medicine and Biomedical and Behavioural Research, *Making Health Care Decisions* (1982).

40. US President's Commission, above, n. 39.

41. British Paediatric Association, 'Guidelines on Research on Children', in *Archives of Disease in Childhood*, 55 (1980), 75–7.

42. See references in nn. 21, 39, and 41 above.

43. Family Court Act, amendment to child abuse prevention and treatment, 98 stat. 1749 and section 233, USA (1984); Macklin, R., *Hastings Centre Report*, 18/1 (1988), 15–20. Parents are required to consent to medically recommended treatment or blood transfusions for their children aged under 18, unless the child is 'emancipated' (has left home). New York State Public Health Law 2504.

44. English law is fully discussed in Kennedy (above, n. 30), 52–118: 'The doctor, the pill and the 15-year-old girl'.

45. Scottish Law Commission, Consultative Memorandum No. 65, *Legal Capacity and Responsibility of Minors and Pupils*, 47, 48, 51.

46. Family Law Reform Act, London, 1969, sect. 8.

47. I thank the Children's Legal Centre, London, for this information.

48. Information from the Children's Legal Centre.

49. Confidentiality for minors is discussed in Gaylin, Macklin (above, n. 18).

50. The Law Reform Commission of Western Australia, *Discussion Paper on Medical Treatment for Minors* (1988), p. 48, proposes that the statutory scheme should provide that children of 13 or over are presumed to be sufficiently mature to consent to medical treatment. The Canadian Law is the Public Health Protection Act, Quebec Statute, ch. 42, sect. 36.

51. Woolf, J., in *Gillick* v. *West Norfolk & Wisbeach AHA* (1985) 3 All ER 373.

52. Lord Scarman, 421 (above, n. 51).

53. Lord Fraser, 410, and Lord Scarman (above, n. 51).

54. Hoggett, B., 'Parents, Children and Medical Treatment: the Legal Issues', in *Rights and Wrongs in Medicine*, ed. Byrne, P. (London, King's Fund, 1986), 158–76.

55. Such as in the Alexandra Case, in *Re B* [1981] 1 WLR 1421. A Down's syndrome baby was made a ward of court and had a life-saving operation to which her parents had refused to consent.

56. Practices were first widely publicized by Duff, R., Campbell, A., 'Moral and Ethical Dilemmas in the Special Care Nursery', *New England Journal of Medicine*, 289 (1973), 885–94.

57. See above, n. 53.

58. Benson, P., Roth, L., Wislade, W., 'Informed consent in psychiatric research', *Social Science & Medicine*, 20/12 (1985), 1331–41.

59. See above, nn. 21, 30, 39.

60. McLean, S., *A Patient's Right to Know* (Aldershot, Dartmouth, 1989), 31–55.

61. In my present research interviewing children having surgery, children below around nine to ten years tend to prefer their parents to choose.

62. Goldstein, J. makes this point in 'Medical Care for the Child at Risk', in Gaylin, W., Macklin, R., *Who Speaks for the Child?* (New York, Plenum, 1982), 166.

63. See above, n. 54.

64. See above, n. 55.

65. Kaufman, C., 'Informed Consent and Patient Decision-making: two Decades of Research', *Social Science & Medicine*, 17/21 (1983), 1657–64; and King, J., *Informed Consent: a Review of the Empirical Evidence* (London: Institute of Medical Ethics Supplement no. 3, 1986).

66. LeBaron, S., Reyher, J., Stack, J., 'Paternalist vs Egalitarian Physician Styles', *Journal of Family Practice*, 21/1 (1985), 56–62.

67. Klaus, M., 'Commentary: Ethical Decision Making in Neonatal Intensive Care, Communicating with Parents', *Birth*, 13/3 (1985), 175.

68. Miles, M., Carter, M., 'Coping Strategies used by Parents during their Child's Hospitalization in an Intensive Care Unit', *Child Health Care*, 14/1 (1985), 14–21.

69. See above, n. 65.

70. See above, n. 68.

71. Gouldner, A., *The Coming Crisis in Western Sociology* (London, Heinemann, 1977), considers awareness at length.

72. Gouldner, p. 103.

73. Bion's theories recounted in Hoxter, S., 'Play and Communication', in Boston, M., Daws, D. (eds.), *The child psychotherapist and problems of young people* (London, Wildwood House, 1977), 214.

74. Ibid.

75. Alderson, P., Comer, B., *Nursing Satisfaction Study*, report of a survey of views of paediatric nurses at the Brompton Hospital. I also attended nurse support meetings and interviewed nurses.

76. Anand, K., Sippel, W., Aynsley-Green, A., 'Randomised Trial of Fentanyl Anaesthesia', *Lancet* (Jan. 1987), 243–8.

77. Anand, K. *et al.*, letter to *Lancet* (Mar. 1987), 750.

78. Hatch, D., 'Analgesia in the Neonate', *British Medical Journal*, 294 (1987), 920.

79. Anon., 'Pain, Anaesthesia and Babies', *Lancet* (Dec. 1987), 543; Scanlon, J., 'Barbarism', *Perinatal Press*, 9 (1985), 103–4; Rana, S., 'Pain—a Subject Ignored', *Pediatrics*, 79 (1987), 309–10. Pain relief is not used in many Canadian neonatal units: Magnet, S., Kluge, E., *Withholding Treatment from Defective Newborns* (Quebec, Brown Legal Publications, 1985).

80. See above, n. 76.

81. Ibid.

82. Wilkinson, D., letter to *Lancet* (Mar. 1987), 720.

83. Lenard, H., letter to *Lancet* (Mar. 1987), 720.

84. The ventilator tube prevents patients from making vocal sounds.

85. Chapman, C., 'New Directions in the Understanding and Management of Pain', *Social Science & Medicine*, 19/12 (1984), 1261–77; see also Edwards, R., 'Pain and the Ethics of Pain Management', *Social Science & Medicine*, 18/6 (1984), 515–23.

86. Gooch, J., 'Who Should Manage Pain?', *Professional Nurse* (Mar. 1989), 295–6.

87. Butler, N., 'The Issue of Medically Caused Pain in Infants', *Children's Health Care*, 18/2 (1989), 70–4.

88. 'Policy for Self-administration of Medicines in the Paediatric Unit', *Society of Paediatric Nursing Newsletter*, 19 (1988), 5–6; 'A Welcome on the Wards', *National Association for the Welfare of Children in Hospital Update*, 21 (1987), 1; 'Providing Family-centred Care', *NAWCH Update*, 23 (1988), 4.

89. See above, n. 9.

90. Lisa has atrioventricular septal defect but not Down's syndrome.

91. Paediatric cardiologists have written very clear and informative material for parents, such as Olive Scott's coloured sheets on heart defects (London, British

Heart Foundation) and *Heart Children* by Philip Rees and others (Biggleswade, Heart Line Association, 1989).

92. Siegel, B.; see above n. 7.

93. *Hansard* (Feb. 1989), col. 278 in response to a parliamentary question on changing the law about Jehovah's Witnesses' consent to blood transfusions.

94. There are many statements about parents' need to be together when they are told bad news, such as, Woolley, H., Stein, A., Forrest, G., Baum, J., 'Imparting Diagnosis of Life Threatening Illness in Children', *British Medical Journal*, 298 (1989), 1623–6.

95. Maguire, P., Faulkner, A., 'Improve the counselling skills of doctors and nurses in cancer care', *British Medical Journal*, 297 (1988), 847–9.

Chapter 7. Voluntary consent

1. Janet had an atrioventricular septal (or canal) defect. There are three options: corrective surgery repairs the walls separating the four chambers, and reconstructs two heart valves; palliative surgery (banding) reduces the effects of the defect, by reducing the pressure of blood flowing to the lungs, but carries a high risk and an uncertain future; no surgery means that if the child survives the first difficult years while her lungs adapt to the defect, she can expect years of reasonable health. Gradually the pressure on the lungs increases until the lung disease becomes fatally severe. The decision has to be made early in life, before the lungs become so diseased that surgery would do more harm than good.

2. Bull, C., Rigby, M., Shinebourne, E., 'Should Management of Complete Atrioventricular Canal Defect be Influenced by Coexistent Down's Syndrome?', *Lancet*, i (18 May 1985), 1147, and correspondence *Lancet* (12 Oct. 1985), 834–5.

3. Nuremberg Code 1947 in Duncan, A., Dunstan, G., Welbourn, R. (eds.), *Dictionary of Medical Ethics* (London, Darton, Longman & Todd, 1981), 130–2.

4. Faden, R., Beauchamp, T., *A History and Theory of Informed Consent* (New York, OUP, 1986), 257.

5. Nuremberg Code.

6. The analogy raises debates about the nature of the self, free will, and whether, like flotsam, we are entirely driven by extraneous forces. If we are, consent, and indeed life-saving surgery, would hardly matter in so relativist a view. I have therefore taken the view that there are some fundamental impulses which are integral to the self, and that consent is voluntary when it is in harmony with them.

7. Delight, E., Goodall, J., 'Babies with Spina Bifida Treated Without Surgery', *British Medical Journal*, 297 (1988), 1230–3.

8. Goodall, J., 'Balancing Options in Neonatal Care', *Archives of Disease in Childhood*, 59 (1984), 88–9.

9. Alderson, P., Comer, B., Rees, S., *Care of Children who have died at the Brompton Hospital and Care of their Families*, a report of the views of bereaved parents and paediatric nurses (1986).

10. Jurow, R., Paul, R., 'Caesarean Delivery for Fetal Distress without Maternal Consent', *Obstetrics & Gynecology*, 63 (1984), 586–90.

11. Klaus, M., Kennell, J., *Maternal and Infant Bonding* (St Louis, C. Mosby, 1976),

associated separation of mothers and babies in hospital with increased incidence of later child abuse.

12. *Slater* v. *Baker and Stapleton* (1767) 94 ER 60.

13. A detailed history is given in Faden, R., Beauchamp, T., *A History and Theory of Informed Consent* (New York, OUP, 1986). The authors stress the importance of changing meanings of 'consent'. The current democratic meaning would not be recognized only a few decades ago, far less centuries ago when, for instance, Thomas Aquinas used the term.

14. Justice Cardozo in *Schloendorff* v. *Society of New York Hospitals* 211 NY 125 (1914).

15. Hippocratic Oath in *Dictionary of Medical Ethics* (above, n. 3), 210.

16. See above, n. 3.

17. Beecher, H., *Research and the Individual* (Boston, Little Brown, 1970), reports serious abuses in American medical research in the 1970s; Hamblin, T., 'A shocking American report with lessons for us all', *British Medical Journal*, 295 (11 July 1987), 73, discusses radioactive experiments affecting humans, 1945–71, carried out 'simply to satisfy scientific curiosity'; Holmes, H. criticizes unethical American research on children in Thailand which would not be permitted in the United States, in 'Can Clinical Research be both Ethical and Scientific?', *Hypatia*, 4/2 (1989), 156–68. The research is reported by McBride, J., 'Asian Children may quell Nutritional Controversy', *Agricultural Research* (Feb. 1988), 11.

18. Lifton, R., *The Nazi Doctors* (London, Macmillan, 1986).

19. Declaration of Helsinki *The World Medical Association Handbook of Declarations* (Fernay-Voltaire, 1986). The 1964 version was revised in 1983).

20. Declaration of Lisbon (1981) in *WMA Handbook*.

21. Declaration of Helsinki.

22. National Commission for the Protection of Human Subjects of Biomedical and Behavioural Research, *The Belmont Report* (1979).

23. The debate is in the medical, legal, and bioethics works listed through this book.

24. Lewis, *The Humanitarian Theory of Punishment*, 6 Res Judicate 224, 228 (1952).

25. National Commission for the Protection of Human Subjects of Biomedical and Behavioural Research, *Research Involving Children: Report and Recommendations*, Washington DC, DHEW, (1977), 77–10004.

26. Taylor, K., Kelner, M., 'Informed Consent: the Physicians' Perspective', *Social Science & Medicine*, 24/2 (1987), 135–43.

27. Kaufmann, C., 'Informed Consent and Patient Decision Making: Two Decades of Research', *Social Science & Medicine*, 17/21 (1983), 1657–64; King, J., *Informed Consent* (London, Institute of Medical Ethics Bulletin Supplement no. 3, 1986).

28. Baum, M., Zilkha, K., Houghton, J., 'Ethics of Clinical Research: Lessons for the Future', *British Medical Journal*, 299 (1989), 251–3. See also, Tobias, J., 'Informed Consent and Controlled Trials', letter to the *Lancet* (Dec. 1988), 1194. This approach is influenced by guidelines from the 1960s, such as those of the Medical Research Council and the Royal College of Physicians still in force in the late 1980s.

29. Research trials may require patients' consent to: (*a*) all the available options

equally; (*b*) leaving the choice of treatment to the clinician or to random allocation; (*c*) remaining ignorant of the selected treatment; (*d*) being treated by a clinician who does not know the selected treatment (in a double-blind trial).

30. Clough, F., 'The validation of meaning in illness-treatment situations', in Hall, D., Stacey, M. (eds.), *Beyond Separation* (London, Routledge, 1979); Kelley, M., 'Loss and grief reactions as responses to surgery', *Journal of Advanced Nursing*, 10 (1985), 517–25.

31. Thomas, E., 'Research Without Consent Continues in the UK', *Institute of Medical Ethics Bulletin*, 40 (1988), 13–15. The debate continued in autumn issues of the *Bulletin*, *Lancet*, and *Observer*.

32. See Tobias (above, n. 28).

33. See above, n. 31.

34. Siegel, B., *Love, Medicine and Miracles* (London, Rider, 1986). Examples of patients' active partnership in healing are also seen in their self-help groups which promote health in its widest sense of emotional and social (if not always physical) well-being. See Alderson, P., Ritchie, S., Kingsmill, S., 'A Friend at Hand: Report on Cancer Self-help Groups', *Nursing Standard*, 3/23 (1989), 30–2.

35. Wilson, R., Hart, A., Dawes, P., 'Mastectomy or Conservation: the Patient's Choice', *British Medical Journal*, 297 (1988), 1167–9.

36. *Positively Healthy News* (Jan. 1989), 1, reports the AIDS trials.

37. Zelen, M., 'A New Design for Randomized Trials', *New England Journal of Medicine*, 300/22 (1979), 1242–5, proposes asking for patients' consent after they have been randomized. Criticisms are discussed in Marquis, D., 'An Ethical Problem Concerning Recent Therapeutic Research on Breast Cancer', *Hypatia*, 4/2 (1989), 140–55. Kennedy, I., 'The Law and Ethics of Informed Consent and Randomized Controlled Trials', *Treat Me Right* (Oxford, OUP, 1988), 213–24, is also critical of these trials.

38. Keller, E., *Reflections on Gender and Science* (New Haven, Yale, 1985). Several of the following references are discussed in this book.

39. Goodfield, J., *An Imagined World* (New York, Harper and Row, 1981), 63, 69, 213.

40. See Keller (above, n. 38), chapter on 'Dynamic objectivity'.

41. Ibid. 96.

42. Kinmouth, A., Lindsey, M., Baum, J., 'Social and Emotional Complications in a Clinical Trial among Adolescents with Diabetes Mellitus', *British Medical Journal*, 286 (1983), 952–4.

43. Keller (above, n. 38), chapter on 'Dynamic autonomy'.

44. Freud, S., *Civilisation and its Discontents* (New York, Anchor Press, 1930); Piaget, J., *The Child's Conception of the World* (Totowa, NJ, Littlefield, Adams, 1972).

45. Winnicott, D., *Playing and Reality* (New York, Basic Books, 1971). Dorothy Dinnerstein, Nancy Choderow, Carol Gilligan, and others are concerned with differences between men's and women's reactions, and how these may have been influenced by their differing childhood experiences. Rather than suggest that types of behaviour and values are divided between men and women, I attempt to review what have been labelled as broadly 'masculine' and 'feminine' principles which are held by both men and women although often with markedly different emphases.

46. Kohlberg, L., *The Philosophy of Moral Development* (San Francisco, Harper and Row, 1971); Erikson, E., *Identity, Youth and Crisis* (New York, W. W. Norton, 1968).
47. Keller (above, n. 38), 82.
48. Winnicott (above, n. 45), 65.
49. Schachtel, E., *Metamorphosis* (New York, Basic Books, 1959).
50. Shapiro, D., *Neurotic Styles* (New York, Basic Books, 1965).
51. Keller (above, n. 38), 121, commenting on Shapiro's words.
52. Ibid. 117.
53. Moe, K., 'Should Nazi Research Data be Cited?', *Hastings Center Report*, 14/6 (1984), 5–7, discusses cruel but useful research on hypothermia; Brykczyńska, G., *Ethics in Paediatric Nursing* (London, Chapman and Hall, 1989), 131–2, advocates learning from the hunger disease studies made in Jewish children's wards in Warsaw in 1942. The studies were republished in Winick, M. (ed.), *Hunger Disease: Current Concepts in Nutrition* (New York, Wiley, 1979), 17.
54. Trusted, J., *The Logic of Scientific Inference: an Introduction* (London, Macmillan, 1979), 22. The presidential address for the Obstetric Section of the Royal Society of Medicine, 2 Dec. 1988, reviewed developments over the last 30 years, noting several times that beneficial knowledge had been gained through methods which would not now be permitted by ethics committees.
55. See above, n. 1.
56. Jane, D., Stratford, S., *Current Approaches to Down's Syndrome* (London, Cassell, 1985).
57. In 1980 Dr Arthur was prosecuted for 'helping a Down's syndrome baby to die'. The parents thought that this was in their son's best interests although he did not have any fatal defect. Dr Arthur was found not guilty of attempted murder. The case made public and formal dilemmas which had previously tended to be treated privately and informally.
58. The Nuremberg Code (see above, n. 3).
59. Lukes, S., *Power, a Radical View* (London, Macmillan, 1974).

Chapter 8. Trust between doctors and families

1. Brewin, T., 'Truth, Trust and Paternalism', *Lancet* (Aug. 1985), 228.
2. Dunstan, G., Seller, M., *Consent in Medicine* (Oxford, OUP and King's Fund, 1983), 111.
3. Hilary Graham pointed out that experiences such as caring, which like trust involve thinking and feeling, 'slip between the tight conceptual categories of the social sciences [within] the deficiency of a scientific apparatus which is blind to the very phenomena we wish to make visible'. Caring is fragmented into its two parts, labour and love, so that 'interlocking features are dismantled' and 'its most distinctive and compelling qualities have been lost'. Graham, H., 'Caring: a Labour of Love', in Finch, J. (ed.), *A Labour of Love: Women, Work and Caring* (London, Routledge, 1983).
4. Jacobs, R., 'The Meaning of Hospital: Denial of Emotions', in Hall, D., Stacey, M. (eds.), *Beyond Separation* (London, Routledge, 1979).
5. Two examples from a wide literature are Ehrenrich, B., English, D., *For Her Own Good: 150 Years of the Experts' Advice to Women* (London, Pluto Press, 1979).

and Foucault, M., *The Birth of the Clinic* (London, Tavistock, 1976).

6. Siegel, B., *Love, Medicine and Miracles* (London, Rider, 1988), 14.
7. Maguire, P., 'Barriers to the Psychological Care of the Dying', *British Medical Journal*, 291 (1984), 178–83.
8. Kohrman, A., 'Selective Nontreatment of Handicapped Newborns: a Critical Essay', *Social Science & Medicine*, 20/11 (1985), 1091–5.
9. Buber, M., 'Distance and Relation', *Psychiatry*, 29 (1957), 97–104.
10. Alderson, P., Comer, B., Rees, S., *Care of Children who have died at the Brompton Hospital and Care of their Families*: A report of the views of bereaved parents and the paediatric nurses (1986).
11. See n. 6 above.
12. Royal College of Nursing, 'Policy for Self-administration of Medicines in the Paediatric Unit, *Society of Paediatric Nursing Newsletter*, 19 (Summer 1989).
13. See n. 8 above.
14. Ibid.
15. Ibid.
16. Watzlavic, P., Beavin, J., Jackson, D., *Pragmatics of Human Communication* (New York, W. W. Norton, 1967), 195.
17. Ibid. 83.
18. A baby's normal respiration rate is about forty.
19. Popper, K., *The Logic of Scientific Discovery* (London, Routledge, 1959).
20. Donne, J., Satire 3 *On religion*.
21. Numbers 22.
22. MacKenna, R., *Is There Anyone There?* (London, Collins, 1987).

Chapter 9. Ethical medicine and bioethics

1. Tom was a patient at a third hospital linked to both the hospitals I observed. Some consultants would be unlikely to consider him for surgery.
2. Beauchamp, T., Childress, J., *Principles of Biomedical Ethics* (New York, OUP, 1983) is a standard American text, Gillon, R., *Philosophical Medical Ethics* (Chichester, Wiley, 1986) is a standard British text. They promote principles which are embodied in the *Belmont Report* (National Commission for the Protection of Human Subjects of Biomedical and Behavioural Research, Washington DC, 1979). For rights theory see Rawls, J., *A Theory of Justice* (New York, OUP, 1973).
3. See references in n. 2.
4. Kant, I., 'Groundwork of the Metaphysic of Morals', in Paton, H., *The Moral Law* (London, Hutchinson, 1948), 84.
5. Ibid. 99.
6. Smart, J., Williams, B., *Utilitarianism* (Cambridge, CUP, 1973), make many other points for and against utilitarianism.
7. Templeman, L., in *Re B* [1981] 1 WLR 1424.
8. Grimshaw, J., *Feminism and Philosophy* (Brighton, Wheatsheaf, 1986), 31.
9. Weir, R., *Selective Non-treatment of Handicapped Newborns* (New York, OUP, 1984).
10. Raphael, D., *Problems of Politics and Philosophy* (London, Macmillan, 1976), 8.
11. Above, n. 8, pp. 22–5.

12. Hare, R., 'Abortion and the Golden Rule', in Baker, R., Elliston, F. (eds.), *Philosophy and Sex* (New York, Prometheus Books, 1975), quoted in Grimshaw, above, n. 8.

13. See n. 8 above.

14. See n. 10 above, p. 8.

15. World Medical Association, *Handbook of Declarations* (Fernay-Voltaire, 1986), 4.

16. Shapiro, D., *Neurotic Styles* (New York, Basic Books, 1965), 36.

17. Keller, E., *Reflections on Gender and Science* (New Haven, Yale, 1985), 121.

18. Kant, I. (n. 4 above), 68, 89, 95–6.

19. Mendus, S., 'Kant: an Honest but Narrow-minded Bourgeois?', in *Women in Western Political Philosophy*, ed. Kennedy, E., Mendus, S. (Brighton, Wheatsheaf, 1987), 21–43.

20. Locke, J., *An Essay Concerning Human Understanding* (1690), Bk. 2, p. 27.

21. Midgely, M., *Beast and Man* (Brighton, Harvester, 1979), examines amazingly complex instincts.

22. Kant, I., in Paton, H. (above, n. 4), 90.

23. Harris, J., *The Value of Life* (London, Routledge, 1985); Tooley, M., *Abortion and Infanticide* (Oxford, OUP, 1983).

24. Oswin, M., *The Empty Hours* (London, Allen Lane, 1971).

25. Harris, J. (above, n. 23), 19–23.

26. Stern, D., *The First Relationship: Infant and Mother* (London, Fontana, 1977), and other books in the series 'The Developing Child'.

27. Russell, B., *Collected Short Stories* (New York, Simon and Schuster, 1972), 33.

28. See above, n. 4, p. 84.

29. Beauchamp, T., Childress, J., *Principles of Biomedical Ethics* (New York, OUP, 1983).

30. Charles, L. *et al.*, *Informed Consent: a Study of Decision Making in Psychiatry* (New York, Guilford Press, 1984), 1.

31. Ibid. 1.

32. MacIntyre, A., *After Virtue* (London, Duckworth, 1985), 35.

33. *Metaphysic of Morals*, sect. 46, pp. 139–40, in Reiss, H. (ed.), trans. Nisbet, H., *Kant's Political Writings* (Cambridge, CUP, 1970); and see above, n. 4, p. 25.

34. Grimshaw, J. (above, n. 8), discusses Locke's views on women on p. 50.

35. See above, n. 4.

36. Seidler, V., *Kant, Respect and Injustice* (London, Routledge, 1986), 120.

37. Miller, A., *For Your Own Good: the Roots of Violence in Child-rearing* (London, Virago, 1987).

38. MacIntyre, A., *A Short History of Ethics* (New York, Macmillan, 1966), 208. Eichmann claimed to have been educated on the moral basis of the categorical imperative.

39. Kant, I., *Metaphysics of Morals*, Pt. 2, trans. Gregor, M. (London, Harper and Row, 1964).

40. Kennedy, I., *Treat Me Right* (Oxford, OUP, 1988), 177.

41. Hoggett, B., 'Parents, Children and Medical Treatment: the Legal Issues', in *Rights and Wrongs in Medicine*, ed. Byrne, P. (London, King's Fund, 1986), 165. 'In the case of an adult [consenting to medical treatment] it is axiomatic that

understanding, not wisdom, is all that is required for a man may go to the devil if he chooses.'

42. This is fully discussed in Seidler, V. (above, n. 36).

43. Paul Ramsey endorses a common view when he says: 'man's propensity to overreach his joint adventurer . . . makes consent necessary'. Ramsey, P., *The Patient as Person* (New Haven, Yale University Press, 1970), 5.

44. See above, n. 29, pp. 148–50.

45. Searle, J., 'Mind and Body', Inter-Collegiate Lecture, London University (16 May 1989).

46. Auger, M., 'Mononuclear phagocytes', *British Medical Journal*, 298 (1989), 546.

47. Jung, C., *Memories, Dreams and Reflections* (London, Fontana 1983), 199. For detailed discussion of learning about illness through weakness see Bennet, G., *The Wound and the Doctor* (London, Secker and Warburg, 1987).

48. Freidson, E., *Profession of Medicine* (New York, Dodd Mead, 1970).

49. Raphael, D., *Problems of Politics and Philosophy* (London, Macmillan, 1976), 8.

50. Chiswick, M., lecture to the London Medical Group (Jan. 1989) on 'Withdrawing Neonatal Treatment'.

51. See above, n. 32, p. 143.

52. Brody, B., *Moral Theory and Moral Judgements in Medical Ethics* (Dordrecht, Kluwer, 1988).

53. Giddens, A., *Sociology: a Brief but Critical Introduction* (London, Macmillan, 1982), 60.

54. Gouldner, A., *The Coming Crisis in Western Sociology* (London, Heinemann, 1977), 505.

55. Williams, B., *Morality: an Introduction to Ethics* (Cambridge, CUP, 1972), 9.

56. Williams, B., *Ethics and the Limits of Philosophy* (London, Fontana, 1985), 195–6.

57. Gramsci, A., *Selections from the Prison Notebooks*, ed. Hoare, Q., Nowell Smith, G. (London, Lawrence and Wishart, 1971), 333 f.

58. Ibid. 333.

59. Kohlberg, L., *The Philosophy of Moral Development* (San Francisco, Harper and Row, 1981).

60. Gilligan, C., *In a Different Voice* (Cambridge, Mass., Harvard, 1982), 22.

61. Ibid. 18 f.

62. Jung, C., *Aspects of the Feminine* (Princeton University Press, 1982).

63. Gilligan (above, n. 60), 22.

64. Ibid. 19.

65. Gilligan, C., Wiggins, G., 'The Origins of Morality in Early Childhood Relationships' (unpublished paper, Harvard University, 1986), 15.

66. Gilligan (above, n. 60), 149.

67. Gilligan, C., Wiggins, G. (above, n. 65), 1–4.

68. Pellegrino, E., Thomasma, D., *For the Patient's Good* (New York, OUP, 1988).

69. Ibid. 205.

70. Gilligan (above, n. 60), 49.

71. Loc. cit.

72. Bennett, G., *The Wound and the Doctor* (London, Secker and Warburg, 1987); and Siegel, B., *Love, Medicine and Miracles* (London, Rider, 1986).

73. Above, n. 67, p. 1.

Chapter 10. Proxy consent

1. Some of these issues are considered in Gaylin, W., Macklin, R. (eds.), *Who Speaks for the Child? The Problems of Proxy Consent* (New York, Plenum Press, 1982); Nicholson, R. (ed.), *Medical Research with Children: Ethics, Law and Practice* (Oxford, OUP, 1986).

2. My present research is on children's consent from their point of view.

3. The incident happened in Apr. 1989 and was reported in *Medical Ethics Advisor*, 5/6 (Atlanta, 1989), 69–73.

4. Second International Conference on Health Law and Ethics, London (July 1989).

5. Dunstan, G., Shinebourne, E. (eds.), *Doctors' Decisions: Ethical Conflicts in Medical Practice* (Oxford, OUP, 1989).

6. Byrne, P., 'Authority, Social Policy, and the Doctor–Patient Relationship', in Dunstan and Shinebourne (above, n. 5), 240, 253.

7. Warnock, M., 'Universities: the New Civil Service?', *New Society* (12 Feb. 1988), 24.

8. Gladwin, T., *Cultural and Logical Process*, pp. 112–17, discussed in McMillan, C., *Women, Reason and Nature* (Oxford, Basil Blackwell, 1982).

9. Tillyard, E., *The Elizabethan World Picture* (Harmondsworth, Penguin, 1963); Merchant, C., *The Death of Nature* (London, Wildwood House, 1982). Merchant analyses many texts including those in nn. 10–14 below.

10. Giambattista della Porta, *Magiae Naturalis* (Naples, 1558).

11. Descartes, R., *Principles of Philosophy* (1644).

12. Hobbes, J., *Leviathan* (1651).

13. Harvey, W., *Exercitatio de Generatione Animalium* (1628).

14. Newton, I., *Philosophiae Naturalis Principia Mathematica* (1687).

15. Shakespeare, W., *Much Ado about Nothing*, IV. i.

16. Kennedy, I., *Treat Me Right* (Oxford, OUP, 1988).

17. Harris, J., Review of *Treat Me Right* in *Journal of Medical Ethics*, 15/1 (1989), 48–9.

18. Faden, R., Beauchamp, T., *A History and Theory of Informed Consent* (New York, OUP, 1985).

19. Denning, L., in *Hewere* v. *Bryant* [1970] 1 QB 357.

20. See above, n. 16.

21. Pellegrino, E., Thomasma, D., *For the Patient's Good* (New York, OUP, 1988).

22. Of many examples, there are the parents whose criticisms of inadequate anaesthesia during babies' surgery were discounted as emotional over-reactions, cf. Butler, N., in *Children's Health Care*, Journal of the American Association for the Care of Children's Health, 18/2 (1989), 70–4; Baruch, G., 'Moral Tales', *Sociology of Health & Illness*, 3/3 (1981), 275–95, on parents' accounts as constructs and stories.

23. Robertson, J., *Young Children in Hospital* (London, Tavistock, 1970). *Laura* was filmed in 1961.

24. Amanda's mother, quoted in Fradd, E., 'Tug of love', *Nursing Times*, 84/41 (1988), 32–5.

25. Gibran, K., *The Prophet*.

26. Hare, R., *The Language of Morals* (Oxford, OUP, 1952).

27. Mitchell, M., 'The Costs of Survival', *Health Service Journal*, 97 (1987).

28. Dominica, F., 'Reflections on Death in Childhood', *British Medical Journal*, 294 (1987) 108–10.

29. Dickens, M., *Miracles of Courage* (London, David and Charles, 1985).

30. Bentovim, A., 'Psychological and Social Aspects of Cardiac Disease in Children', in Graham, G., Rossi, E. (eds.), *Heart Disease in Infants and Children* (London, Edward Arnold, 1980).

31. See above, n. 24.

32. Gilligan, C., *In a Different Voice* (Cambridge, Mass., Harvard, 1982), 29.

Index of children

Index